UTAH TRAILS

SOUTHWEST REGION

PETER MASSEY
AND JEANNE WILSON

ADLER
PUBLISHING

Acknowledgements

Many people and organizations have made major contributions to the research and production of this book. We owe them all special thanks for their assistance.

First, we would like to thank the following people who have played major roles in the production of this book and have been key to completing it in a timely fashion.

Cover Design Concept: **Rudy Ramos**
Editing and Proofreading: **Jeff Campbell, Alice Levine**
Graphic Design and Maps: **Deborah Rust**

We would also like to thank the many people at the Bureau of Land Management offices throughout Utah, who spent countless hours assisting us. In particular, we would like to thank Jeanie Linn at the Hanksville Field Office.

Staff at many offices of the National Forest Service also provided us with valuable assistance, particularly the offices in Price, Ferron, Teasdale, and Richfield.

We received a great deal of assistance from many other people and organizations. We would like to thank the Utah State Historical Society, the Denver Public Library Western History Department, Kari Murphy at the Moab to Monument Valley Film Commission, and the Moab Historical Society.

The book includes many photos, and we are most thankful to the Bushducks—Donald McGann and Maggie Pinder, and Alan Barnett and Tara Thompson at the Utah State Historical Society.

With a project of this size countless hours are spent researching and recording the trail information, and we would like to thank Carol and Gary Martin of the Virginian Motel in Moab for providing a base camp for our researchers and for their helpful trail suggestions.

We would also like to draw our readers' attention to the website (www.bush-ducks.com) of our senior researchers, the Bushducks—Donald McGann and Maggie Pinder. It provides information on current 4WD trail conditions and offers their valuable assistance to anyone who is planning a backcountry itinerary.

Publisher's Note: Every effort has been taken to ensure that the information in this book is accurate at press time. Please visit our website to advise us of any changes or corrections you find. We also welcome recommendations for new 4WD trails or other suggestions to improve the information in this book.

Adler Publishing Company, Inc.
1601 Pacific Coast Highway, Suite 290
Hermosa Beach, CA 90254
Phone: 800-660-5107
Fax: 310-698-0709
4WDbooks.com

Contents

Before You Go   **7**

Southwest Regional Map   **24**

Trail #1:   Indian Spring Trail   28

Trail #2:   Scarecrow Peak Trail   31

Trail #3:   Hell Hole Pass Trail   35

Trail #4:   TV Towers Jeep Trail   37

Trail #5:   Joshua Tree Loop   39

Trail #6:   The Divide Trail   43

Trail #7:   Hurricane Cliffs Trail   46

Trail #8:   Smithsonian Butte Trail   49

Trail #9:   Grafton Mesa Trail   53

Trail #10: Elephant Butte Trail   54

Trail #11: The Barracks Trail   58

Trail #12: Moquith Mountains Trail   60

Trail #13: Hog Canyon Trail   62

Trail #14: John R Flat Trail   65

Trail #15: Skutumpah Road   70

Trail #16: Cottonwood Canyon Road   78

Trail #17: Paria River Valley Trail   84

Trail #18: Smoky Mountain Road   86

Trail #19: Alstrom Point Trail   94

Trail #20: Nipple Creek and Tibbet Canyon Trail   96

Trail #21: Smoky Hollow Trail   101

Trail #22: Hole-in-the-Rock Trail   104

Trail #23: Hells Backbone Trail   110

Trail #24: McGath Lake Trail   115

Trail #25: Road Draw Road   118

Trail #26: Posey Lake Road   120

Trail #27: Boulder Tops Road   125

Trail #28: Bowns Point Trail   129

Trail #29: Spectacle Lake Trail   132

Trail #30: Purple and Blue Lakes Trail   135

Trail #31: Dark Valley Trail   137

Trail #32: Chokecherry Point Trail   140

Trail #33: Griffin Road   143

Trail #34: Escalante Summit Trail   147

Trail #35: Corn Creek Road   150

Trail #36: Powell Point Trail   152

Trail #37: Barney Top Trail   155

Trail #38: Tantalus Creek Trail   158

Trail #39: Notom Road   162

Trail #40: Burr Trail   167

Trail #41: Upper Muley Twist Trail   175

Trail #42: Wolverine Loop   176

Trail #43: Clay Point Road   182

Trail #44: Shootering Canyon Trail   185

Trail #45: Stanton Pass Trail   189

Trail #46: Pennell Creek Bench Trail   192

Trail #47: Bull Creek Pass Trail   194

Trail #48: Copper Ridge Trail   200

Trail #49: Town Wash and Bull Mountain Trail   204

Selected Further Reading   **209**

Before You Go

Why a 4WD Does It Better

The design and engineering of 4WD vehicles provide them with many advantages over normal cars when you head off the paved road:

- improved distribution of power to all four wheels;
- a transmission transfer case, which provides low-range gear selection for greater pulling power and for crawling over difficult terrain;
- high ground clearance;
- less overhang of the vehicle's body past the wheels, which provides better front- and rear-clearance when crossing gullies and ridges;
- large-lug, wide-tread tires;
- rugged construction (including under-body skid plates on many models).

If you plan to do off-highway touring, all of these considerations are important whether you are evaluating the capabilities of your current 4WD or are looking to buy one; each is considered in detail in this chapter.

To explore the most difficult trails described in this book, you will need a 4WD vehicle that is well rated in each of the above features. If you own a 2WD sport utility vehicle, a lighter car-type SUV, or a pickup truck, your ability to explore the more difficult trails will depend on conditions and your level of experience.

A word of caution: Whatever type of 4WD vehicle you drive, understand that it is not invincible or indestructible. Nor can it go everywhere. A 4WD has a much higher center of gravity and weighs more than a car, and so has its own consequent limitations.

Experience is the only way to learn what your vehicle can and cannot do. Therefore, if you are inexperienced, we strongly recommend that you start with trails that have lower difficulty ratings. As you develop an understanding of your vehicle and of your own

taste for adventure, you can safely tackle the more challenging trails.

One way to beef up your knowledge quickly, while avoiding the costly and sometimes dangerous lessons learned from on-the-road mistakes, is to undertake a 4WD course taught by a professional. Look in the Yellow Pages for courses in your area.

Using This Book

Route Planning

The regional map on pages 24 and 27 provide a convenient overview of the trails in the Southwest Region of Utah. Each 4WD trail is shown, as are major highways and towns, to help you plan various routes by connecting a series of 4WD trails and paved roads.

As you plan your overall route, you will probably want to utilize as many 4WD trails as possible. However, check the difficulty rating and time required for each trail before finalizing your plans. You don't want to be stuck 50 miles from the highway—at sunset and without camping gear, since your trip was supposed to be over hours ago—when you discover that your vehicle can't handle a certain difficult passage.

Difficulty Ratings

We use a point system to rate the difficulty of each trail. Any such system is subjective, and your experience of the trails will vary depending on your skill and the road conditions at the time. Indeed, any amount of rain may make the trails much more difficult, if not completely impassable.

We have rated the 4WD trails on a scale of 1 to 10—1 being passable for a normal passenger vehicle in good conditions and 10 requiring a heavily modified vehicle and an experienced driver who expects to encounter vehicle damage. Because this book is designed for owners of unmodified 4WD vehicles—who we assume do not want to damage their vehicles—most of the trails are rated 5 or lower. A few trails are included that rate as high as 7, while those rated 8 to 10 are beyond the scope of this book.

This is not to say that the moderate-rated trails are easy. We strongly recommend that inexperienced drivers not tackle trails rated at 4 or higher until they have undertaken a number of the lower-rated ones, so that they can gauge their skill level and prepare for the difficulty of the higher-rated trails.

In assessing the trails, we have always assumed good road conditions (dry road surface, good visibility, and so on). The factors influencing our ratings are as follows:

■ obstacles such as rocks, mud, ruts, sand, slickrock, and stream crossings;

■ the stability of the road surface;

■ the width of the road and the vehicle clearance between trees or rocks;

■ the steepness of the road;

■ the margin for driver error (for example, a very high, open shelf road would be rated more difficult even if it was not very steep and had a stable surface).

The following is a guide to the ratings.

Rating 1: The trail is graded dirt but suitable for a normal passenger vehicle. It usually has gentle grades, is fairly wide, and has very shallow water crossings (if any).

Rating 2: High-clearance vehicles are preferred but not necessary. These trails are dirt roads, but they may have rocks, grades, water crossings, or ruts that make clearance a concern in a normal passenger vehicle. The trails are fairly wide, making passing possible at almost any point along the trail. Mud is not a concern under normal weather conditions.

Rating 3: High-clearance 4WDs are preferred, but any high-clearance vehicle is acceptable. Expect a rough road surface; mud and sand are possible but will be easily passable. You may encounter rocks up to 6 inches in diameter, a loose road surface, and shelf roads, though these will be wide enough for passing or will have adequate pull-offs.

Rating 4: High-clearance 4WDs are recommended, though most stock SUVs are acceptable. Expect a rough road surface with rocks larger than 6 inches, but there

will be a reasonable driving line available. Patches of mud are possible but can be readily negotiated; sand may be deep and require lower tire pressures. There may be stream crossings up to 12 inches deep, substantial sections of single-lane shelf road, moderate grades, and sections of moderately loose road surface.

Rating 5: High-clearance 4WDs are required. These trails have either a rough, rutted surface, rocks up to 9 inches, mud and deep sand that may be impassable for inexperienced drivers, or stream crossings up to 18 inches deep. Certain sections may be steep enough to cause traction problems, and you may encounter very narrow shelf roads with steep drop-offs and tight clearance between rocks or trees.

Rating 6: These trails are for experienced four-wheel drivers only. They are potentially dangerous, with large rocks, ruts, or terraces that may need to be negotiated. They may also have stream crossings at least 18 inches deep, involve rapid currents, unstable stream bottoms, or difficult access; steep slopes, loose surfaces, and narrow clearances; or very narrow sections of shelf road with steep drop-offs and possibly challenging road surfaces.

Rating 7: Skilled, experienced four-wheel drivers only. These trails include very challenging sections with extremely steep grades, loose surfaces, large rocks, deep ruts, and/or tight clearances. Mud or sand may necessitate winching.

Rating 8 and above: Stock vehicles are likely to be damaged, and drivers may find the trail impassable. Highly skilled, experienced four-wheel drivers only.

Scenic Ratings

If rating the degree of difficulty is subjective, rating scenic beauty is guaranteed to lead to arguments. Utah contains a spectacular variety of scenery—from its grand canyons and towering mountains and buttes to its seemingly endless desert country. Despite the subjectivity of attempting a comparative rating of diverse scenery, we have tried to provide a guide to the relative scenic quality of the various trails. The ratings are based on a scale of 1 to 10, with 10 being the most attractive.

Remoteness Ratings

Many trails in this region are in remote mountain or desert country; sometimes the trails are seldom traveled, and the likelihood is low that another vehicle will appear within a reasonable time to assist you if you get stuck or break down. We have included a ranking for remoteness of +0 through +2. Extreme summer temperatures can make a breakdown in the more remote areas a life-threatening experience. Prepare carefully before tackling the higher-rated, more remote trails (see Special Preparations for Remote Travel, page 11). For trails with a high remoteness rating, consider traveling with a second vehicle.

Estimated Driving Times

In calculating driving times, we have not allowed for stops. Your actual driving time may be considerably longer depending on the number and duration of the stops you make. Add more time if you prefer to drive more slowly than good conditions allow.

Current Road Information

All the 4WD trails described in this book may become impassable in poor weather conditions. Storms can alter roads, remove tracks, and create impassable washes. Most of the trails described, even easy 2WD trails, can quickly become impassable even to 4WD vehicles after only a small amount of rain. For each trail, we have provided a phone number for obtaining current information about conditions.

Abbreviations

The route directions for the 4WD trails use a series of abbreviations as follows:

SO	CONTINUE STRAIGHT ON
TL	TURN LEFT
TR	TURN RIGHT
BL	BEAR LEFT
BR	BEAR RIGHT
UT	U-TURN

Using Route Directions

For every trail, we describe and pinpoint (by odometer reading) nearly every significant feature along the route—such as intersections, streams, washes, gates, cattle guards, and so on—and provide directions from these landmarks. Odometer readings will vary from vehicle to vehicle, so you should allow for slight variations. Be aware that trails can quickly change in the desert. A new trail may be cut around a washout, a faint trail can be graded by the county, or a well-used trail may fall into disuse. All these factors will affect the accuracy of the given directions.

If you diverge from the route, zero your trip meter upon your return and continue along the route, making the necessary adjustment to the point-to-point odometer readings. In the directions, we regularly reset the odometer readings—at significant landmarks or popular lookouts and spur trails—so that you won't have to recalculate for too long.

Most of the trails can be started from either end, and the route directions include both directions of travel; reverse directions are printed in blue below the main directions. When traveling in reverse, read from the bottom of the table and work up.

Route directions include cross-references whenever two 4WD trails included in this book connect; these cross-references allow for an easy change of route or destination.

Each trail includes periodic latitude and longitude readings to facilitate using a global positioning system (GPS) receiver. These readings may also assist you in finding your location on the maps. The GPS coordinates are given in the format dd°mm.mm'. To save time when loading coordinates into your GPS receiver, you may wish to include only one decimal place, since in Utah, the first decimal place equals about 165 yards and the second only about 16 yards.

Map References

We recommend that you supplement the information in this book with more-detailed maps. For each trail, we list the sheet maps and road atlases that provide the best detail for the area. Typically, the following references are given:

- Bureau of Land Management Maps
- U.S. Forest Service Maps
- Utah Travel Council Maps, Department of Geography, University of Utah—regions 1 through 5,
- *Utah Atlas & Gazetteer,* 4th ed. (Freeport, Maine: DeLorme Mapping, 2000)—Scale 1:250,000,
- Maptech-Terrain Navigator Topo Maps—Scale 1:100,000 and 1:24,000,
- *Trails Illustrated* Topo Maps; National Geographic Maps—Various scales, but all contain good detail.

We recommend the *Trails Illustrated* series of maps as the best for navigating these trails. They are reliable, easy to read, and printed on nearly indestructible plastic paper. However, this series covers only a few of the 4WD trails described in this book.

The DeLorme Atlas has the advantage of providing you with maps of the state at a reasonable price. Although its 4WD trail information doesn't go beyond what we provide, it is useful if you wish to explore the hundreds of side roads.

U.S. Forest Service maps lack the topographic detail of the other sheet maps and, in our experience, are occasionally out of date. They have the advantage of covering a broad area and are useful in identifying land use and travel restrictions. These maps are most useful for the longer trails.

Utah Travel Council maps cover Utah in five regions. They provide good overviews with a handful of 4WD trails, although with little specific detail. Four of Utah's five regions are currently available: Southwestern #4, Southeastern #5, Northern #1, and Northeastern #3. Central map #2 has been out of print for several years and it is yet undetermined when it will be available.

In our opinion, the best single option by far is the Terrain Navigator series of maps published on CD-ROM by Maptech. These CD-ROMs contain an amazing level of detail because they include the entire set of 1,941 U.S. Geological Survey topographical maps of Utah at the 1:24,000 scale and all 71 maps at the 1:100,000

scale. These maps offer many advantages over normal maps:

- GPS coordinates for any location can be found and loaded into your GPS receiver. Conversely, if you have your GPS coordinates, your location on the map can be pinpointed instantly.
- Towns, rivers, passes, mountains, and many other sites are indexed by name so that they can be located quickly.
- 4WD trails can be marked and profiled for elevation changes and distances from point to point.
- Customized maps can be printed out.

Maptech uses seven CD-ROMs to cover the entire state of Utah; they can be purchased individually or as part of a two-state package at a heavily discounted price. The CD-ROMs can be used with a laptop computer and a GPS receiver in your vehicle to monitor your location on the map and navigate directly from the display.

All these maps should be available through good map stores. The Maptech CD-ROMs are available directly from the company (800-627-7236, or on the internet at www.maptech.com).

Backcountry Driving Rules and Permits

Four-wheel driving involves special driving techniques and road rules. This section is an introduction for 4WD beginners.

4WD Road Rules

To help ensure that these trails remain open and available for all four-wheel drivers to enjoy, it is important to minimize your impact on the environment and not be a safety risk to yourself or anyone else. Remember that the 4WD clubs in Utah fight a constant battle with the government and various lobby groups to retain the access that currently exists.

The fundamental rule when traversing the 4WD trails described in this book is to use common sense. In addition, special road rules for 4WD trails apply:

- Vehicles traveling uphill have the

right of way.

■ If you are moving more slowly than the vehicle behind you, pull over to let the other vehicle by.

■ Park out of the way in a safe place. Blocking a track may restrict access for emergency vehicles as well as for other recreationalists. Set the parking brake—don't rely on leaving the transmission in park. Manual transmissions should be left in the lowest gear.

Tread Lightly!

Remember the rules of the Tread Lightly!® program:

■ Be informed. Obtain maps, regulations, and other information from the forest service or from other public land agencies. Learn the rules and follow them.

■ Resist the urge to pioneer a new road or trail or to cut across a switchback. Stay on constructed tracks and avoid running over young trees, shrubs, and grasses, damaging or killing them. Don't drive across alpine tundra; this fragile environment can take years to recover.

■ Stay off soft, wet roads and 4WD trails readily torn up by vehicles. Repairing the damage is expensive, and quite often authorities find it easier to close the road rather than repair it.

■ Travel around meadows, steep hillsides, stream banks, and lake shores that are easily scarred by churning wheels.

■ Stay away from wild animals that are rearing young or suffering from a food shortage. Do not camp close to the water sources of domestic or wild animals.

■ Obey gate closures and regulatory signs.

■ Preserve America's heritage by not disturbing old mining camps, ghost towns, or other historical features. Leave historic sites, Native American rock art, ruins, and artifacts in place and untouched.

■ Carry out all your trash, and even that of others.

■ Stay out of designated wilderness areas. They are closed to all vehicles. It is your responsibility to know where the boundaries are.

■ Get permission to cross private land. Leave livestock alone. Respect landowners' rights.

Report violations of these rules to help keep these 4WD trails open and to ensure that others will have the opportunity to visit these backcountry sites. Many groups are actively seeking to close these public lands to vehicles, thereby denying access to those who are unable, or perhaps merely unwilling, to hike long distances. This magnificent countryside is owned by, and should be available to, all Americans.

Special Preparations for Remote Travel

Due to the remoteness of some areas in Utah and the very high summer temperatures, you should take some special precautions to ensure that you don't end up in a life-threatening situation:

■ When planning a trip into the desert, always inform someone as to where you are going, your route, and when you expect to return. Stick to your plan.

■ Carry and drink at least one gallon of water per person per day of your trip. (Plastic gallon jugs are handy and portable.)

■ Be sure your vehicle is in good condition with a sound battery, good hoses, spare tire, spare fan belts, necessary tools, and reserve gasoline and oil. Other spare parts and extra radiator water are also valuable. If traveling in pairs, share the common spares and carry a greater variety.

■ Keep an eye on the sky. Flash floods can occur in a wash any time you see thunderheads—even when it's not raining a drop where you are.

■ If you are caught in a dust storm while driving, get off the road and turn off your lights. Turn on the emergency flashers and back into the wind to reduce windshield pitting by sand particles.

■ Test trails on foot before driving through washes and sandy areas. One minute of walking may save hours of hard work getting your vehicle unstuck.

■ If your vehicle breaks down, stay near

it. Your emergency supplies are there. Your car has many other items useful in an emergency. Raise your hood and trunk lid to denote "help needed." Remember, a vehicle can be seen for miles, but a person on foot is very difficult to spot from a distance.

■ When you're not moving, use available shade or erect shade from tarps, blankets, or seat covers—anything to reduce the direct rays of the sun.

■ Do not sit or lie directly on the ground. It may be 30 degrees hotter than the air.

■ Leave a disabled vehicle only if you are positive of the route and the distance to help. Leave a note for rescuers that gives the time you left and the direction you are taking.

■ If you must walk, rest for at least 10 minutes out of each hour. If you are not normally physically active, rest up to 30 minutes out of each hour. Find shade, sit down, and prop up your feet. Adjust your shoes and socks, but do not remove your shoes—you may not be able to get them back on swollen feet.

■ If you have water, drink it. Do not ration it.

■ If water is limited, keep your mouth closed. Do not talk, eat, smoke, drink alcohol, or take salt.

■ Keep your clothing on despite the heat. It helps to keep your body temperature down and reduces your body's dehydration rate. Cover your head. If you don't have a hat, improvise a head covering.

■ If you are stalled or lost, set signal fires. Set smoky fires in the daytime and bright ones at night. Three fires in a triangle denote "help needed."

■ A roadway is a sign of civilization. If you find a road, stay on it.

■ When hiking in the desert, equip each person, especially children, with a police-type whistle. It makes a distinctive noise with little effort. Three blasts denote "help needed."

■ To avoid poisonous creatures, put your hands or feet only where your eyes can see. One insect to be aware of in Southen

Utah is the Africanized honeybee. Though indistinguishable from its European counterpart, these bees are far more aggressive and can be a threat. They have been known to give chase of up to a mile and even wait for people who have escaped into the water to come up for air. The best thing to do if attacked is to cover your face and head with clothing and run to the nearest enclosed shelter. Keep an eye on your pet if you notice a number of bees in the area, as many have been killed by Africanized honeybees.

■ Avoid unnecessary contact with wildlife. Some mice in Utah carry the deadly hantavirus, a pulmonary syndrome fatal in 60 to 70 percent of human cases. Fortunately the disease is very rare—as of May 2006, only 24 cases had been reported in Utah and 438 nationwide—but caution is still advised. Other rodents may transmit bubonic plague, the same epidemic that killed one-third of Europe's population in the 1300s. Be especially wary near sick animals and keep pets, especially cats, away from wildlife and their fleas. Another creature to watch for is the western black-legged tick, the carrier of Lyme disease. Wearing clothing that covers legs and arms, tucking pants into boots, and using insect repellent are good ways to avoid fleas and ticks.

Obtaining Permits

Backcountry permits, which usually cost a fee, are required for certain activities on public lands in Utah, whether the area is a national park, state park, national monument, Indian reservation, or BLM land.

Restrictions may require a permit for all overnight stays, which can include backpacking and 4WD or bicycle camping. Permits may also be required for day use by vehicles, horses, hikers, or bikes in some areas.

When possible, we include information about fees and permit requirements and where permits may be obtained, but these regulations change constantly. If in doubt, check with the most likely governing agency.

Assessing Your Vehicle's Off-Road Ability

Many issues come into play when evaluating your 4WD vehicle, although most of the 4WDs on the market are suitable for even the roughest trails described in this book. Engine power will be adequate in even the least-powerful modern vehicle. However, some vehicles are less suited to off-highway driving than others, and some of the newest, carlike sport utility vehicles simply are not designed for off-highway touring. The following information should enable you to identify the good, the bad, and the ugly.

Differing 4WD Systems

All 4WD systems have one thing in common: The engine provides power to all four wheels rather than to only two, as is typical in most standard cars. However, there are a number of differences in the way power is applied to the wheels.

The other feature that distinguishes nearly all 4WDs from normal passenger vehicles is that the gearboxes have high and low ratios that effectively double the number of gears. The high range is comparable to the range on a passenger car. The low range provides lower speed and more power, which is useful when towing heavy loads, driving up steep hills, or crawling over rocks. When driving downhill, the 4WD's low range increases engine braking.

Various makes and models of SUVs offer different drive systems, but these differences center on two issues: the way power is applied to the other wheels if one or more wheels slip, and the ability to select between 2WD and 4WD.

Normal driving requires that all four wheels be able to turn at different speeds; this allows the vehicle to turn without scrubbing its tires. In a 2WD vehicle, the front wheels (or rear wheels in a front-wheel-drive vehicle) are not powered by the engine and thus are free to turn individually at any speed. The rear wheels, powered by the engine, are only able to turn at different speeds because of the differential, which applies power to the faster-turning wheel.

This standard method of applying traction has certain weaknesses. First, when power is applied to only one set of wheels, the other set cannot help the vehicle gain traction. Second, when one powered wheel loses traction, it spins, but the other powered wheel doesn't turn. This happens because the differential applies all the engine power to the faster-turning wheel and no power to the other wheels, which still have traction. All 4WD systems are designed to overcome these two weaknesses. However, different 4WDs address this common objective in different ways.

Full-Time 4WD. For a vehicle to remain in 4WD all the time without scrubbing the tires, all the wheels must be able to rotate at different speeds. A full-time 4WD system allows this to happen by using three differentials. One is located between the rear wheels, as in a normal passenger car, to allow the rear wheels to rotate at different speeds. The second is located between the front wheels in exactly the same way. The third differential is located between the front and rear wheels to allow different rotational speeds between the front and rear sets of wheels. In nearly all vehicles with full-time 4WD, the center differential operates only in high range. In low range, it is completely locked. This is not a disadvantage because when using low range the additional traction is normally desired and the deterioration of steering response will be less noticeable due to the vehicle traveling at a slower speed.

Part-Time 4WD. A part-time 4WD system does not have the center differential located between the front and rear wheels. Consequently, the front and rear drive shafts are both driven at the same speed and with the same power at all times when in 4WD.

This system provides improved traction because when one or both of the front or rear wheels slips, the engine continues to provide power to the other set. However, because such a system doesn't allow a difference in speed between the front and rear sets of wheels, the tires scrub when turning, placing additional strain on the whole drive system.

Therefore, such a system can be used only in slippery conditions; otherwise, the ability to steer the vehicle will deteriorate and the tires will quickly wear out.

Some vehicles, such as Jeeps with Selectrac and Mitsubishi Monteros with Active Trac 4WD, offer both full-time and part-time 4WD in high range.

Manual Systems to Switch Between 2WD and 4WD. There are three manual systems for switching between 2WD and 4WD. The most basic requires stopping and getting out of the vehicle to lock the front hubs manually before selecting 4WD. The second requires you to stop, but you change to 4WD by merely throwing a lever inside the vehicle (the hubs lock automatically). The third allows shifting between 2WD and 4WD high range while the vehicle is moving. Any 4WD that does not offer the option of driving in 2WD must have a full-time 4WD system.

AutomatedSwitching Between 2WD and 4WD. Advances in technology are leading to greater automation in the selection of two- or four-wheel drive. When operating in high range, these high-tech systems use sensors to monitor the rotation of each wheel. When any slippage is detected, the vehicle switches the proportion of power from the wheel(s) that is slipping to the wheels that retain grip. The proportion of power supplied to each wheel is therefore infinitely variable as opposed to the original systems where the vehicle was either in two-wheel drive or four-wheel drive.

In recent years, this process has been spurred on by many of the manufacturers of luxury vehicles entering the SUV market—Mercedes, BMW, Cadillac, Lincoln, and Lexus have joined Range Rover in this segment.

Manufacturers of these higher-priced vehicles have led the way in introducing sophisticated computer-controlled 4WD systems. Although each of the manufacturers has its own approach to this issue, all the systems automatically vary the allocation of power between the wheels within milliseconds of the sensors' detecting wheel slippage.

Limiting Wheel Slippage

All 4WDs employ various systems to limit wheel slippage and transfer power to the wheels that still have traction. These systems may completely lock the differentials or they may allow limited slippage before transferring power back to the wheels that retain traction.

Lockers completely eliminate the operation of one or more differentials. A locker on the center differential switches between full-time and part-time 4WD. Lockers on the front or rear differentials ensure that power remains equally applied to each set of wheels regardless of whether both have traction. Lockers may be controlled manually, by a switch or a lever in the vehicle, or they may be automatic.

The Toyota Land Cruiser offers the option of having manual lockers on all three differentials, while other brands such as the Mitsubishi Montero offer manual lockers on the center and rear differential. Manual lockers are the most controllable and effective devices for ensuring that power is provided to the wheels with traction. However, because they allow absolutely no slippage, they must be used only on slippery surfaces.

An alternative method for getting power to the wheels that have traction is to allow limited wheel slippage. Systems that work this way may be called limited-slip differentials, posi-traction systems, or in the center differential, viscous couplings. The advantage of these systems is that the limited difference they allow in rotational speed between wheels enables such systems to be used when driving on a dry surface. All full-time 4WD systems allow limited slippage in the center differential.

For off-highway use, a manually locking differential is the best of the above systems, but it is the most expensive. Limited-slip differentials are the cheapest but also the least satisfactory, as they require one wheel to be slipping at 2 to 3 mph before power is transferred to the other wheel. For the center differential, the best system combines a locking differential and, to enable full-time use, a viscous coupling.

Tires

The tires that came with your 4WD vehicle may be satisfactory, but many 4WDs are fitted with passenger-car tires. These are unlikely to be the best choice because they are less rugged and more likely to puncture on rocky trails. They are particularly prone to sidewall damage as well. Passenger vehicle tires also have a less aggressive tread pattern than specialized 4WD tires, and provide less traction in mud.

For information on purchasing tires better suited to off-highway conditions, see Special 4WD Equipment, page 20.

Clearance

Road clearances vary considerably among different 4WD vehicles—from less than 7 inches to more than 10 inches. Special vehicles may have far greater clearance. For instance, the Hummer has a 16-inch ground clearance. High ground clearance is particularly advantageous on the rockier or more rutted 4WD trails in this book.

When evaluating the ground clearance of your vehicle, you need to take into account the clearance of the bodywork between the wheels on each side of the vehicle. This is particularly relevant for crawling over larger rocks. Vehicles with sidesteps have significantly lower clearance than those without.

Another factor affecting clearance is the approach and departure angles of your vehicle—that is, the maximum angle the ground can slope without the front of the vehicle hitting the ridge on approach or the rear of the vehicle hitting on departure. Mounting a winch or tow hitch to your vehicle is likely to reduce your angle of approach or departure.

If you do a lot of driving on rocky trails, you will inevitably hit the bottom of the vehicle sooner or later. When this happens, you will be far less likely to damage vulnerable areas such as the oil pan and gas tank if your vehicle is fitted with skid plates. Most manufacturers offer skid plates as an option. They are worth every penny.

Maneuverability

When you tackle tight switchbacks, you will quickly appreciate that maneuverability is an important criterion when assessing 4WD vehicles. Where a full-size vehicle may be forced to go back and forth a number of times to get around a sharp turn, a small 4WD might go straight around. This is not only easier, it's safer.

If you have a full-size vehicle, all is not lost. We have traveled many of the trails in this book in a Suburban. That is not to say that some of these trails wouldn't have been easier to negotiate in a smaller vehicle! We have noted in the route descriptions if a trail is not suitable for larger vehicles.

In Summary

Using the criteria above, you can evaluate how well your 4WD will handle off-road touring, and if you haven't yet purchased your vehicle, you can use these criteria to help select one. Choosing the best 4WD system is, at least partly, subjective. It is also a matter of your budget. However, for the type of off-highway driving covered in this book, we make the following recommendations:

■ Select a 4WD system that offers low range and, at a minimum, has some form of limited slip differential on the rear axle.

■ Use light truck, all-terrain tires as the standard tires on your vehicle. For sand and slickrock, these will be the ideal choice. If conditions are likely to be muddy, or if traction will be improved by a tread pattern that will give more bite, consider an additional set of mud tires.

■ For maximum clearance, select a vehicle with 16-inch wheels or at least choose the tallest tires that your vehicle can accommodate. Note that if you install tires with a diameter greater than standard, the odometer will under calculate the distance you have traveled. Your engine braking and gear ratios will also be affected.

■ If you are going to try the rockier 4WD trails, don't install a sidestep or low-hanging front bar. If you have the option, have under-body skid plates mounted.

■ Remember that many of the obstacles

you encounter on backcountry trails are more difficult to navigate in a full-size vehicle than in a compact 4WD.

Four-Wheel Driving Techniques

Safe four-wheel driving requires that you observe certain golden rules:

- Size up the situation in advance.
- Be careful and take your time.
- Maintain smooth, steady power and momentum.
- Engage 4WD and low-range gears before you get into a tight situation.
- Steer toward high spots, trying to put the wheel over large rocks.
- Straddle ruts.
- Use gears and not just the brakes to hold the vehicle when driving downhill. On very steep slopes, chock the wheels if you park your vehicle.
- Watch for logging and mining trucks and smaller recreational vehicles, such as all-terrain vehicles (ATVs).
- Wear your seat belt and secure all luggage, especially heavy items such as tool boxes or coolers. Heavy items should be secured by ratchet tie-down straps rather than elastic-type straps, which are not strong enough to hold heavy items if the vehicle rolls.

Utah's 4WD trails have a number of common obstacles, and the following provides an introduction to the techniques required to surmount them.

Rocks. Tire selection is important in negotiating rocks. Select a multiple-ply, tough sidewall, light-truck tire with a large-lug tread.

As you approach a rocky stretch, get into 4WD low range to give yourself maximum slow-speed control. Speed is rarely necessary, since traction on a rocky surface is usually good. Plan ahead and select the line you wish to take. If a rock appears to be larger than the clearance of your vehicle, don't try to straddle it. Check to see that it is not higher than the frame of your vehicle once you get a wheel over it. Put a wheel up on the rock and slowly climb it, then gently drop over the other

side using the brake to ensure a smooth landing. Bouncing the car over rocks increases the likelihood of damage, because the body's clearance is reduced by the suspension compressing. Running boards also significantly reduce your clearance in this respect. It is often helpful to use a "spotter" outside the vehicle to assist you with the best wheel placement.

Steep Uphill Grades. Consider walking the trail to ensure that the steep hill before you is passable, especially if it is clear that backtracking is going to be a problem.

Select 4WD low range to ensure that you have adequate power to pull up the hill. If the wheels begin to lose traction, turn the steering wheel gently from side to side to give the wheels a chance to regain traction.

If you lose momentum, but the car is not in danger of sliding, use the foot brake, switch off the ignition, leave the vehicle in gear (if manual transmission) or park (if automatic), engage the parking brake, and get out to examine the situation. See if you can remove any obstacles, and figure out the line you need to take. Reversing a couple of yards and starting again may allow you to get better traction and momentum.

If halfway up, you decide a stretch of road is impassably steep, back down the trail. Trying to turn the vehicle around on a steep hill is extremely dangerous; you will very likely cause it to roll over.

Steep Downhill Grades. Again, consider walking the trail to ensure that a steep downhill is passable, especially if it is clear that backtracking uphill is going to be a problem.

Select 4WD low range and use first gear to maximize braking assistance from the engine. If the surface is loose and you are losing traction, change up to second or third gear. Do not use the brakes if you can avoid it, but don't let the vehicle's speed get out of control. Feather (lightly pump) the brakes if you slip while braking. For vehicles fitted with an antilock breaking system, apply even pressure if you start to slip; the ABS helps keep vehicles on line.

Travel very slowly over rock ledges or ruts. Attempt to tackle these diagonally, letting one wheel down at a time.

If the back of the vehicle begins to slide

around, gently apply the throttle and correct the steering. If the rear of the vehicle starts to slide sideways, do not apply the brakes.

Sand. As with most off-highway situations, your tires are the key to your ability to cross sand. It is difficult to tell how well a particular tire will handle in sand just by looking at it, so be guided by the manufacturer and your dealer.

The key to driving in soft sand is floatation, which is achieved by a combination of low tire pressure and momentum. Before crossing a stretch of sand, reduce your tire pressure to between 15 and 20 pounds. If necessary, you can safely go to as low as 12 pounds. As you cross, maintain momentum so that your vehicle rides on the top of the soft sand without digging in or stalling. This may require plenty of engine power. Avoid using the brakes if possible; removing your foot from the accelerator alone is normally enough to slow or stop. Using the brakes digs the vehicle deep in the sand.

Pump the tires back up as soon as you are out of the sand to avoid damaging the tires and the rims. Pumping the tires back up requires a high-quality air compressor. Even then, it is a slow process.

In the backcountry of Utah, sandy conditions are commonplace. You will therefore find a good compressor most useful.

Slickrock. When you encounter slickrock, first assess the correct direction of the trail. It is easy to lose sight of the trail on slickrock, because there are seldom any developed edges. Often the way is marked with small rock cairns, which are simply rocks stacked high enough to make a landmark.

All-terrain tires with tighter tread are more suited to slickrock than the more open, luggier type tires. As with rocks, a multiple-ply sidewall is important. In dry conditions, slickrock offers pavement-type grip. In rain or snow, you will soon learn how it got its name. Even the best tires may not get an adequate grip. Walk steep sections first; if you are slipping on foot, chances are your vehicle will slip, too.

Slickrock is characterized by ledges and long sections of "pavement." Follow the guidelines for travel over rocks. Refrain from speeding over flat-looking sections, because you may hit an unexpected crevice or water pocket, and vehicles bend easier than slickrock! Turns and ledges can be tight, and vehicles with smaller overhangs and better maneuverability are at a distinct advantage—hence the popularity of the compacts in the slickrock mecca of Moab, Utah.

On the steepest sections, engage low range and pick a straight line up or down the slope. Do not attempt to traverse a steep slope sideways.

Mud. Muddy trails are easily damaged, so they should be avoided if possible. But if you must traverse a section of mud, your success will depend heavily on whether you have open-lugged mud tires or chains. Thick mud fills the tighter tread on normal tires, leaving the tire with no more grip than if it were bald. If the muddy stretch is only a few yards long, the momentum of your vehicle may allow you to get through regardless.

If the muddy track is very steep, uphill or downhill, or off camber, do not attempt it. Your vehicle is likely to skid in such conditions, and you may roll or slip off the edge of the road. Also, check to see that the mud has a reasonably firm base. Tackling deep mud is definitely not recommended unless you have a vehicle-mounted winch—and even then—be cautious, because the winch may not get you out. Finally, check to see that no ruts are too deep for the ground clearance of your vehicle.

When you decide you can get through and have selected the best route, use the following techniques to cross through the mud:

- Avoid making detours off existing tracks to minimize environmental damage.
- Select 4WD low range and a suitable gear; momentum is the key to success, so use a high enough gear to build up sufficient speed.
- Avoid accelerating heavily, so as to minimize wheel spinning and to provide maximum traction.
- Follow existing wheel ruts, unless they are too deep for the clearance of your vehicle.
- To correct slides, turn the steering wheel in the direction that the rear wheels are skidding, but don't be too aggressive or you'll overcorrect and lose control again.

■ If the vehicle comes to a stop, don't continue to accelerate, as you will only spin your wheels and dig yourself into a rut. Try backing out and having another go.

■ Be prepared to turn back before reaching the point of no return.

Stream Crossings. By crossing a stream that is too deep, drivers risk far more than water flowing in and ruining the interior of their vehicles. Water sucked into the engine's air intake will seriously damage the engine. Likewise, water that seeps into the air vent on the transmission or differential will mix with the lubricant and may lead to serious problems in due course.

Even worse, if the water is deep or fast flowing, it could easily carry your vehicle downstream, endangering the lives of everyone in the vehicle.

Some 4WD manuals tell you what fording depth the vehicle can negotiate safely. If your vehicle's owner's manual does not include this information, your local dealer may be able to assist. If you don't know, then avoid crossing through water that is more than a foot or so deep.

The first rule for crossing a stream is to know what you are getting into. You need to ascertain how deep the water is, whether there are any large rocks or holes, if the bottom is solid enough to avoid bogging down the vehicle, and whether the entry and exit points are negotiable. This may take some time and involve getting wet, but you take a great risk by crossing a stream without first properly assessing the situation.

The secret to water crossings is to keep moving, but not too fast. If you go too fast, you may drown the electrics, causing the vehicle to stall midstream. In shallow water (where the surface of the water is below the bumper), your primary concern is to safely negotiate the bottom of the stream, to avoid any rock damage, and to maintain momentum if there is a danger of getting stuck or of slipping on the exit.

In deeper water (between 18 and 30 inches), the objective is to create a small bow wave in front of the moving vehicle. This requires a speed that is approximately walking pace. The bow wave reduces the depth of the water around the engine compartment. If the water's surface reaches your tailpipe, select a gear that will maintain moderate engine revs to avoid water backing up into the exhaust; and do not change gears midstream.

Crossing water deeper than 25 to 30 inches requires more extensive preparation of the vehicle and should be attempted only by experienced drivers.

Snow. The trails in this book that receive heavy snowfall are closed in winter. Therefore, the snow conditions that you are most likely to encounter are an occasional snowdrift that has not yet melted or fresh snow from an unexpected storm. Getting through such conditions depends on the depth of the snow, its consistency, the stability of the underlying surface, and your vehicle.

If the snow is no deeper than about 9 inches and there is solid ground beneath it, crossing the snow should not be a problem. In deeper snow that seems solid enough to support your vehicle, be extremely cautious: If you break through a drift, you are likely to be stuck, and if conditions are bad, you may have a long wait.

The tires you use for off-highway driving, with a wide tread pattern, are probably suitable for these snow conditions. Nonetheless, it is wise to carry chains (preferably for all four wheels), and if you have a vehicle-mounted winch, even better.

Vehicle Recovery Methods

If you do enough four-wheel driving, you are sure to get stuck sooner or later. The following techniques will help you get back on the go. The most suitable method will depend on the equipment available and the situation you are in—whether you are stuck in sand, mud, or snow, or are high-centered or unable to negotiate a hill.

Towing. Use a nylon yank strap of the type discussed in the Special 4WD Equipment section below. This type of strap will stretch 15 to 25 percent, and the elasticity will assist in extracting the vehicle.

Attach the strap only to a frame-mounted tow point. Ensure that the driver of the stuck vehicle is ready, take up all but about 6 feet of slack, then move the towing vehicle away at a moderate speed (in most circumstances this means using 4WD low range in second gear) so that the elasticity of the strap is employed in the way it is meant to be. Don't take off like a bat out of hell or you risk breaking the strap or damaging a vehicle.

Never join two yank straps together with a shackle. If one strap breaks, the shackle will become a lethal missile aimed at one of the vehicles (and anyone inside). For the same reason, never attach a yank strap to the tow ball on either vehicle.

Jacking. Jacking the vehicle allows you to pack rocks, dirt, or logs under the wheel or to use your shovel to remove an obstacle. However, the standard vehicle jack is unlikely to be of as much assistance as a high-lift jack. We highly recommend purchasing a good high-lift jack as a basic accessory if you decide that you are going to do a lot of serious, off-highway four-wheel driving. Remember a high-lift jack is of limited use if your vehicle does not have an appropriate jacking point. Some brush bars have two built-in forward jacking points.

Tire Chains. Tire chains can be of assistance in both mud and snow. Cable-type chains provide much less grip than link-type chains. There are also dedicated mud chains with larger, heavier links than on normal snow chains. It is best to have chains fitted to all four wheels.

Once you are bogged down is not the best time to try to fit the chains; if at all possible, try to predict their need and have them on the tires before trouble arises. An easy way to affix chains is to place two small cubes of wood under the center of the stretched-out chain. When you drive your tires up on the blocks of wood, it is easier to stretch the chains over the tires because the pressure is off of them.

Winching. Most recreational four-wheel drivers do not have a winch. But if you get serious about four-wheel driving, this is probably the first major accessory you should consider buying.

Under normal circumstances, a winch would be warranted only for the more difficult 4WD trails in this book. Having a winch is certainly comforting when you see a difficult section of road ahead and have to decide whether to risk it or turn back. Also, major obstacles can appear when you least expect them, even on trails that are otherwise easy.

Owning a winch is not a panacea to all your recovery problems. Winching depends on the availability of a good anchor point, and electric winches may not work if they are submerged in a stream. Despite these constraints, no accessory is more useful than a high-quality, powerful winch when you get into a difficult situation.

If you acquire a winch, learn to use it properly; take the time to study your owner's manual. Incorrect operation can be extremely dangerous and may cause damage to the winch or to your anchor points, which are usually trees.

Navigation by the Global Positioning System (GPS)

Although this book is designed so that each trail can be navigated simply by following the detailed directions provided, nothing makes navigation easier than a GPS receiver.

The global positioning system (GPS) consists of a network of 24 satellites, nearly 13,000 miles in space, in six different orbital paths. The satellites are constantly moving at about 8,500 miles per hour and make two complete orbits around the earth every 24 hours.

Each satellite is constantly transmitting data, including its identification number, its operational health, and the date and time. It also transmits its location and the location of every other satellite in the network.

By comparing the time the signal was transmitted to the time it is received, a GPS receiver calculates how far away each satellite is. With a sufficient number of signals, the receiver can then triangulate its location. With three or more satellites, the receiver can determine latitude and longitude coordinates. With four or more, it can calculate elevation. By constantly making these calculations, it can determine speed and direction. To facilitate these calculations, the time data broadcast by GPS is accurate to within 40 billionths of a second.

The U.S. military uses the system to provide positions accurate to within half an inch. When the system was first established, civilian receivers were deliberately fed slightly erroneous information in order to effectively deny military applications to hostile countries or terrorists—a practice called selective availability (SA). However on May 1, 2000, in response to the growing importance of the system for civilian applications, the U.S. government stopped intentionally downgrading GPS data. The military gave its support to this change once new technology made it possible to selectively degrade the system within any defined geographical area on demand. This new feature of the system has made it safe to have higher-quality signals available for civilian use. Now, instead of the civilian-use signal having a margin of error between 20 and 70 yards, it is only about one-tenth of that.

A GPS receiver offers the four-wheeler numerous benefits:

■ You can track to any point for which you know the longitude and latitude coordinates with no chance of heading in the wrong direction or getting lost. Most receivers provide an extremely easy-to-understand graphic display to keep you on track.

■ It works in all weather conditions.

■ It automatically records your route for easy backtracking.

■ You can record and name any location, so that you can relocate it with ease. This may include your campsite, a fishing spot, or even a silver mine you discover!

■ It displays your position, enabling you to pinpoint your location on a map.

■ By interfacing the GPS receiver directly to a portable computer, you can monitor and record your location as you travel (using the appropriate map software) or print the route you took.

However, remember that GPS units can fail, batteries can go flat, and tree cover and tight canyons can block the signals. Never rely entirely on GPS for navigation. Always carry a compass for backup.

Special 4WD Equipment

Tires

When 4WD touring, you will likely encounter a variety of terrain: rocks, mud, talus, slickrock, sand, gravel, dirt, and bitumen. The immense array of tires on the market includes many specifically targeted at one or another of these types of terrain, as well as tires designed to adequately handle a range of terrain.

Every four-wheel driver seems to have a preference when it comes to tire selection, but most people undertaking the 4WD trails in this book will need tires that can handle all of the above types of terrain adequately.

The first requirement is to select rugged, light-truck tires rather than passenger-vehicle tires. Check the size data on the sidewall: it should have "LT" rather than "P" before the number. Among light-truck tires, you must choose between tires that are designated "all-terrain" and more-aggressive, wider-tread mud tires. Either type will be adequate, especially on rocks, gravel, talus, or dirt. Although mud tires have an advantage in muddy conditions and soft snow, all-terrain tires perform better on slickrock, in sand, and particularly on ice and paved roads.

When selecting tires, remember that they affect not just traction but also cornering ability, braking distances, fuel consumption, and noise levels. It pays to get good advice before making your decision.

Global Positioning System Receivers

GPS receivers have come down in price considerably in the past few years and are rapidly becoming indispensable navigational tools. Many higher-priced cars now offer integrated GPS receivers, and within the next few years, receivers will become available on most models.

Battery-powered, hand-held units that meet the needs of off-highway driving currently range from less than $100 to a little over $300 and continue to come down in price. Some high-end units feature maps that are incorporated in the display, either from a built-in database or from interchangeable memory cards. Currently, only a few of these maps include 4WD trails.

If you are considering purchasing a GPS unit, keep the following in mind:

■ Price. The very cheapest units are likely outdated and very limited in their display features. Expect to pay from $125 to $300.

■ The display. Compare the graphic display of one unit with another. Some are much easier to decipher or offer more alternative displays.

■ The controls. GPS receivers have many functions, and they need to have good, simple controls.

■ Vehicle mounting. To be useful, the unit needs to be placed where it can be read easily by both the driver and the navigator. Check that the unit can be conveniently located in your vehicle. Different units have different shapes and different mounting systems.

■ Map data. More and more units have map data built in. Some have the ability to download maps from a computer. Such maps are normally sold on a CD-ROM. GPS units have a finite storage capacity and having the ability to download maps covering a narrower geographical region means that the amount of data relating to that specific region can be greater.

■ The number of routes and the number of sites (or "waypoints") per route that can be stored in memory. For off-highway use, it is important to be able to store plenty of waypoints so that you do not have to load coordinates into the machine as frequently. Having plenty of memory also ensures that you can automatically store your present location without fear that the memory is full.

■ Waypoint storage. The better units store up to 500 waypoints and 20 reversible routes of up to 30 waypoints each. Also consider the number of characters a GPS receiver allows you to use to name waypoints. When you try to recall a waypoint, you may have difficulty recognizing names restricted to only a few characters.

■ Automatic route storing. Most units automatically store your route as you go along and enable you to display it in reverse to make backtracking easy.

After you have selected a unit, a number of optional extras are also worth considering:

■ A cigarette lighter electrical adapter. Despite GPS units becoming more power efficient, protracted in-vehicle use still makes this accessory a necessity.

■ A vehicle-mounted antenna, which will improve reception under difficult conditions. (The GPS unit can only "see" through the windows of your vehicle; it cannot monitor satellites through a metal roof.) Having a vehicle-mounted antenna also means that you do not have to consider reception when locating the receiver in your vehicle.

■ An in-car mounting system. If you are going to do a lot of touring using the GPS, consider attaching a bracket on the dash rather than relying on a Velcro mount.

■ A computer-link cable and digital maps. Data from your GPS receiver can be downloaded to your PC; maps and waypoints can be downloaded from your PC; or if you have a laptop computer, you can monitor your route as you go along, using one of a number of inexpensive map software products on the market.

Yank Straps

Yank straps are industrial-strength versions of the flimsy tow straps carried by the local discount store. They are 20 to 30 feet long and 2 to 3 inches wide, made of heavy nylon, rated to at least 20,000 pounds, and have looped ends.

Do not use tow straps with metal hooks in the ends (the hooks can become missiles in the event the strap breaks free). Likewise, never join two yank straps together using a shackle.

CB Radios

If you are stuck, injured, or just want to know the conditions up ahead, a citizen's band (CB) radio can be invaluable. CB radios are relatively inexpensive and do not require an Federal Communications Comission license. Their range is limited, especially in very hilly country, as their transmission patterns basically follow lines of sight. Range can be improved using single sideband (SSB) transmission, an option on more expensive units. Range is even better on vehicle-mounted units that have been professionally fitted to ensure that the antenna and cabling are matched appropriately.

Winches

There are three main options when it comes to winches: manual winches, removable electric winches, and vehicle-mounted electric winches.

If you have a full-size 4WD vehicle—which can weigh in excess of 7,000 pounds when loaded—a manual winch is of limited use without a lot of effort and considerable time. However, a manual winch is a very handy and inexpensive accessory if you have a small 4WD. Typically, manual winches are rated to pull about 5,500 pounds.

An electric winch can be mounted to your vehicle's trailer hitch to enable it to be removed, relocated to the front of your vehicle (if you have a hitch installed), or moved to another vehicle. Although this is a very useful feature, a winch is heavy, so relocating one can be a two-person job. Consider that 5,000-pound-rated winches weigh only about 55 pounds, while 12,000-pound-rated models weigh around 140 pounds. Therefore, the larger models are best permanently front-mounted. Unfortunately, this position limits their ability to winch the vehicle backward.

When choosing among electric winches, be aware that they are rated for their maximum capacity on the first wind of the cable around the drum. As layers of cable wind onto the drum, they increase its diameter and thus decrease the maximum load the winch can handle. This decrease is significant: A winch rated to pull 8,000 pounds on a bare drum may only handle 6,500 pounds on the second layer, 5,750 pounds on the third layer, and 5,000 pounds on the fourth. Electric winches also draw a high level of current and may necessitate upgrading the battery in your 4WD or adding a second battery.

There is a wide range of mounting options—from a simple, body-mounted frame that holds the winch to heavy-duty winch bars that replace the original bumper and incorporate brush bars and mounts for auxiliary lights.

If you buy a winch, either electric or manual, you will also need quite a range of addi-

tional equipment so that you can operate it correctly:

- at least one choker chain with hooks on each end,
- winch extension straps or cables,
- shackles,
- a receiver shackle,
- a snatch block,
- a tree protector,
- gloves.

Grill/Brush Bars and Winch Bars

Brush bars protect the front of the vehicle from scratches and minor bumps; they also provide a solid mount for auxiliary lights and often high-lift jacking points. The level of protection they provide depends on how solid they are and whether they are securely mounted onto the frame of the vehicle. Lighter models attach in front of the standard bumper, but the more substantial units replace the bumper. Prices range from about $150 to $450.

Winch bars replace the bumper and usually integrate a solid brush bar with a heavy-duty winch mount. Some have the brush bar as an optional extra to the winch bar component. Manufacturers such as Warn, ARB, and TJM offer a wide range of integrated winch bars. These are significantly more expensive, starting at about $650.

Remember that installing heavy equipment on the front of the vehicle may necessitate increasing the front suspension rating to cope with the additional weight.

Portable Air Compressors

Most portable air compressors on the market are flimsy models that plug into the cigarette lighter and are sold at the local discount store. These are of very limited use for four-wheel driving. They are very slow to inflate the large tires of a 4WD vehicle; for instance, to reinflate from 15 to 35 pounds typically takes about 10 minutes for each tire. They are also unlikely to be rated for continuous use, which means that they will overheat and cut off before completing the job. If you're lucky, they will start up again when they have cooled down, but this means that you are unlikely to reinflate your tires in less than an hour.

The easiest way to identify a useful air compressor is by the price—good ones cost $200 or more. Many of the quality units feature a Thomas-brand pump and are built to last. Another good unit is sold by ARB. All these pumps draw between 15 and 20 amps and thus should not be plugged into the cigarette lighter socket but attached to the vehicle's battery with clips. The ARB unit can be permanently mounted under the hood. Quick-Air makes a range of units including a 10-amp compressor that can be plugged into the cigarette lighter socket and performs well.

Auxiliary Driving Lights

There is a vast array of auxiliary lights on the market today and selecting the best lights for your purpose can be a confusing process.

Auxiliary lights greatly improve visibility in adverse weather conditions. Driving lights provide a strong, moderately wide beam to supplement headlamp high beams, giving improved lighting in the distance and to the sides of the main beam. Fog lamps throw a wide-dispersion, flat beam; and spots provide a high-power, narrow beam to improve lighting range directly in front of the vehicle. Rear-mounted auxiliary lights provide greatly improved visibility for backing up.

For off-highway use, you will need quality lights with strong mounting brackets. Some high-powered off-highway lights are not approved by the Department of Transportation for use on public roads.

Roof Racks

Roof racks can be excellent for storing gear, as well as providing easy access for certain weatherproof items. However, they raise the center of gravity on the vehicle, which can substantially alter the rollover angle. A roof rack is best used for lightweight objects that are well-strapped down. Heavy recovery gear and other bulky items should be packed low in the vehicle's interior to lower the center of gravity and stabilize the vehicle.

A roof rack should allow for safe and secure packing of items and be sturdy enough

Packing Checklist

Before embarking on any 4WD adventure, whether a lazy Sunday drive on an easy trail or a challenging climb over rugged terrain, be prepared. The following checklist will help you gather the items you need.

Essential

- ❑ Rain gear
- ❑ Small shovel or multipurpose ax, pick, shovel, and sledgehammer
- ❑ Heavy-duty yank strap
- ❑ Spare tire that matches the other tires on the vehicle
- ❑ Working jack and base plate for soft ground
- ❑ Maps
- ❑ Emergency medical kit, including sun protection and insect repellent
- ❑ Bottled water
- ❑ Blankets or space blankets
- ❑ Parka, gloves, and boots
- ❑ Spare vehicle key
- ❑ Jumper leads
- ❑ Heavy-duty flashlight
- ❑ Multipurpose tool, such as a Leatherman
- ❑ Emergency food—high-energy bars or similar

Worth Considering

- ❑ Global Positioning System (GPS) receiver
- ❑ Cell phone
- ❑ A set of light-truck, off-highway tires and matching spare
- ❑ High-lift jack
- ❑ Additional tool kit
- ❑ CB radio
- ❑ Portable air compressor
- ❑ Tire gauge
- ❑ Tire-sealing kit
- ❑ Tire chains
- ❑ Handsaw and ax
- ❑ Binoculars
- ❑ Firearms
- ❑ Whistle
- ❑ Flares
- ❑ Vehicle fire extinguisher
- ❑ Gasoline, engine oil, and other vehicle fluids
- ❑ Portable hand winch
- ❑ Electric cooler

If Your Credit Cards Aren't Maxed Out

- ❑ Electric, vehicle-mounted winch and associated recovery straps, shackles, and snatch blocks
- ❑ Auxiliary lights
- ❑ Locking differential(s)

Trails in the Southwest Region

- **SW01** Indian Spring Trail *(page 28)*
- **SW02** Scarecrow Peak trail *(page 31)*
- **SW03** Hell Hole Pass Trail *(page 35)*
- **SW04** TV Towers Jeep Trail *(page 37)*
- **SW05** Joshua Tree Loop *(page 39)*
- **SW06** The Divide Trail *(page 43)*
- **SW07** Hurricane Cliffs Trail *(page 46)*
- **SW08** Smithsonian Butte Trail *(page 49)*
- **SW09** Grafton Mesa Trail *(page 53)*
- **SW10** Elephant Butte Trail *(page 54)*
- **SW11** The Barracks Trail *(page 58)*
- **SW12** Moquith Mountains Trail *(page 60)*
- **SW13** Hog Canyon Trail *(page 62)*
- **SW14** John R Flat Trail *(page 65)*
- **SW15** Skutumpah Road *(page 70)*
- **SW16** Cottonwood Canyon Road *(page 78)*
- **SW17** Paria River Valley Trail *(page 84)*
- **SW33** Griffin Road *(page 143)*
- **SW34** Escalante Summit Trail *(page 147)*
- **SW35** Corn Creek Road *(page 150)*
- **SW36** Powell Point Trail *(page 152)*
- **SW37** Barney Top Trail *(page 155)*

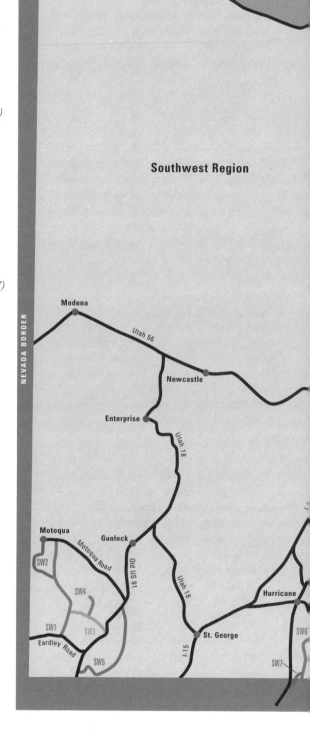

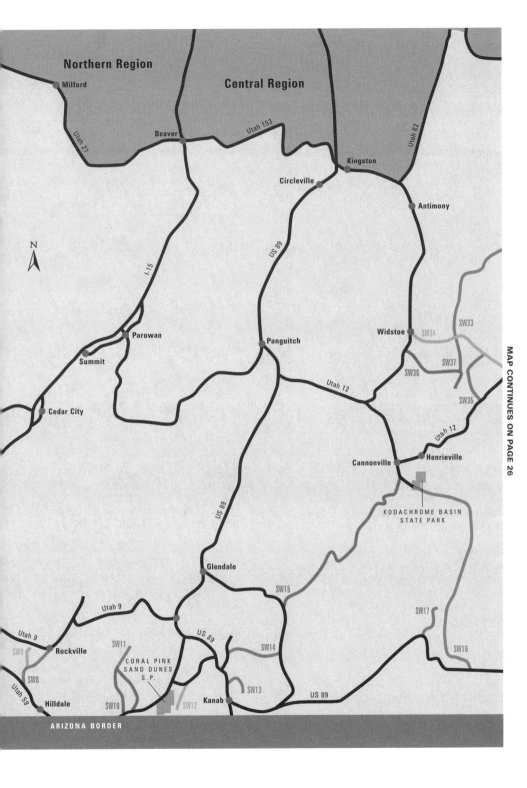

- SW15 Skutumpah Road *(page 70)*
- SW16 Cottonwood Canyon Road *(page 78)*
- SW17 Paria River Valley Trail *(page 84)*
- SW18 Smoky Mountain Road *(page 86)*
- SW19 Alstrom Point Trail *(page 94)*
- SW20 Nipple Creek and Tibbet Canyon Trail *(page 96)*
- SW21 Smoky Hollow Trail *(page 101)*
- SW22 Hole-in-the-Rock Trail *(page 104)*
- SW23 Hells Backbone Trail *(page 110)*
- SW24 McGath Lake Trail *(page 115)*
- SW25 Road Draw Road *(page 118)*
- SW26 Posey Lake Road *(page 120)*
- SW27 Boulder Tops Road *(page 125)*
- SW28 Bowns Point Trail *(page 129)*
- SW29 Spectacle Lake Trail *(page 132)*
- SW30 Purple and Blue Lakes Trail *(page 135)*
- SW31 Dark Valley Trail *(page 137)*
- SW32 Chokecherry Point Trail *(page 140)*
- SW33 Griffin Road *(page 143)*
- SW34 Escalante Summit Trail *(page 147)*
- SW35 Corn Creek Road *(page 150)*
- SW36 Powell Point Trail *(page 152)*
- SW37 Barney Top Trail *(page 155)*
- SW38 Tantalus Creek Trail *(page 158)*
- SW39 Notom Road *(page 162)*
- SW40 Burr Trail *(page 167)*
- SW41 Upper Muley Twist Trail *(page 175)*
- SW42 Wolverine Loop *(page 176)*
- SW43 Clay Point Road *(page 182)*
- SW44 Shootering Canyon Trail *(page 185)*
- SW45 Stanton Pass Trail *(page 189)*
- SW46 Pennell Creek Bench Trail *(page 192)*
- SW47 Bull Creek Pass Trail *(page 194)*
- SW48 Copper Ridge Trail *(page 200)*
- SW49 Town Wash & Bull Mountain Trail *(page 204)*

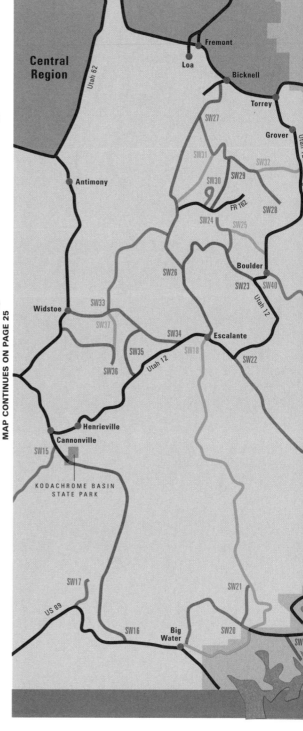

MAP CONTINUES ON PAGE 25

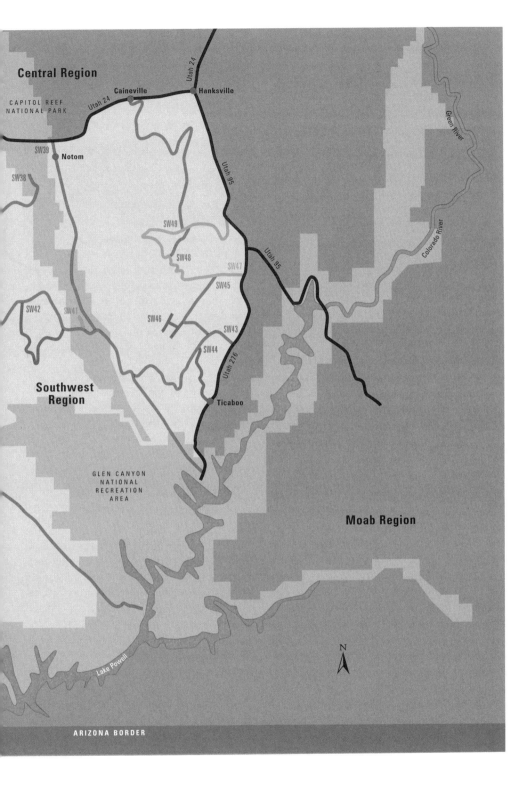

Central Region

CAPITOL REEF
NATIONAL PARK

Caineville

Hanksville

Utah 24

Utah 24

SW39

Notom

SW38

Utah 95

SW49

SW48

SW47

Utah 95

SW45

SW42

SW41

SW46

SW43

SW44

Utah 276

Southwest
Region

Ticaboo

GLEN CANYON
NATIONAL
RECREATION
AREA

Moab Region

Green River

Colorado River

Lake Powell

ARIZONA BORDER

N

Indian Spring Trail

STARTING POINT Eardley Road
FINISHING POINT Motoqua Road, 14.4 miles west of Old US 91
TOTAL MILEAGE 17.4 miles
UNPAVED MILEAGE 17.4 miles
DRIVING TIME 1 hour
ELEVATION RANGE 3,200–4,500 feet
USUALLY OPEN Year-round
DIFFICULTY RATING 2
SCENIC RATING 8
REMOTENESS RATING +1

Special Attractions
- Dense Joshua tree forest.
- Far-ranging views across Beaver Dam Wash into Nevada.
- Remote, lightly traveled trail along the western edge of the Beaver Dam Mountains.

Description
If you want to see Joshua trees and plenty of them in a rugged desert setting, then this is your trail! The meandering trail skirts the western edge of the Beaver Dam Mountains, running across the alluvial fan that slopes down to the Beaver Dam Wash.

To get to the start of the trail, turn west off Old US 91 down Eardley Road. The junction is marked by a sign for the High

A large patch of Joshua trees along Indian Spring Trail

Signpost and water tank at Indian Spring

Desert Game Ranch, but has no directional sign. It leaves immediately south of Castle Cliff, 4.5 miles north of the Arizona state line. The start of Indian Spring Trail is 4.4 miles from this junction.

The trail undulates to the north, crossing many deep washes. Many trails lead off, mainly to springs used by ranchers, but a couple of longer ones such as Horse Canyon Trail lead partway up the eroded canyons in the Beaver Dam Mountains.

After 5.1 miles, Southwest #3: Hell Hole Pass Trail leads east over Hell Hole Pass to rejoin Old US 91. The Indian Spring tank, which gives this trail its name, is at the junction.

The Joshua trees become more prolific the farther north you go; when you reach the turnoff for Southwest #2: Scarecrow Peak Trail, they are a dense forest of mature trees, interspersed with golden chollas. Joshua trees are a member of the lily family and are related to yuccas, which they somewhat resemble. Their upstretched arms reminded the Mormon pioneers, who named them, of the biblical Joshua, whose arms were upstretched to heaven.

Many animals and birds—including coyotes, mule deer, prairie falcons, golden eagles, rattlesnakes, and the endangered desert tortoise—make their home along the Beaver Dam Mountains, and if you are lucky, you will see some of them along this route.

The trail finishes on the graded dirt Motoqua Road, which is at the lower end of the Burnt Canyon ATV trail system, a popular network of trails suitable for ATVs, motorbikes, and 4WDs.

Current Road Information

BLM St. George Field Office
345 East Riverside Drive
St. George, UT 84790
(435) 688-3200

Map References

BLM   St. George
USFS   Dixie National Forest: Pine Valley
        Ranger District (incomplete)
USGS   1:24,000   Castle Cliff, West Mt.
        Peak, Motoqua
        1:100,000 St. George
Maptech CD-ROM: Escalante/Dixie
        National Forest
Utah Atlas & Gazetteer, p. 16
Utah Travel Council #4

Route Directions

▼ 0.0   On Eardley Road, 4.4 miles from Old
         US 91, turn north on small graded dirt
         road, following sign for Motoqua Road,
         and zero trip meter. To find Eardley
         Road from Old US 91, look for intersec-
         tion at Castle Cliff and follow sign for
         the High Desert Game Ranch.
5.1 ▲   Trail ends at Eardley Road. Turn left for
         Old US 91.
         GPS: N 37°05.64' W 113°57.17'

▼ 0.6   SO Cross through wash.
4.5 ▲   SO Cross through wash.

▼ 1.0   SO Faint track on left.
4.1 ▲   SO Faint track on right.

▼ 1.2   SO Old corral on right—only the uprights
            remain.
3.9 ▲   SO Old corral on left—only the uprights
            remain.

▼ 1.4   SO Cross through wash, with track on
            right up wash.
3.7 ▲   SO Cross through wash, with track on left
            up wash.

▼ 1.5   SO Track on left to Middle Spring Pipeline
            and storage tank.
3.6 ▲   SO Track on right to Middle Spring Pipeline
            and storage tank.
         GPS: N 37°06.86' W 113°56.91'

▼ 2.3   SO Track on left.
2.8 ▲   SO Track on right.

▼ 2.5   SO Cross through Reber Wash.
2.6 ▲   SO Cross through Reber Wash.

▼ 2.6   BL Track on right.
2.5 ▲   SO Track on left.

▼ 2.8   SO Two entrances to track on right.
2.3 ▲   SO Two entrances to track on left.

▼ 3.1   SO Faint track on right.
2.0 ▲   SO Faint track on left.

▼ 3.5   SO Track on right.
1.6 ▲   SO Track on left.

▼ 3.6   SO Track on right.
1.5 ▲   SO Track on left.

▼ 3.8   SO Track on right to tank.
1.3 ▲   BR Track on left to tank.
         GPS: N 37°08.22' W 113°56.10'

▼ 3.9   SO Cross through wash, then track on left.
1.2 ▲   SO Track on right, then cross through
            wash.

▼ 4.0   SO Track on right.
1.1 ▲   SO Track on left.

▼ 4.1   SO Cross through wash.
1.0 ▲   SO Cross through wash.

▼ 4.4   SO Cross through wash.
0.7 ▲   SO Cross through wash.

▼ 4.8   SO Track on right.
0.3 ▲   SO Track on left.
         GPS: N 37°08.89' W 113°55.83'

▼ 4.9   SO Cross through wash.

SW Trail #1: Indian Spring Trail

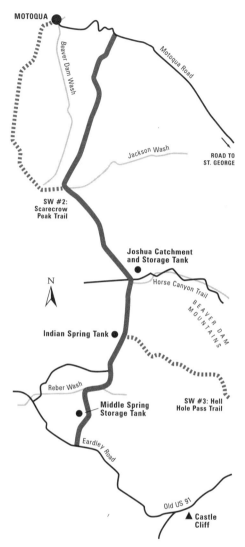

Zero trip meter at the second.
GPS: N 37°09.17' W 113°55.75'

▼ 0.1 SO Indian Spring tank is on the left, marked by sign. Washed out track on right.
2.4 ▲ SO Indian Spring tank is on the right, marked by sign. Washed out track on left.

▼ 0.4 SO Track on right.
2.1 ▲ SO Track on left.

▼ 0.8 SO Track on right.
1.7 ▲ SO Track on left.

▼ 1.0 SO Track on right.
1.5 ▲ SO Track on left.

▼ 1.1 SO Cross through wash.
1.4 ▲ SO Cross through wash.

▼ 1.3 SO Faint track on right.
1.2 ▲ SO Faint track on left.

▼ 1.4 SO Track on right and left, then cattle guard.
1.1 ▲ SO Cattle guard, then track on right and left.

▼ 1.8 SO Track on left.
0.7 ▲ SO Track on right.

▼ 1.9 SO Cross through wash.
0.6 ▲ SO Cross through wash.
GPS: N 37°10.51' W 113°55.89'

▼ 2.5 SO Track on right is Horse Canyon Trail, marked by BLM sign, leading into the Beaver Dam Mountains. Also track on left. Zero trip meter.
0.0 ▲   Continue toward Indian Spring.

▼ 0.0   Continue toward Motoqua Road.
3.8 ▲ SO Track on left is Horse Canyon Trail, marked by BLM sign, leading into the Beaver Dam Mountains. Also track on right. Zero trip meter.
GPS: N 37°10.91' W 113°55.84'

▼ 0.1 SO Cattle guard, then Joshua catchment and storage tank on right, then track on right.
3.7 ▲ SO Track on left, then Joshua catchment

0.2 ▲ SO Cross through wash.

▼ 5.1 SO Track on left, followed by track on right; this is Southwest #3: Hell Hole Pass Trail. Zero trip meter.
0.0 ▲ BL Continue south toward Eardley Road. Immediately bear left at fork following Hell Hole Pass Trail.

▼ 0.0   Continue north, passing second entrance to Hell Hole Pass Trail.
2.5 ▲ SO Two tracks to left are one end of Southwest #3: Hell Hole Pass Trail.

and storage tank on left, followed by cattle guard.

GPS: N 37°11.05′ W 113°55.87′

▼ 1.5   SO Track on left to power lines.
2.3 ▲   SO Track on right to power lines.

▼ 1.6   SO Cross through wash.
2.2 ▲   SO Cross through wash.

▼ 1.7   SO Track on right at power lines, then cross over natural gas pipeline.
2.1 ▲   SO Cross over natural gas pipeline, then track on left at power lines.

▼ 3.4   SO Faint track on left, then cattle guard.
0.4 ▲   SO Cattle guard, then faint track on right.

▼ 3.8   SO Track on left is Southwest #2: Scarecrow Peak Trail, signed to Jackson Well. Zero trip meter.
0.0 ▲   Continue toward Indian Spring.

▼ 0.0   Continue toward Motoqua Road.
6.0 ▲   SO Track on right is Southwest #2: Scarecrow Peak Trail, signed to Jackson Well. Zero trip meter.

GPS: N 37°13.45′ W 113°58.69′

▼ 0.2   SO Cross through Jackson Wash.
5.8 ▲   SO Cross through Jackson Wash.

▼ 0.4   SO Track on left.
5.6 ▲   SO Track on right.

▼ 1.8   SO Cross through wash, then climb ridge with views left to Beaver Dam Wash.
4.2 ▲   SO Descend ridge with views right to Beaver Dam Wash, then cross through wash.

▼ 4.8   SO Cattle guard, then track on right.
1.2 ▲   SO Track on left, then cattle guard.

GPS: N 37°17.42′ W 113°57.94′

▼ 4.9   SO Track on left.
1.1 ▲   SO Track on right.

▼ 6.0   End at intersection with the major graded dirt Motoqua Road. Turn left for the settlement of Motoqua, turn right

for Old US 91 and St. George.
0.0 ▲   On Motoqua Road, 14.4 miles west of Old US 91, zero trip meter and turn southeast on the graded dirt road, following the sign for Indian Spring and Eardley Road.

GPS: N 37°18.44′ W 113°57.50′

Scarecrow Peak Trail

STARTING POINT Motoqua
FINISHING POINT Southwest #1: Indian Spring Trail, 6 miles south of Motoqua Road
TOTAL MILEAGE 13.1 miles
UNPAVED MILEAGE 13.1 miles
DRIVING TIME 1 hour .
ELEVATION RANGE 3,000–3,800 feet
USUALLY OPEN Year-round
DIFFICULTY RATING 2
SCENIC RATING 7
REMOTENESS RATING +1

Special Attractions
- Joshua tree forests.
- Scarecrow Peak and Beaver Dam Wash.
- Views into two states—Utah and Nevada.

Description
This easy trail links the lower end of the Burnt Canyon ATV trail system with Southwest #1: Indian Spring Trail, passing through a remote,

Joshua trees dot the desert landscape

Jackson Well

scenic area of the Mojave Desert as it does. The trail leaves from the small settlement of Motoqua; to get there, take Motoqua Road from Old US 91 in the Shivwits Indian Reservation. The trail immediately crosses Beaver Dam Wash, the lowest elevation in Utah, and climbs a ridge to the Nevada state line. The line is unmarked, except for a fence line, and the trail follows alongside it for nearly 3 miles, passing through large stands of mature Joshua trees.

The trail then drops down a wash, winds around the bulk of Scarecrow Peak (4,398 feet), and then crosses the wide, sandy Beaver Dam Wash again. After passing Jackson Well, the trail finishes at Southwest #1: Indian Spring Trail, 6 miles south of Motoqua Road.

Current Road Information
BLM St. George Field Office
345 East Riverside Drive
St. George, UT 84790
(435) 688-3200

Map References
BLM   St. George
USFS Dixie National Forest: Pine Valley
      Ranger District (incomplete)
USGS 1:24,000   West Mt. Peak,
      Scarecrow Peak, Dodge Spring,
      Motoqua
      1:100,000 St. George
Maptech CD-ROM: Escalante/Dixie
      National Forest
Utah Atlas & Gazetteer, p. 16
Utah Travel Council #4

Route Directions

▼ 0.0   In Motoqua, at the junction before Beaver Dam Wash, zero trip meter and continue north along the graded dirt road following the sign to the Utah/Nevada state line. The settlement of Motoqua is to the right.
1.1 ▲   Trail ends at the settlement of Motoqua. Continue along Motoqua Road to reach Old US 91 and St. George.
          GPS: N 37°18.59′ W 113°59.77′

▼ 0.1   SO Cross through Beaver Dam Wash.
1.0 ▲   SO Cross through Beaver Dam Wash.

▼ 0.2   SO Corral on left.
0.9 ▲   SO Corral on right.

▼ 0.5   SO Track on left.
0.6 ▲   SO Track on right.

▼ 0.6   SO Cattle guard.
0.5 ▲   SO Cattle guard.

▼ 1.0   SO Track on right is signed to Dodge Spring, then cross over wash.
0.1 ▲   SO Cross over wash, then track on left is signed to Dodge Spring.

▼ 1.1   TL Turn left onto unmarked, smaller graded dirt road and zero trip meter.
0.0 ▲   Continue toward Motoqua.
          GPS: N 37°18.29′ W 114°00.48′

UTAH'S DIXIE

Brigham Young sought a self-sustaining state where Mormons could freely practice their beliefs. With this in mind, missionaries and sojourners scouted the land and discovered the region that would become known as "Utah's Dixie." A. P. Hardy was returning back to the Santa Clara area with provisions for his fellow missionaries when Sister Nancy Anderson gave him some cottonseeds and the idea of growing them. Sure enough, the cotton grew abundantly. Settlers in 1857 took that knowledge with them as they founded the town of Washington in southern Utah. As a southern, cotton producing area, the nickname "Dixie" seemed appropriate. The name caught on and has since stuck to the region around present-day Washington County. In 1911, St. George Stake Academy was founded and just a couple of years later the nickname was literally set in stone. Students painted the word "Dixie" on the nearby rock outcropping and since then St. George Stake Academy has been known as Dixie College.

Utah's Dixie is a superb example of the state's varying climate and geography. The area is approximately 2,500 feet lower than the Great Basin, and the county stays warm during the winter. Because of this unique, almost semi-tropical climate, such crops as cotton, grapes, peaches, and tobacco grow readily. A proud Dixie culture also flourishes in the area, as well as in the less temperate towns of Kolob, Pine Valley, and Enterprise.

▼ 0.0   Continue toward the Nevada state line.

4.0 ▲   TR   Turn right onto larger graded dirt road and zero trip meter.

▼ 0.1   SO   Cattle guard.

3.9 ▲   SO   Cattle guard.

▼ 0.2   SO   Cross through wash, then track on left.

3.8 ▲   SO   Track on right, then cross through wash.

▼ 0.8   SO   Cross through wash.

3.2 ▲   SO   Cross through wash.

▼ 0.9   SO   Cross through wash.

3.1 ▲   SO   Cross through wash.

▼ 1.0   SO   Track on right, then cross through wash.

3.0 ▲   SO   Cross through wash, then track on left.

▼ 1.1   SO   Cross through wash.

2.9 ▲   SO   Cross through wash.

▼ 1.4   SO   Cross through wash.

2.6 ▲   SO   Cross through wash.

▼ 1.7   SO   Cross through smaller wash.

2.3 ▲   SO   Cross through smaller wash.

▼ 1.8   BR   Track swings right, away from main wash.

2.2 ▲   BL   Track swings left and joins main wash.

GPS: N 37°16.88′ W 114°01.13′

▼ 2.2   BL   Track on right.

1.8 ▲   SO   Track on left.

GPS: N 37°17.07′ W 114°01.48′

SW Trail #2: Scarecrow Peak Trail

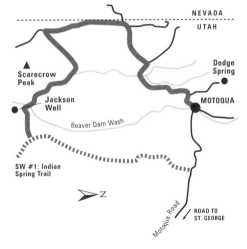

▼ 2.9   SO Track on left.
1.1 ▲   SO Track on right.

▼ 3.1   SO Track on right, then cross through
            wash.
0.9 ▲   SO Cross through wash, then track on
            left.

▼ 3.6   SO Track on right.
0.4 ▲   SO Track on left.
            GPS: N 37°16.55′ W 114°02.70′

▼ 3.7   SO Track on right, then cross through
            wash.
0.3 ▲   SO Cross through wash, then track on
            left.

▼ 4.0   TL Nevada state line (unmarked). Turn left
            in front of cattle guard and follow along
            the fence line. Zero trip meter.
0.0 ▲   Continue toward Motoqua.
            GPS: N 37°16.38′ W 114°03.06′

▼ 0.0   Proceed south along state line.
2.8 ▲   TR Turn right at intersection and leave
            state line. Track on left crosses a
            cattle guard into Nevada. Zero trip
            meter.

▼ 2.8   TL Turn sharp left, immediately in front of
            water tank and zero trip meter.
0.0 ▲   The fence on left is Nevada state line.
            Proceed north along state line.
            GPS: N 37°13.88′ W 114°02.73′

▼ 0.0   Proceed away from state line.
4.2 ▲   TR Turn sharp right, immediately in front
            of water tank and zero trip meter.

▼ 0.6   SO Track on right.
3.6 ▲   SO Track on left.

▼ 1.5   SO Track on left, then trail drops toward
            wash.
2.7 ▲   SO Trail climbs away from wash, then
            track on right.
            GPS: N 37°14.85′ W 114°01.53′

▼ 1.7   SO Enter wash.

2.5 ▲   SO Exit wash.

▼ 1.9   TR Track on left. Exit wash.
2.3 ▲   BL Enter wash. Track on right.

▼ 2.1   SO Cross through wash.
2.1 ▲   SO Cross through wash.

▼ 2.2   SO Trail drops to wash. Views south to
            Beaver Dam Mountains.
2.0 ▲   SO Trail climbs away from wash.

▼ 2.3   SO Cross through wash.
1.9 ▲   SO Cross through wash.

▼ 3.8   SO Edge of Beaver Dam Wash. Cross
            through wide wash.
0.4 ▲   SO Cross through Beaver Dam Wash.
            GPS: N 37°13.58′ W 113°59.94′

▼ 4.2   TR Pass through wire gate. Jackson Well
            windmill is on right next to the corral.
            Zero trip meter.
0.0 ▲   Continue toward Nevada state line.
            GPS: N 37°13.29′ W 113°59.80′

▼ 0.0   Continue toward Southwest #1:
            Indian Spring Trail, climbing away
            from wash.
1.0 ▲   TL Jackson Well windmill is on left next
            to the corral. Zero trip meter and turn
            sharp left through the wire gate next to
            corral.

▼ 0.2   SO End of climb away from Beaver Dam
            Wash.
0.8 ▲   SO Trail descends to Beaver Dam Wash.

▼ 1.0   Trail ends at Southwest #1: Indian
            Spring Trail. Turn left to join Motoqua
            Road for St. George, turn right to con-
            tinue along Indian Spring Trail to Old
            US 91.
0.0 ▲   On Southwest #1: Indian Spring
            Trail, 6 miles south of Motoqua Road,
            turn west on graded dirt road at the
            sign for Jackson Well and zero trip
            meter.
            GPS: N 37°13.45′ W 113°58.69′

Hell Hole Pass Trail

STARTING POINT Old US 91, 0.9 miles south of Shivwits Indian Reservation
FINISHING POINT Southwest #1: Indian Spring Trail
TOTAL MILEAGE 7.9 miles
UNPAVED MILEAGE 7.9 miles
DRIVING TIME 45 minutes
ELEVATION RANGE 4,400–6,300 feet
USUALLY OPEN Year-round
DIFFICULTY RATING 3
SCENIC RATING 7
REMOTENESS RATING +1

Special Attractions
■ Extensive views west into Nevada.
■ Hell Hole Pass through the Beaver Dam Mountains.

Description
Hell Hole Pass is one of only a few small dirt roads that cross the Beaver Dam Mountains. The trail leaves Old US 91 south of the Shivwits Indian Reservation and immediately winds its way up toward the pass. The grade is moderately steep for the most part; the trail climbs a total of 1,900 feet from the highway to the pass. The surface is good, there are no large rocks, and although sections are loose, on the whole traction is good. There are some good views as the trail climbs—back to the east over St. George, the long Hurricane Cliffs escarpment, Sand Mountain, and as far as Zion National Park.

Leading off from the top of the pass is the challenging Southwest #4: TV Towers Jeep Trail, a steep, difficult spur trail that leads to stunning views. As Hell Hole Pass Trail descends into Indian Canyon, the trail standard drops somewhat, and the single-width ungraded trail becomes slightly sandy as it follows Indian Creek through the trees. There are a couple of small, sheltered campsites along the descent. The rockiest section is in the wash itself, as the trail rounds a point in a narrow valley—extra wide vehi-

Looking down through Indian Canyon

cles will find it tight but passable.

As Indian Spring spills out onto the sloping alluvial fan above the spring itself, the views spread out to the west into Nevada. The trail finishes at Indian Spring, which is marked by a large metal water tank; this north-south dirt road is Southwest #1: Indian Spring Trail. The original track is washed out, and the new route finishes just below the spring. A sign at the spring gives the distance south to Old US 91.

Current Road Information
BLM St. George Field Office
345 East Riverside Drive
St. George, UT 84790
(435) 688-3200

Map References
BLM   St. George
USGS 1:24,000   Jarvis Peak, Shivwits, West Mt. Peak
          1:100,000 St. George
Maptech CD-ROM: Escalante/Dixie National Forest
Utah Atlas & Gazetteer, p. 16
Utah Travel Council #4 (incomplete)

Route Directions

▼ 0.0   From Old US 91, 0.9 miles south of the Shivwits Indian Reservation, turn west on unmarked graded road, and zero trip meter. Cross cattle guard.

SW Trail #3: Hell Hole Pass Trail

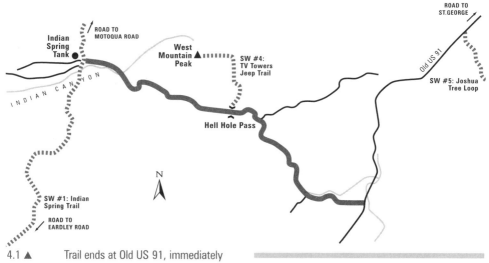

4.1 ▲   Trail ends at Old US 91, immediately south of the Shivwits Indian Reservation. Turn left for St. George, turn right for Littlefield, Arizona.
GPS: N 37°06.70' W 113°49.27'

▼ 0.1   SO   Track on left.
4.0 ▲   SO   Track on right.

▼ 0.2   SO   Track on left.
3.9 ▲   SO   Track on right.

▼ 0.6   SO   Track on right opposite concrete foundations.
3.5 ▲   SO   Track on left opposite concrete foundations.
GPS: N 37°06.77' W 113°49.92'

▼ 0.8   SO   Track on right.
3.3 ▲   SO   Track on left.

▼ 1.1   SO   Faint track on left. Main trail climbs toward the pass.
3.0 ▲   SO   Faint track on right.

▼ 2.1   SO   Tracks on left and right.
2.0 ▲   SO   Tracks on left and right.
GPS: N 37°07.48' W 113°51.01'

▼ 2.8   SO   Faint track on left, then track on right.
1.3 ▲   SO   Track on left, then faint track on right.

▼ 2.9   SO   Track on left to viewpoint.
1.2 ▲   SO   Track on right to viewpoint.

▼ 3.4   SO   Cross through wash, then track on left.
0.7 ▲   SO   Track on right, then cross through wash.

▼ 3.7   SO   Cross over wash.
0.4 ▲   SO   Cross over wash.

▼ 4.1   BL   Saddle at Hell Hole Pass. Track on right is Southwest #4: TV Towers Jeep Trail. Also a small track on left. Zero trip meter.
0.0 ▲   Descend from saddle toward Old US 91.
GPS: N 37°08.27' W 113°52.24'

▼ 0.0   Descend from saddle, following sign for Indian Spring.
3.8 ▲   SO   Saddle at Hell Hole Pass. Track back to left is Southwest #4: TV Towers Jeep Trail. Also a small track on right. Zero trip meter.

▼ 0.6   SO   Cross through wash.
3.2 ▲   SO   Cross through wash.
GPS: N 37°08.39' W 113°52.92'

▼ 0.8   SO   Cross through Indian Creek Wash.
3.0 ▲   SO   Cross through Indian Creek Wash.

▼ 1.0	SO	Views ahead of West Mountain Peak.
2.8 ▲	SO	Views to left of West Mountain Peak.

▼ 1.4	SO	Track on left, then concrete tank on left.
2.4 ▲	SO	Concrete tank on right, then track on right.

GPS: N 37°08.51' W 113°53.64'

▼ 2.3	SO	Enter Indian Creek Wash.
1.5 ▲	SO	Exit Indian Creek Wash.

▼ 2.4	SO	Exit Indian Creek Wash.
1.4 ▲	SO	Enter Indian Creek Wash.

▼ 2.7	SO	Concrete tank on left.
1.1 ▲	SO	Concrete tank on right.

▼ 2.8	SO	Cross through wash.
1.0 ▲	SO	Cross through wash.

▼ 3.0	BL	Cross through wash, then track on right.
0.8 ▲	SO	Track on left, then cross through wash.

GPS: N 37°08.99' W 113°54.89'

▼ 3.1	SO	Track on right.
0.7 ▲	SO	Track on left.

▼ 3.6	BL	Two tracks on right.
0.2 ▲	SO	Two tracks on left.

▼ 3.8	BR	Track on left, then trail ends at T-intersection with graded dirt Southwest #1: Indian Spring Trail, immediately south of Indian Spring tank. Turn right for Motoqua Road, turn left for Eardley Road.
0.0 ▲		On Southwest #1: Indian Spring Trail, 5.1 miles north of Eardley Road and just south of Indian Spring tank, zero trip meter and turn east on unmarked road. The original road is washed out and marked by a sign giving distances to Eardley Road and Old US 91.

GPS: N 37°09.13' W 113°55.74'

TV Towers Jeep Trail

STARTING POINT Hell Hole Pass on Southwest #3: Hell Hole Pass Trail
FINISHING POINT TV Towers on West Mountain Peak
TOTAL MILEAGE 2.5 miles
UNPAVED MILEAGE 2.5 miles
DRIVING TIME 30 minutes (one-way)
ELEVATION RANGE 6,100–7,600 feet
USUALLY OPEN March to December
DIFFICULTY RATING 6
SCENIC RATING 9
REMOTENESS RATING +1

Special Attractions

■ Panoramic views from West Mountain Peak into three states.
■ Steep climb up exciting, rugged trail.

Description

Don't be fooled by the easy, graded start of this spur trail! It leaves from the top of Hell Hole Pass on Southwest #3: Hell Hole Pass Trail and climbs to the very top of West Mountain Peak, over a thousand feet higher than the pass.

The trail starts off easy enough, climbing steadily toward the TV towers. At the 1.9 mark though, it earns its Jeep trail status as it abruptly becomes a lot steeper, with some very loose rubble and rock. Most vehicles

Rocky switchbacks near the top of TV Towers Jeep Trail

will spin wheels here as they try to climb. The trail is shelf road for the remainder of the climb, most of it wide enough not to cause any concern, although there are limited passing places. After the first TV tower is reached, the trail runs briefly across a ridge with massive drops on either side. This looks particularly scary coming back down, when the steep descent aims your vehicle directly off the cliff edge.

However, the final climb to the tower makes it worthwhile. At the top, there are panoramic views stretching in all directions and into three states. Nevada is west, Arizona south, and Utah north and east. To the west, you can see the route down from Hell Hole Pass and the wide sandy Beaver Dam Wash, the lowest point in Utah at only 2,000 feet above sea level. Beyond that in Nevada are the Tule Springs Hills and the Mormon and the Meadow Dam Mountains. To the north, you can see Square Top Mountain, the cone-shaped Jackson Peak, and the Bull Valley Mountains. To the east is the sprawl of St. George in the valley, with Zion National Park, the Hurricane Cliffs, and the pink sands of Sand Mountain beyond. Pine Valley Mountain is northeast.

West Mountain Peak, at 7,746 feet, often has snow at the highest elevations in winter. It may be passable during dry winter months, but do not attempt this trail if there is snow on the ground, or in wet weather because of the steepness and looseness of the trail.

View from the telecommunications tower at the top of the trail

SW Trail #4: TV Towers Jeep Trail

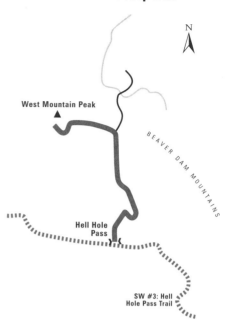

Current Road Information
BLM St. George Field Office
345 East Riverside Drive
St. George, UT 84790
(435) 688-3200

Map References
BLM   St. George (incomplete)
USGS 1:24,000   Shivwits, West Mt. Peak
1:100,000 St. George (incomplete)
Maptech CD-ROM: Escalante/Dixie
National Forest
Utah Atlas & Gazetteer, p. 16

Route Directions

▼ 0.0   On Southwest #3: Hell Hole Pass Trail, from the saddle of Hell Hole Pass at the cattle guard, turn northwest on graded road following sign for TV Towers Jeep Trail and zero trip meter.
GPS: N 37°08.27' W 113°52.24'

▼ 0.2 SO Cross through small wash.
▼ 0.4 SO Track on left.
▼ 0.9 SO Saddle. TV towers are visible ahead.
GPS: N 37°09.24' W 113°52.34'

▼ 1.4 SO Track on right.

▼ 1.8 SO Cross through wash.

▼ 1.9 SO Track climbs steeply and is rougher and rockier.

▼ 2.2 SO Pass first TV tower on left.

▼ 2.3 SO Cross over narrow ridge with drops on either side.

▼ 2.4 BL Start of loop around TV towers at end of trail.

▼ 2.5 End of loop; various viewpoints around loop.

GPS: N 37°09.33' W 113°52.98'

Joshua Tree Loop

STARTING POINT Old US 91, 1 mile south of Motoqua Road, in Shivwits Indian Reservation

FINISHING POINT Old US 91, 1.8 miles north of the Arizona state line

TOTAL MILEAGE 17.9 miles

UNPAVED MILEAGE 17.1 miles

DRIVING TIME 1.5 hours

ELEVATION RANGE 3,000–4,800 feet

USUALLY OPEN Year-round

DIFFICULTY RATING 2

SCENIC RATING 7

REMOTENESS RATING +0

Special Attractions
■ Joshua tree forest.
■ Views of the Beaver Dam Mountains.
■ Mojave Desert vegetation and desert tortoise habitat.

History
The Apex Mine, situated along this trail, has been extracting copper since 1890. A smelter was built in St. George, on Diagonal Street, to process the metal after the mine was acquired by the Woolley, Lund and Judd Company. After World War I, the need for copper declined, and it remained low until World War II, when the Apex picked up production again.

Joshua trees line this section of the Joshua Tree Loop. Southern Utah has the northernmost climate able to sustain this type of tree.

The trail passes through the Woodbury Desert Study Area, a 3,040-acre area fenced off in 1977 to study the elusive desert tortoise, an endangered species. The area is named after Dr. Woodbury, who, along with Dr. Hardy, did pioneering research of the tortoise between 1936 and 1948. The fenced area allows the study of the plant and animal communities of this unusual region.

Description
This trail is shown on some atlases as the Joshua Tree Scenic Loop Drive, and the southern end of the road passes through large stands of Joshua trees.

As well as Joshua trees, this trail offers many views of the Beaver Dam Mountains; this range marks the divide between the Mojave Desert and the Great Basin. Areas surrounding these mountains support plants and animals from both communities. Joshua trees, creosote bushes, and desert tortoises—all representatives of the Mojave Desert community—mingle with collared lizards and sagebrush. In addition, you are likely to see prairie falcons, golden eagles, rattlesnakes, Gambel's quails, and mule deer along this drive and the others in the region.

The trail leaves the highway south of Shivwits on the Indian reservation, and the first part of the trail crosses reservation land. Please respect the privacy of reservation residents by remaining on the major thoroughfare. The first section of the trail is a wide graded gravel road, as it is used by Apex Operations, which has a large plant near the start of the trail and a mine farther down, although the mine appears to be little used these days.

After leaving the Shivwits Reservation, the trail crosses into BLM land. Tracks to the left lead down to St. George via the open land of Blake's Lambing Grounds. To the west, Mount Jarvis rises up to 6,500 feet. Once you pass the turn to the Apex Mine (there's no public access to the workings), the trail gets narrower and slightly rougher as it travels through Mine Valley and Cedar Pockets before cresting Bulldog Pass. There is hiking access to the Beaver Dam Wilderness Area to the east.

The Joshua trees enter the landscape after

The Beaver Dam Mountains provide a dramatic backdrop for this old corral

Bulldog Pass, and the farther south you go the more abundant they become. They are densest after the trail passes through Bulldog Gap at the mouth of Bulldog Canyon.

Unfortunately, a fire in 1999 destroyed many of the trees, especially in the upper areas of Bulldog Canyon. The trees are putting out new shoots, but it will be a while before they recover fully. The fire did not affect the lower areas of the trail or the Woodbury Desert Study Area, and the Joshua trees are especially prolific in the fenced area.

The trail finishes back on Old US 91, just north of the Arizona state line. In dry weather a carefully driven passenger car could make the trip, although high clearance is definitely preferable.

Current Road Information

BLM St. George Field Office
345 East Riverside Drive
St. George, UT 84790
(435) 688-3200

Map References

BLM   St. George
USFS Dixie National Forest: Pine Valley
      Ranger District (incomplete)
USGS 1:24,000   Shivwits, Jarvis Peak,
      Castle Cliff
      1:100,000 St. George
Maptech CD-ROM: Escalante/Dixie
      National Forest
Utah Atlas & Gazetteer, p. 16
Utah Travel Council #4

Route Directions

▼ 0.0   From Old US 91 in the Shivwits Indian
         Reservation, 1 mile south of Motoqua
         Road, turn southeast on paved road at
         the large sign for Apex Operations and
         cross cattle guard. Zero trip meter.
7.2 ▲   Trail ends at Old US 91 in the Shivwits
         Indian Reservation. Turn right for
         St. George, turn left for Littlefield,
         Arizona.
         GPS: N 37°09.76' W 113°47.01'

▼ 0.5   SO Apex Operations site on left.

| 6.7 ▲ | SO | Apex Operations site on right. |

| ▼ 0.8 | SO | Road is now graded gravel. Beware of heavy mining trucks using the road. |
| 6.4 ▲ | SO | Road is now paved. |

| ▼ 2.6 | SO | Cross over Wittwer Canyon wash. |
| 4.6 ▲ | SO | Cross over Wittwer Canyon wash. |

▼ 3.0	SO	Cattle guard. Leaving the Shivwits Indian Reservation (no sign).
4.2 ▲	SO	Cattle guard. Entering the Shivwits Indian Reservation (no sign).
		GPS: N 37°07.47′ W 113°45.80′

| ▼ 5.2 | SO | Track on left. |
| 2.0 ▲ | SO | Track on right. |

| ▼ 5.3 | SO | Track on right, then track on left to corral. |
| 1.9 ▲ | SO | Track on right to corral, then track on left. |

▼ 5.4	SO	Cattle guard, then track on left to corral.
1.8 ▲	SO	Track on right to corral, then cattle guard.
		GPS: N 37°05.67′ W 113°45.98′

| ▼ 5.6 | SO | Track on right. |
| 1.6 ▲ | SO | Track on left. |

▼ 5.8	SO	Track on left is Hollow Wash Road.
1.4 ▲	SO	Track on right is Hollow Wash Road.
		GPS: N 37°05.29′ W 113°45.93′

▼ 7.2	SO	Major graded road to the left; zero trip meter. Continue straight, following sign for Bulldog Canyon and Cedar Pockets Wash.
0.0 ▲		Continue toward Shivwits Indian Reservation.
		GPS: N 37°04.18′ W 113°46.30′

| ▼ 0.0 | | Continue toward Bulldog Canyon. Small track immediately on right. |
| 0.8 ▲ | SO | Small track on left, then major graded road to the right; zero trip meter. Continue straight, following sign for Old US 91. |

SW Trail #5: Joshua Tree Loop

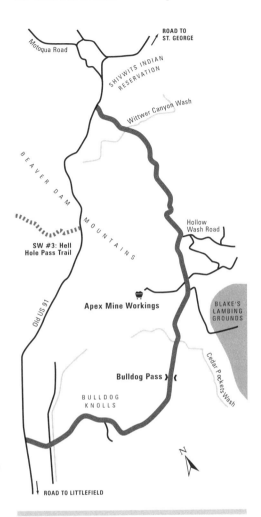

| ▼ 0.1 | SO | Cattle guard. |
| 0.7 ▲ | SO | Cattle guard. |

▼ 0.2	BL	Large track on right to the Apex Mine workings (no access). Also small track on right. Main trail is now narrower and graded dirt.
0.6 ▲	BR	Large track on left to the Apex Mine workings (no access). Also small track on left. Main trail is now wider and graded gravel road.
		GPS: N 37°04.03′ W 113°46.47′

| ▼ 0.6 | SO | Track on right. |
| 0.2 ▲ | SO | Track on left. |

▼ 0.8	SO	Track on left to Blake's Lambing Grounds, signed to Bloomington. Zero trip meter.
0.0 ▲		Continue toward the Apex Mine.
		GPS: N 37°03.59′ W 113°46.56′

▼ 0.0		Continue toward Bulldog Pass.
9.0 ▲	SO	Track on right to Blake's Lambing Grounds, signed to Bloomington. Zero trip meter.

▼ 0.1	SO	Corral on right, then track on left.
8.9 ▲	SO	Track on right, then corral on left.

▼ 0.7	SO	Track on left.
8.3 ▲	SO	Track on right.

▼ 1.0	SO	Cattle guard on rise, then track on left.
8.0 ▲	SO	Track on right, then cattle guard on rise.
		GPS: N 37°03.05′ W 113°47.38′

▼ 1.6	SO	Track on left.
7.4 ▲	SO	Track on right.
		GPS: N 37°02.51′ W 113°47.53′

▼ 1.7	SO	Track on left.
7.3 ▲	SO	Track on right.

▼ 1.8	SO	Cross through Cedar Pockets Wash, then track on right.
7.2 ▲	SO	Track on left, then cross through Cedar Pockets Wash.

▼ 1.9	SO	Track on left.
7.1 ▲	SO	Track on right.

▼ 2.2	SO	Track on left.
6.8 ▲	SO	Track on right.

▼ 2.5	SO	Track on left.
6.5 ▲	SO	Track on right.
		GPS: N 37°01.86′ W 113°48.08′

▼ 2.7	SO	Bulldog Pass. Trail descends into Bulldog Canyon. Joshua trees appear in increasing numbers.
6.3 ▲	SO	Bulldog Pass. Trail leaves Bulldog Canyon. Joshua trees peter out.

▼ 3.5	SO	Cross through wash.
5.5 ▲	SO	Cross through wash.

▼ 3.6	SO	Track on left.
5.4 ▲	SO	Track on right.

▼ 3.9	SO	Faint track on right.
5.1 ▲	SO	Faint track on left.

▼ 4.0	SO	Track on left.
5.0 ▲	SO	Track on right.

▼ 4.1	SO	Cross through wash.
4.9 ▲	SO	Cross through wash.

▼ 4.2	SO	Track on left.
4.8 ▲	SO	Track on right.

▼ 4.3	SO	Cattle guard and cattletank on right.
4.7 ▲	SO	Cattle guard and cattletank on left.
		GPS: N 37°00.78′ W 113°49.33′

▼ 4.5	SO	Cross through wash.
4.5 ▲	SO	Cross through wash.

▼ 4.6	SO	Faint track on left.
4.4 ▲	SO	Faint track on right.

▼ 5.2	SO	Track on left.
3.8 ▲	SO	Track on right.

▼ 5.6	SO	Track on right.
3.4 ▲	SO	Track on left.

▼ 5.9	SO	Track on left.
3.1 ▲	SO	Track on right.

▼ 6.4	SO	Cattle guard in Bulldog Gap.
2.6 ▲	SO	Cattle guard in Bulldog Gap.

▼ 6.6	SO	Cross through wash.
2.4 ▲	SO	Cross through wash.

▼ 6.8	SO	Track on left.
2.2 ▲	SO	Track on right.
		GPS: N 37°01.25′ W 113°51.50′

▼ 6.9	SO	Cross through wash.

2.1 ▲	SO	Cross through wash.
▼ 7.2	SO	Track on right.
1.8 ▲	SO	Track on left.
▼ 7.5	SO	Track on right, then cross through wash, and second track on right to campsite.
1.5 ▲	SO	Track on left to campsite, then cross through wash and second track on left.
▼ 7.6	SO	Entering Woodbury Desert Study Area over cattle guard.
1.4 ▲	SO	Leaving Woodbury Desert Study Area over cattle guard.
▼ 8.5	SO	Cross through wash.
0.5 ▲	SO	Cross through wash.
▼ 8.9	SO	Cross through wash.
0.1 ▲	SO	Cross through wash.
▼ 9.0	SO	Camping area on right, then track on right, cattle guard, and track on left. Exiting Woodbury Desert Study Area. Information board at exit. Zero trip meter.
0.0 ▲		Continue toward Bulldog Gap.
		GPS: N 37°01.09' W 113°53.49'
▼ 0.0		Continue toward Old US 91.
0.9 ▲	SO	Track on right. Entering Woodbury Desert Study Area. Information board at entrance. Cattle guard, then camping area and track on left. Zero trip meter.
▼ 0.1	SO	Track on right.
0.8 ▲	SO	Track on left.
▼ 0.8	SO	Track on right.
0.1 ▲	SO	Track on left.
▼ 0.9		Trail ends at paved Old US 91. Turn left for Littlefield, Arizona; turn right for St. George.
0.0 ▲		On Old US 91, 1.8 miles north of the Arizona state line, turn southeast on graded dirt road at the sign for the Woodbury Desert Study Area and zero trip meter.
		GPS: N 37°01.60' W 113°54.35'

The Divide Trail

STARTING POINT Arizona-Utah state line
FINISHING POINT Utah 59, 3.2 miles east of Hurricane
TOTAL MILEAGE 11.6 miles
UNPAVED MILEAGE 11.6 miles
DRIVING TIME 1 hour
ELEVATION RANGE 3,900–4,800 feet
USUALLY OPEN Year-round
DIFFICULTY RATING 1
SCENIC RATING 6
REMOTENESS RATING +1

Special Attractions

- Access point to the historic Honeymoon Trail.
- Little Creek Mountain Mesa and the Divide.
- Alternative route down to the Arizona Strip.

Description

This graded dirt road connects Utah 59 with the Arizona Strip district. In dry weather, it is an easy scenic drive that passes through a wide-bottomed valley, with the Hurricane Cliffs on the west and Little Creek Mountain rising up to the east. It also provides access to the historic Honeymoon Trail, and adventurous driv-

A view of the trail with Little Creek Mountain in the background

ers can make a loop drive from Hurricane by combining this easy trail with the 6-rated Southwest #7: Hurricane Cliffs Trail.

To reach the start of the trail, drive south on Utah 59 into Arizona (where it becomes Arizona 389), past Colorado City, to the junction with county highway 237. Turn right onto county highway 237 and proceed southwest to the junction with Navajo Trail Road. Turn right here and drive west to the junction with Arizona BLM road #1015. Turn right and head north toward Utah. The trail commences on the Arizona state line, where the Arizona BLM road #1015 crosses into Utah.

You reach the junction with the Hurricane Cliffs Trail, which is part of the long Honeymoon Trail, almost immediately. The Divide Trail heads north for most of its route, rising up to pass through the gap of the Divide. There are many small tracks to the left and right; most are short dead end trails that lead to a viewpoint or campsite, although a few loop around to rejoin the main trail later.

After 8.6 miles, a major track to the right has a BLM sign for Little Creek Mountain. On maps, this climbs onto the mesa to the radio tower, but the track is washed out and impassable to vehicles. Access to Little Creek Mountain is via Apple Valley, farther east on Utah 59.

The trail finishes at Utah 59, 3.2 miles from Hurricane.

A signpost along the trail

Current Road Information
BLM St. George Field Office
345 East Riverside Drive
St. George, UT 84790
(435) 688-3200

Map References
BLM   St. George
USGS 1:24,000   The Divide, Little Creek
    Mt., Virgin, Hurricane
    1:100,000 St. George
Maptech CD-ROM: Escalante/Dixie
    National Forest
Utah Atlas & Gazetteer, p. 17
Utah Travel Council #4

Route Directions

▼ 0.0   Trail commences on the Arizona-Utah
         state line. In Arizona, the road is
         marked as BLM road #1015. Zero trip
         meter at the border fence and proceed
         north into Utah.
8.6 ▲   Trail ends at Arizona-Utah state line.
         Continuing straight leads to the
         Arizona Strip.
         GPS: N 37°00.00′ W 113°16.42′

▼ 0.1 SO Track on left is Southwest #7: Hurricane
         Cliffs Trail, part of the Honeymoon Trail.
8.5 ▲ SO Track on right is Southwest #7:
         Hurricane Cliffs Trail, part of the
         Honeymoon Trail.
         GPS: N 37°00.10 W 113°16.46′

▼ 0.3 SO Track on left joins the Honeymoon Trail
         and the Hurricane Cliffs Trail.
8.3 ▲ SO Track on right joins the Honeymoon
         Trail and the Hurricane Cliffs Trail.

▼ 0.4 SO Track on right. Little Creek Mountain is
         large mesa ahead on right.
8.2 ▲ SO Track on left.

▼ 1.3 SO Cattle guard, then major road on right.
7.3 ▲ SO Major road on left, then cattle guard.
         GPS: N 37°01.14′ W 113°16.15′

▼ 1.6 SO Cross over wash.
7.0 ▲ SO Cross over wash.

▼ 1.8   SO   Track on right, then cross through wash.
6.8 ▲   SO   Cross through wash, then track on left.

▼ 1.9   SO   Track on left.
6.7 ▲   SO   Track on right.

▼ 2.6   SO   Track on left.
6.0 ▲   SO   Track on right.

▼ 3.2   SO   Faint track on left. Trail passes through The Divide.
5.4 ▲   SO   Trail passes through The Divide. Faint track on right.
         GPS: N 37°02.83' W 113°16.32'

▼ 3.4   SO   Track on left.
5.2 ▲   SO   Track on right.

▼ 3.8   SO   Old sign on left, "Ashby's Blvd."
4.8 ▲   SO   Old sign on right, "Ashby's Blvd."

▼ 3.9   SO   Track on left.
4.7 ▲   SO   Track on right.

▼ 4.1   SO   Track on left, cattle guard, then track on right.
4.5 ▲   SO   Track on left, cattle guard, then track on right.

▼ 4.6   SO   Cross over wash.
4.0 ▲   SO   Cross over wash.

▼ 6.0   SO   Track on right. Gooseberry Mesa is directly ahead.
2.6 ▲   SO   Track on left.

▼ 7.8   SO   Track on left.
0.8 ▲   SO   Track on right.

▼ 8.3   SO   Track on left.
0.3 ▲   SO   Track on right.

▼ 8.4   SO   Cattle guard.
0.2 ▲   SO   Cattle guard.

▼ 8.6   SO   Track on right is signed to Little Creek Mountain, but road is washed out; no vehicle access. Zero trip meter at sign.
0.0 ▲   Continue toward the Arizona state line.

SW Trail #6: The Divide Trail

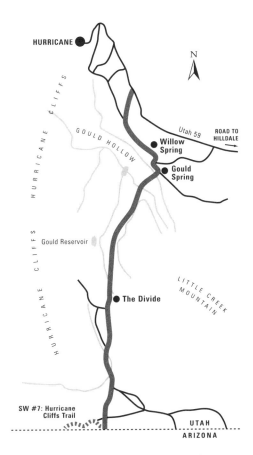

Little Creek Mountain is on left.
GPS: N 37°07.03' W 113°14.49'

▼ 0.0   Continue toward Utah 59.
3.0 ▲   SO   Track on left is signed to Little Creek Mountain, but road is washed out; no vehicle access. Zero trip meter at sign.

▼ 0.1   SO   Cross through Gould Wash.
2.9 ▲   SO   Cross through Gould Wash.

▼ 0.2   SO   Faint track on right.
2.8 ▲   SO   Faint track on left.

▼ 0.3   SO   Track on left.
2.7 ▲   SO   Track on right.

▼ 1.9   BR   Corral on right, two tracks on left.
1.1 ▲   SO   Corral on left, two tracks on right.

| ▼ 2.1 | SO | Cattle guard. |
| 0.9 ▲ | SO | Cattle guard. |

| ▼ 3.0 | | Trail ends on Utah 59, 0.1 miles southeast of mile marker 19. Turn left for Hurricane, right for Hilldale. |
| 0.0 ▲ | | On Utah 59, 0.1 miles southeast of mile marker 19, 3.2 miles east of Hurricane, zero trip meter and turn south on unsigned, graded dirt road. |

GPS: N 37°09.28' W 113°15.45'

SOUTHWEST REGION TRAIL #7

Hurricane Cliffs Trail

STARTING POINT 11 miles south of Hurricane Airport, 0.4 miles south of Arizona state line

FINISHING POINT Southwest #6: The Divide Trail, at the Arizona state line

TOTAL MILEAGE 2.7 miles

UNPAVED MILEAGE 2.7 miles

DRIVING TIME 45 minutes

ELEVATION RANGE 3,400–4,400 feet

USUALLY OPEN Year-round

DIFFICULTY RATING 6

SCENIC RATING 9

REMOTENESS RATING +1

Special Attractions

- Section of the historic Honeymoon Trail.
- Exciting, challenging climb up Hurricane Cliffs.
- Desert cactus vegetation.

History

The Hurricane Cliffs lie along the north-south Hurricane fault line. Movement of this fault caused the lands east of the fault to lift by hundreds of feet, which left a basin to the west. The Hurricane Cliffs extend down into the Arizona Strip and present an almost unbroken face for more than 200 miles.

The Honeymoon Trail is an early Mormon route, constructed by John D. Lee, that led from the Mormon colonies along the Arizona Strip north to St. George. In the late 1800s, many Mormons were settling the remote areas of southwest Utah and the Arizona Strip district. Some were moving by choice, others at the direction of the Mormon Church, which was actively encouraging and directing pioneers into this remote region. Still others were quietly relocating there in an effort to evade the federal government in its crackdown on polygamists.

St. George Temple, the first Mormon temple built west of the Mississippi, was opened in 1877, a full 16 years before the better known temple in Salt Lake City. After St. George Temple opened, a steady stream of Mormons began to make the long trek from their settlements along the Arizona Strip to St. George to be married. They traveled in groups, and the route they traveled became known as the Honeymoon Trail. Most of this trail is still visible today and can be traveled in a 4WD.

This trail follows the section of the Honeymoon Trail that descends the Hurricane Cliffs, and it connects with the much easier Southwest #6: The Divide Trail to make a loop back to Hurricane.

Description

Getting to the start of this trail is a slight challenge in itself, as none of the roads are

Climbing the switchbacks along the Hurricane Cliffs Trail

Looking back toward the mesas in Arizona from Hurricane Cliffs

marked! From Utah 9, on the west side of Hurricane, turn south on the signed road to the airport. Follow this due south, then before entering the airport itself, swing right, then left. The graded road continues due south, closely following the base of the Hurricane Cliffs. After 11 miles from the airport entrance—past the subdivisions and just across the Arizona border (although there is no state line sign)—look for an upright wooden post carved with the words "Honeymoon Trail." The sign is to the left of the trail, where the trail drops down into a creek wash. This is the trail's original entrance, but it is washed out. Zero your trip meter here, and after another 0.1 miles, turn left onto an unmarked but well-used trail.

The trail climbs steeply almost immediately and becomes very steep in places, with low traction on loose rock. For the most part the trail follows an extremely narrow shelf road, where passing places are very limited. The most difficult section is near the top; a narrow, rocky, off-camber section tilts vehicles toward the drop. Those who do not like narrow shelf roads will rate this trail with a high fear factor!

As you climb, the views are stunning: over Sand Mountain to the west, along the face of the sheer Hurricane Cliffs, and south into Arizona over multicolored, banded buttes and mesas.

At the top, the trail is an easygoing two-track as it joins Southwest #6: The Divide Trail.

This trail should not be attempted in slippery conditions.

Current Road Information

BLM St. George Field Office
345 East Riverside Drive
St. George, UT 84790
(435) 688-3200

Map References

BLM   Littlefield (AZ), St. George (UT)
USGS 1:24,000   Rock Canyon (AZ), The Divide (UT)
      1:100,000 Littlefield (AZ), St. George (UT)
Maptech CD-ROM: Grand Canyon (AZ); Escalante/Dixie National Forest (UT)
Utah Atlas & Gazetteer, p. 17

Route Directions

▼ 0.0   11 miles south of Hurricane Airport, on graded dirt road along the base of Hurricane Cliffs, zero trip meter in a wash, next to the Honeymoon Trail

SW Trail #7: Hurricane Cliffs Trail

signpost. Continue south along graded road.

1.5 ▲		Trail ends at graded dirt road, in a wash, south of Hurricane. Continue north to return to Utah 9 via Hurricane Airport. Left leads into Arizona.

GPS: N 36°59.73' W 113°18.54'

▼ 0.1	TL	Turn left onto unmarked, narrow, ungraded, well-used dirt road.
1.4 ▲	TR	Turn right onto graded dirt road.

GPS: N 36°59.69' W 113°18.60'

▼ 0.3	SO	Track on left is the original washed-out trail. Trail climbs steeply along a narrow shelf road.
1.2 ▲	SO	Track on right is the original washed-out trail. End of steep descent.

▼ 0.8	SO	Cross through wash.
0.7 ▲	SO	Cross through wash.

GPS: N 36°59.78' W 113°18.05'

▼ 1.1	SO	Cross over wash.
0.4 ▲	SO	Cross over wash.

▼ 1.2	SO	Cross the Arizona state line (unmarked) at the 37° latitude line.
0.3 ▲	SO	Cross the Arizona state line (unmarked) at the 37° latitude line.

▼ 1.3	SO	Off-camber, loose, rocky short section.
0.2 ▲	SO	Off-camber, loose, rocky short section.

GPS: N 37°00.03' W 113°17.84'

▼ 1.5	TL	T-intersection at end of steep climb. Track on right goes 0.1 miles to viewpoint on the state line. Zero trip meter.
0.0 ▲		Proceed along trail, which quickly drops steeply along a narrow shelf road.

GPS: N 37°00.05' W 113°17.65'

▼ 0.0		Continue toward the Divide Trail and pass through wire gate.
1.2 ▲	TR	Pass through wire gate, then turn right. Track straight on goes 0.1 miles to viewpoint on the state line. Zero trip meter.

▼ 0.2	SO	Track on left to viewpoint.
1.0 ▲	SO	Track on right to viewpoint.

GPS: N 37°00.14' W 113°17.45'

▼ 0.7	SO	Track on left to dam.
0.5 ▲	BL	Track on right to dam.

▼ 0.9	BR	Track on left also joins the Divide Trail.
0.3 ▲	SO	Track on right rejoins the Divide Trail.

GPS: N 37°00.28' W 113°16.71'

▼ 1.2		Trail ends at the T-intersection with Southwest #6: The Divide Trail, just north of the Arizona state line. Turn left on the Divide Trail to Hurricane.
0.0 ▲		On Southwest #6: The Divide Trail, 0.1 miles north of the Arizona state line, turn northwest on dirt trail, marked

with a Honeymoon Trail marker post and zero trip meter. The state line is marked with a cattle guard and a fence but no sign, although BLM road #1015 is marked on the Arizona side.

GPS: N 37°00.10' W 113°16.46'

Smithsonian Butte Trail

STARTING POINT Rockville
FINISHING POINT Utah 59 at Big Plain Junction, 0.1 miles north of mile marker 8
TOTAL MILEAGE 8.9 miles
UNPAVED MILEAGE 8.1 miles
DRIVING TIME 45 minutes
ELEVATION RANGE 3,800–5,000 feet
USUALLY OPEN Year-round
DIFFICULTY RATING 2
SCENIC RATING 9
REMOTENESS RATING +0

Special Attractions

- Views over Zion National Park.
- Grafton ghost town.
- Designated national backcountry byway.

History

When the John Wesley Powell Expedition traveled through Zion, the expedition geologist, Edward Dutton, named Smithsonian Butte after the Smithsonian Institute, which was sponsoring the expedition. Dutton himself has a nearby pass named after him, Dutton Pass, which cuts through the Vermilion Cliffs to the southeast of Smithsonian Butte.

The town at the start of the trail, Rockville, was first settled in 1862 in an attempt by the scattered settlers of the upper Virgin River to band together. The combination of the Indian Wars and repeated flooding made it difficult for individual pioneers to get ahead, so the people gathered and concentrated their efforts in Rockville. The township was originally called Adventure, but the name was changed to Rockville

because of the rocky soils along the Virgin River. The town's single-lane steel bridge was built in 1926, providing a permanent route across the river and replacing the many shaky structures that were constantly having to be rebuilt after floods.

Across the river to the west, Grafton, now a ghost town, was settled in 1859 by folks from nearby Virgin, including Nathan Tenney. Here too, the Virgin River was the bane of the new settlement (for a short time known as Wheeler), and after many of the houses were washed away in 1862, the fledgling township was forced to relocate a mile upstream from the original site. However, on January 8, 1862, with floodwaters still raging, Nathan Tenney's wife went into labor in the family's wagon box. The men of the town succeeded in lifting the wagon out of harm's way and later that night Mr. and Mrs. Tenney became the proud parents of a new son whom they appropriately named Marvelous Flood "Marv" Tenney. Besides repeated flooding of the unpredictable Virgin River, Indian Wars also troubled Grafton, forcing several families to leave the

The larger of the two roads approaching Wire Mesa

Restoration workers visit the old meeting hall

area; the graveyard contains a memorial to a family killed by Indians.

The Virgin River, which enabled Grafton to grow crops, was also the dividing point of the town. Residents would keep horses on both sides of the river—those on the far side for traveling north, those within the town for traveling over Grafton Mesa to the towns to the south. This way, when the river flooded, they were not trapped in town.

By the mid-1880s, Grafton supported 28 families and was the first county seat for Kane County (Grafton is now part of Washington County). The adobe meeting-house, the major building remaining today, was built in 1886 using timber imported from Mount Trumbull on the Arizona Strip, and it was packed and rendered with local clay. This meeting hall, the focal point for the community, was used for dances, church meetings, funerals, and parties as well as religious worship. Residents also helped with the construction of the Hurricane Canal, an ambitious scheme to bring irrigation waters to the Hurricane Bench, which opened up the area for cultivation. In return for their work, these Grafton residents received parcels of land in Hurricane. For many, the temptation to dismantle their homes and rebuild in Hurricane, away from the Virgin River floodplain, was great, and by the early 1920s, Grafton was nearing ghost town status. The final resident moved out in the early 1930s.

Grafton had a brief resurgence when its decaying buildings were used in scenes for the movie *Butch Cassidy and the Sundance Kid* (1969).

Today, Grafton is privately owned, and the remaining buildings are undergoing extensive renovations in conjunction with the Bureau of Land Management. In 2000, the adobe meeting hall was brought back from ruin; it has a new floor, patched adobe, and fresh paint. The oldest building in town, opposite the meeting hall, has been propped up and stabilized for safety, as have some of the other cabins. Visitors are allowed to explore the area, but should not disturb the remains.

Description

Smithsonian Butte Road, a designated national backcountry byway, crosses over the Vermilion Cliffs between Utah 9 and Utah 59. The trail is short and graded road its entire length. It leaves the town of Rockville near the western edge of Zion National Park and immediately crosses the East Fork of the Virgin

Smithsonian Butte

River on the historic steel girder bridge.

After 1.6 miles, you reach a T-intersection. Turn right to go 1.7 miles along a graded dirt road if you want to visit the ghost town of Grafton. You first pass the cemetery on the left, followed by the remains of the town itself.

The main trail follows Horse Valley Wash for a short distance before climbing steeply onto the mesa. This section can be a little rutty and washed out, but high-clearance 2WD vehicles will have no problems in dry weather. The prominent jagged peaks of Eagle Crags can be seen on the left.

Once on the mesa, you'll see the bulk of Smithsonian Butte ahead. The trail continues along the top, passing Southwest #9: Grafton Mesa Trail before dropping gradually down the south side of the Vermilion Cliffs.

The final part of the road crosses over farmland before reaching Utah 59 at Big Plain Junction. The junction appears on maps, but there are no signs for it on the road.

Current Road Information
BLM St. George Field Office
345 East Riverside Drive
St. George, UT 84790
(435) 688-3200

Map References
BLM   St. George
USGS 1:24,000   Smithsonian Butte,
        Springdale West
        1:100,000 St. George
Maptech CD-ROM: Escalante/Dixie
        National Forest
Trails Illustrated, #214 (incomplete)
Utah Atlas & Gazetteer, p. 17
Utah Travel Council #4

Route Directions

▼ 0.0   From Utah 9 at the east end of Rockville, turn south on Bridge Road (200 East Street) and zero trip meter.
1.6 ▲   Trail ends at Utah 9 in Rockville. Turn right for Zion National Park, turn left for Hurricane.
        GPS: N 37°09.66′ W 113°02.23′

▼ 0.1   SO Cross over East Fork Virgin River on steel girder bridge.
1.5 ▲   SO Cross over East Fork Virgin River on steel girder bridge.

▼ 0.3   TR Dirt road continues ahead. Follow the small sign for Grafton and Utah 59.
1.3 ▲   TL Road to the right.

▼ 0.8   SO Road is now graded dirt.
0.8 ▲   SO Road is now paved.

▼ 0.9   SO Cattle guard.
0.7 ▲   SO Cattle guard.

▼ 1.5   SO Cattle guard.
0.1 ▲   SO Cattle guard.

▼ 1.6   TL T-intersection. Right goes 1.7 miles to Grafton ghost town. Turn left and cross over Horse Valley Wash on bridge and zero trip meter.
0.0 ▲   Continue toward Rockville.
        GPS: N 37°09.08′ W 113°03.52′

▼ 0.0   Continue south.
3.5 ▲   TR Cross over Horse Valley Wash on bridge and zero trip meter. Continue straight to go 1.7 miles to Grafton ghost town.

▼ 0.3   SO View of Eagle Crags on left.
3.2 ▲   SO View of Eagle Crags on right.

▼ 0.5   SO Trail climbs to mesa.
3.0 ▲   SO End of descent.

▼ 1.2   SO End of climb.
2.3 ▲   SO Descend to Virgin River.

▼ 1.4   SO Track on right.
2.1 ▲   SO Track on left.
        GPS: N 37°08.04′ W 113°03.81′

▼ 1.5   SO Track on left.
2.0 ▲   SO Track on right.

▼ 1.6   SO Track on left.
1.9 ▲   SO Track on right.

| ▼ 1.8 | SO | Track on right goes out on Wire Mesa. |
| 1.7 ▲ | SO | Track on left goes out on Wire Mesa. |

GPS: N 37°07.88' W 113°04.13'

| ▼ 3.3 | SO | Cross over South Wash. |
| 0.2 ▲ | SO | Cross over South Wash. |

| ▼ 3.5 | SO | Immediately before left-hand swing, track to right is Southwest #9: Grafton Mesa Trail. Parking area at the trailhead. Zero trip meter. |
| 0.0 ▲ | | Continue northeast. |

GPS: N 37°07.85' W 113°05.83'

| ▼ 0.0 | | Continue southwest. |
| 3.8 ▲ | SO | Immediately after right-hand swing, track to left is Southwest #9: Grafton Mesa Trail. Parking area at the trailhead. Zero trip meter. |

| ▼ 0.2 | SO | Track on right. Smithsonian Butte is on left. |
| 3.6 ▲ | SO | Track on left. Smithsonian Butte is on right. |

| ▼ 0.4 | SO | Major track on right. |
| 3.4 ▲ | SO | Major track on left. |

GPS: N 37°07.55' W 113°06.12'

| ▼ 0.5 | SO | Track on left. |
| 3.3 ▲ | SO | Track on right. |

| ▼ 0.7 | SO | Track on left. |
| 3.1 ▲ | SO | Track on right. |

| ▼ 1.1 | SO | Track on right is signed to Gooseberry Mesa. Main trail exits BLM land and crosses farmland. |
| 2.7 ▲ | SO | Track on left is signed to Gooseberry Mesa. Main trail enters BLM land. |

GPS: N 37°07.00' W 113°06.36'

| ▼ 1.3 | SO | Track on left. |
| 2.5 ▲ | SO | Track on right. |

| ▼ 2.3 | SO | Track on left, then cattle guard. |
| 1.5 ▲ | SO | Cattle guard, then track on right. |

| ▼ 2.6 | SO | Cross over Gould Wash. |
| 1.2 ▲ | SO | Cross over Gould Wash. |

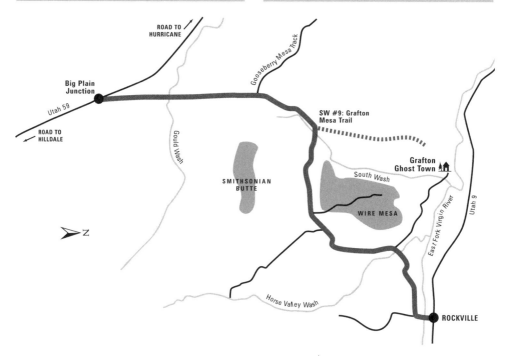

SW Trail #8: Smithsonian Butte Trail

▲ Eagle Crags

▼ 3.3	SO	Corral on right.
0.5 ▲	SO	Corral on left.

▼ 3.8		Trail ends at Utah 59 at Big Plain Junction. Turn right for Hurricane, turn left for Hilldale.
0.0 ▲		On Utah 59 at Big Plain Junction, 0.1 miles north of mile marker 8, turn north on graded dirt road and zero trip meter.
		GPS: N 37°04.55′ W 113°06.36′

SOUTHWEST REGION TRAIL #9

Grafton Mesa Trail

STARTING POINT Southwest #8: Smithsonian Butte Trail, 5.1 miles south of Utah 9
FINISHING POINT Grafton Mesa
TOTAL MILEAGE 1.9 miles
UNPAVED MILEAGE 1.9 miles
DRIVING TIME 30 minutes (one-way)
ELEVATION RANGE 4,300–4,800 feet
USUALLY OPEN Year-round
DIFFICULTY RATING 3
SCENIC RATING 8
REMOTENESS RATING +0

Hiking trail above the old town site of Grafton

Special Attractions
■ Views of Pastry Ridge and Mount Kinesava.
■ Accesses historic hiking trail into Grafton ghost town.

Description
This short spur leads off from Southwest #8: Smithsonian Butte Trail and runs out onto Grafton Mesa. The small trail is rocky and narrow, and the first part runs through the juniper and cedar trees that dot the top of the mesa. When the trees abate, there are wide-ranging views over the eroded Pastry Ridge, so named because of its resemblance to pie crust. The trail gradually descends, passing short spurs, one of which leads to a large pleasant campsite at an oil drilling post with views over Zion National Park.

The lower section of the trail gets narrower, rougher, and slightly brushy; wider vehicles who don't want to risk paint scratches should turn around just before the trail end. The trail then finishes before a wash, with a rocky pour-off into South Wash far below. Immediately north of the wash, you can see the remains of a wagon road leading steeply down from the mesa. The road is well built up around the cliff face; timbers and rocks stabilize a narrow shelf. The start of the trail is washed out and impassable to vehicles, but it is possible to hike. It exits South Wash at the Grafton cemetery. The exact purpose of the trail is unknown, but it was likely a "wood road" for Grafton—a direct trail leading to the top of the mesa to obtain timber for firewood and building material. The Grafton cemetery is visible 700 feet below in the valley.

Current Road Information
BLM St. George Field Office
345 East Riverside Drive
St. George, UT 84790
(435) 688-3200

SW Trail #9: Grafton Mesa Trail

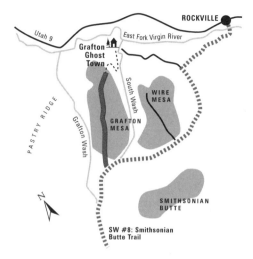

Map References

BLM   St. George
USGS   1:24,000   Springdale West
        1:100,000   St. George
Maptech CD-ROM: Escalante/Dixie
        National Forest
Trails Illustrated, #214
Utah Atlas & Gazetteer, p. 17

Route Directions

▼ 0.0   On Southwest #8: Smithsonian Butte
          Trail, 5.1 miles from Utah 9, zero trip
          meter and turn northeast on a small
          ungraded dirt road. Coming from Utah
          9, turn is immediately before a left-
          hand bend and has a large parking
          area/campsite at the start.
          GPS: N 37°07.85' W 113°05.83'

▼ 0.6   SO Views to the left over Pastry Ridge.
▼ 0.8   SO Small campsite on right, then faint
          track on right.
          GPS: N 37°08.56' W 113°05.61'

▼ 1.1   SO Turnout with view to the left.
▼ 1.4   SO Faint track on right goes 0.1 miles to
          oil drilling post and large campsite
          with views over Zion National Park.
▼ 1.6   SO Faint track on left.
▼ 1.8   SO Turning point for wider vehicles who

want to avoid brushy section of trail.
GPS: N 37°09.34' W 113°05.34'

▼ 1.9   Trail finishes just before a wash and
          rocky pour-off into South Wash. Old hik-
          ing trail continues to Grafton cemetery.
          GPS: N 37°09.42' W 113°05.30'

SOUTHWEST REGION TRAIL #10

Elephant Butte Trail

STARTING POINT Coral Pink Sand Dunes Road,
   4 miles south of state park entrance
FINISHING POINT Coral Pink Sand Dunes
   Road, 5.6 miles south of state park
   entrance
TOTAL MILEAGE 16.4 miles
UNPAVED MILEAGE 16.4 miles
DRIVING TIME 1.5 hours
ELEVATION RANGE 5,600–6,300 feet
USUALLY OPEN Year-round
DIFFICULTY RATING 4 in main direction; 5 in
   reverse
SCENIC RATING 8
REMOTENESS RATING +1

Special Attractions

■ The Elephant Butte and Block Mesas.
■ Views of Zion National Park.
■ Fun, sandy trail.

History

North of Elephant Gap, the trail passes Harris
Flat, with Harris Mountain visible to the
northeast. Harris Ranch was one of the few
prosperous ranches associated with nearby
Shunesburg. The land was purchased from
Chief Shunes of the local Paiute tribe in 1862.
The town of Shunesburg was located to the
northwest, deep in the Parunuweap Canyon
on the East Fork Virgin River. This settlement
was nearly impossible to access from Kanab.
The only way was via the treacherous Shunes
Creek Canyon, a route that became known as
the Wiggle Trail. The Kanab mail carrier
found an ingenious solution, lowering the

mail over the edge of the 1,500-foot cliff in Parunuweap Canyon via wire cable and winch. The people from Shunesburg collected it at the foot of the cliff and continued with it to St. George.

A beautiful view of Elephant Butte at sunset

Although crops were successful in Shunesburg, its location where the East Fork Virgin River exited the deep canyon meant flooding was a constant problem. The final straw was a grasshopper plague in the late 1870s, after which most people left the settlement. A few folks remained to ranch until the turn of the century, and today the site is part of a private ranch.

The famous one-armed geologist John Wesley Powell based his exploration team in Shunesburg while surveying the Parunuweap Canyon, which is now contained within Zion National Park. Powell's main claim to fame was that he was the first explorer of the Colorado River. He, with four boats and a brave crew, made a daring nine-hundred-mile journey that started at the Union Pacific Railroad crossing in Wyoming and ended in Arizona's Grand Canyon. The majestic Lake Powell is named after this stalwart explorer and surveyor.

Description

This formed trail is a lot of fun to drive—with its long, moderately challenging sandy sections—and it appears well used, although you are unlikely to see another vehicle except in hunting season, when the area is popular for its trophy deer (by permit only).

The trail passes through Elephant Gap, an opening in the series of buttes that make up the Block Mesas. The first major junction, a track to the right, leads to the Virgin River. On maps, this trail descends steeply down to the river. However, it is not recommended for vehicles.

After 8 miles, you reach the turnoff for Southwest #11: The Barracks Trail, and the main Elephant Butte Trail doubles back sharply on itself. For the next 3 miles, it follows the course of the wash through abundant sagebrush. This part of the trail can be a little brushy for wider vehicles.

The last few miles of the trail are the most difficult; a couple of deep sand descents have large holes made by vehicles coming up the trail. The easiest direction of travel is the main one described below; traveling around the loop in the reverse direction increases the difficulty rating to a 5.

The entire trail should not pose a problem for stock vehicles, although lower tire pressures are suggested. Note that many of the cattle guards have "sand mats" on either side of them to stop vehicles from wearing deep holes in the sand in front of the cattle guards. The entire trail has good views; the best are of Zion National Park as you approach the apex of the loop.

A cattle guard and sand mats help you along past Elephant Gap

Current Road Information

BLM Kanab Field Office
318 North 100 East
Kanab, UT 84741
(435) 644-4600

Map References

BLM   Kanab
USGS 1:24,000   Elephant Butte
      1:100,000   Kanab
Maptech CD-ROM: Escalante/Dixie
      National Forest
Utah Atlas & Gazetteer, p. 18
Utah Travel Council #4

Route Directions

▼ 0.0   From Coral Pink Sand Dunes Road, 4 miles south of entrance to state park, zero trip meter and turn northwest on ungraded sandy trail. A small gravel parking area is at trailhead.

3.3 ▲   End at Coral Pink Sand Dunes Road, 1.6 miles north of the starting point. Turn left for Coral Pink Sand Dunes State Park and US 89.
        GPS: N 37°01.46' W 112°48.13'

▼ 1.0   SO   Track on right, then two entrances to track on left.
2.3 ▲   SO   Two entrances to track on right, then track on left.

▼ 1.1   SO   Track on left.
2.2 ▲   SO   Track on right.
        GPS: N 37°02.48' W 112°47.95'

▼ 2.2   SO   Track on left.
1.1 ▲   SO   Track on right.

▼ 2.6   SO   Cross through small wash.
0.7 ▲   SO   Cross through small wash.

▼ 2.9   SO   Cattle guard at the south side of Elephant Gap.
0.4 ▲   SO   Cattle guard at the south side of Elephant Gap.
        GPS: N 37°03.95' W 112°48.08'

▼ 3.2   SO   Track on left.

0.1 ▲   SO   Track on right.

▼ 3.3   BL   Track on right goes to the Virgin River (recommended for ATVs only). Zero trip meter.
0.0 ▲   Continue along main sandy trail.
        GPS: N 37°04.28' W 112°48.11'

▼ 0.0   Continue along main sandy trail.
4.7 ▲   SO   Track on left is second entrance to Virgin River trail. Zero trip meter.

▼ 0.3   SO   Track on right is second entrance to Virgin River trail. Continue northwest toward the gap between two buttes. To the right are the Block Mesas and Harris Mountain.
4.4 ▲   BR   Track on left goes to the Virgin River (recommended for ATVs only). To the left are the Block Mesas and Harris Mountain.

▼ 0.6   SO   Pass through gap in the buttes. Track on left and track on right at saddle. Views ahead to Zion National Park.
4.1 ▲   SO   Pass through gap in the buttes. Track on left and track on right at saddle.
        GPS: N 37°04.78' W 112°48.44'

▼ 0.7   SO   Pass through wire gate, then cattle guard.
4.0 ▲   SO   Cattle guard, then pass through wire gate.

▼ 0.8   BR   Track on left. Sandstone Butte on left.
3.9 ▲   SO   Track on right. Sandstone Butte on right.
        GPS: N 37°04.81' W 112°48.72'

▼ 1.9   SO   Faint track on left.
2.8 ▲   SO   Faint track on right.

▼ 2.0   SO   Track on right.
2.7 ▲   SO   Track on left.
        GPS: N 37°05.42' W 112°49.80'

▼ 3.4   SO   Track on right.
1.3 ▲   SO   Track on left.

▼ 3.5   SO   Track on right, then pass through old fence line.

SW Trail #10: Elephant Butte Trail

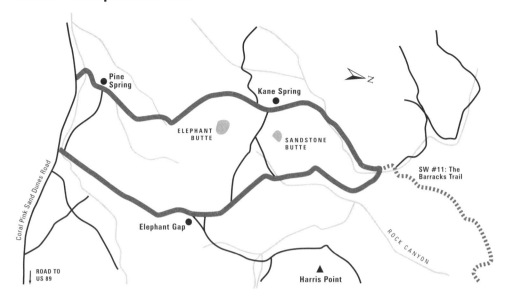

1.2 ▲   SO Pass through old fence line, then track on left.

▼ 4.1 BL Track on right.
0.6 ▲   SO Track on left.

▼ 4.7 TL Ahead is Southwest #11: The Barracks Trail. Turn sharp left in front of small area of white rock. Zero trip meter.
0.0 ▲   Continue back southeast toward Sandstone Butte.
    GPS: N 37°07.24′ W 112°51.09′

▼ 0.0   Continue back southeast following the creek. There is no defined wash, but abundant sagebrush makes trail narrow and brushy for next 3.2 miles.
3.2 ▲ TR Ahead is Southwest #11: The Barracks Trail. Turn sharp right and zero trip meter.

▼ 1.0 SO Pass through fence line.
2.2 ▲ SO Pass through fence line.
    GPS: N 37°06.46′ W 112°51.19′

▼ 1.9 SO Faint track on left.
1.3 ▲ SO Faint track on right.

▼ 2.1 SO Exit creek course.

1.1 ▲   SO Enter creek course. There is no defined wash, but abundant sagebrush.

▼ 2.3 SO Track on right.
0.9 ▲   SO Track on left.
    GPS: N 37°05.49′ W 112°51.72′

▼ 2.5 SO Cross through wash.
0.7 ▲   SO Cross through wash.

▼ 3.2 SO Track on left. Kane Spring and dam on the right. End of brushy section. Zero trip meter.
0.0 ▲   Continue northwest.
    GPS: N 37°04.81′ W 112°51.12′

▼ 0.0   Continue south. Immediately pass second track on left.
5.2 ▲ BL Two tracks on right, Kane Spring and dam on the left. Views ahead to Zion National Park. The trail is narrow and brushy for the next 3.2 miles.

▼ 0.1 SO Cross through wash.
5.1 ▲ SO Cross through wash.

▼ 0.2 SO Intersection. Elephant Butte is on left.
5.0 ▲ SO Intersection. Elephant Butte is on right.
    GPS: N 37°04.58′ W 112°51.16′

| ▼ 0.5 | SO | Track on right. |
| 4.7 ▲ | SO | Track on left. |

GPS: N 37°04.31′ W 112°51.18′

| ▼ 0.6 | SO | Faint track on left. |
| 4.6 ▲ | SO | Faint track on right. |

| ▼ 0.8 | SO | Track on left. |
| 4.4 ▲ | SO | Track on right. |

| ▼ 1.2 | SO | Track on right. |
| 4.0 ▲ | SO | Track on left. |

| ▼ 1.7 | SO | Grassy campsite on left with views of Elephant Butte. |
| 3.5 ▲ | SO | Grassy campsite on right with views of Elephant Butte. |

GPS: N 37°03.43′ W 112°50.59′

| ▼ 1.8 | SO | Faint track on right, then cross through slickrock wash. |
| 3.4 ▲ | SO | Cross through slickrock wash, then faint track on left. |

| ▼ 2.3 | SO | Steep, deep sandy descent. |
| 2.9 ▲ | SO | Top of ascent. |

| ▼ 2.4 | SO | Cross through wash, then track on left. |
| 2.8 ▲ | BL | Track on right, then cross through wash, followed by steep, deep sandy ascent. |

GPS: N 37°03.17′ W 112°49.95′

| ▼ 2.7 | SO | Second loose descent to cross wash. |
| 2.5 ▲ | SO | Cross wash, then loose sandy ascent. |

GPS: N 37°02.93′ W 112°49.86′

| ▼ 2.8 | SO | Track on left. |
| 2.4 ▲ | BL | Track on right. |

GPS: N 37°02.89′ W 112°49.83′

| ▼ 3.1 | SO | Faint track on left, then cattle guard. |
| 2.1 ▲ | SO | Cattle guard, then faint track on right. |

| ▼ 3.2 | SO | Track on left. |
| 2.0 ▲ | BL | Track on right. |

| ▼ 3.8 | SO | Track on right and track on left. |

| 1.4 ▲ | SO | Track on right and track on left. |

GPS: N 37°02.02′ W 112°49.83′

| ▼ 4.2 | SO | Track on left. Pine Spring in Rosy Canyon on the right. |
| 1.0 ▲ | SO | Track on right. Pine Spring in Rosy Canyon on the left. |

GPS: N 37°01.73′ W 112°49.89′

| ▼ 4.4 | SO | Track on left. |
| 0.8 ▲ | SO | Track on right. |

| ▼ 4.8 | BL | Corral on right, then track on left. |
| 0.4 ▲ | SO | Track on right, then corral on left. |

| ▼ 5.0 | BL | Track on right. |
| 0.2 ▲ | BR | Track on left. |

GPS: N 37°01.17′ W 112°50.11′

| ▼ 5.1 | BL | Track on right joins paved road. |
| 0.1 ▲ | SO | Track on left rejoins paved road. |

| ▼ 5.2 | | End at paved Coral Pink Sand Dunes Road, 1.6 miles south of the starting point. Turn left for Coral Pink Sand Dunes State Park and US 89. |
| 0.0 ▲ | | On Coral Pink Sand Dunes Road, 5.6 miles south of the state park entrance, zero trip meter and turn northwest on the unmarked, sandy trail, which briefly parallels paved road. |

GPS: N 37°01.19′ W 112°49.86′

SOUTHWEST REGION TRAIL #11

The Barracks Trail

STARTING POINT Southwest #10: Elephant Butte Trail
FINISHING POINT The Barracks
TOTAL MILEAGE 5.2 miles
UNPAVED MILEAGE 5.2 miles
DRIVING TIME 45 minutes (one-way)
ELEVATION RANGE 5,100–6,200 feet
USUALLY OPEN Year-round
DIFFICULTY RATING 4
SCENIC RATING 8
REMOTENESS RATING +1

Special Attractions

- Views of Zion National Park and the White Cliffs.
- Overlook of the Virgin River.
- Fun, sandy trail.

Description

This short spur trail leads from Southwest #10: Elephant Butte Trail to an overlook of the East Fork Virgin River. The trail is sandy and ungraded, and it winds through scattered vegetation. After 3.3 miles, there is a spectacular, shaded campsite on the edge of the cliff, with views over Zion National Park and the White Cliffs.

After the campsite, a long, very sandy, loose descent leads to a slickrock wash crossing. Don't forget that you have to return this way, so if you are in doubt about your vehicle's ability to climb back up the loose sand, then the campsite makes a good place to stop. The trail descends for the next 1.9 miles to the final viewpoint on a narrow spur. You finish at a small turning circle and rock promontory high above the East Fork Virgin River.

The spur trail is remote, and you are unlikely to see anyone else out here. The BLM warns that it rarely visits the area, so travelers should be completely self-sufficient.

A sandy section of The Barracks Trail

View of Zion National Park from a campsite along The Barracks Trail

Current Road Information

BLM Kanab Field Office
318 North 100 East
Kanab, UT 84741
(435) 644-4600

Map References

BLM   Kanab
USGS 1:24,000   The Barracks, Elephant
           Butte
           1:100,000 Kanab
Maptech CD-ROM: Escalante/Dixie
           National Forest
Utah Atlas & Gazetteer, p. 18
Utah Travel Council #4

Route Directions

▼ 0.0   From Southwest #10: Elephant Butte
           Trail, at the farthest point of the loop, 8
           miles from the start of the trail, turn
           northwest on unmarked trail and zero
           trip meter.
           GPS: N 37°07.24' W 112°51.09'

SW Trail #11: The Barracks Trail

▼ 0.3   BR   Track on left.
▼ 0.7   SO   Pass through wire gate.
         GPS: N 37°07.75' W 112°51.18'

▼ 1.1   SO   Track on right.
         GPS: N 37°08.14' W 112°51.14'

▼ 3.3   SO   Excellent campsite on left. Trail drops toward Rock Canyon.
         GPS: N 37°09.83' W 112°50.49'

▼ 4.0   SO   Cross through wash.
         GPS: N 37°09.73' W 112°50.06'

▼ 4.9   SO   Cross through rocky slickrock wash.
         GPS: N 37°10.06' W 112°50.06'

▼ 5.2   Trail ends at viewpoint over the East Fork Virgin River.
         GPS: N 37°10.16' W 112°49.43'

Moquith Mountains Trail

STARTING POINT Hancock Road, 5.5 miles southwest of US 89
FINISHING POINT Moquith Mountains
TOTAL MILEAGE 8 miles
UNPAVED MILEAGE 8 miles
DRIVING TIME 45 minutes (one-way)
ELEVATION RANGE 6,000–7,000 feet
USUALLY OPEN Year-round
DIFFICULTY RATING 4
SCENIC RATING 8
REMOTENESS RATING +1

Special Attractions
- Coral Pink Sand Dunes State Park.
- Indian Canyon Pictographs Trail.
- Fun, sandy trail with great views into Water Canyon.

Description
The dramatic pinkish red dunes of the Coral Pink Sand Dunes State Park are a major feature on this trail. Wind funnels through the Moccasin and Moquith Mountains, carrying particles of pink sand from the region's Navajo sandstone; as the air pressure drops, the grains fall to form the dunes. The dunes were one of the reasons that Kanab was once known as the most inaccessible town in the United States, and they have been the setting for their share of movies: *Arabian Nights* was filmed here in 1942, *Mackenna's Gold* in 1969, and *One Little Indian* in 1973. A conservation area within the dunes protects the coral pink beetle in its only known habitat.

The trail remains outside the boundary of the state park, but it provides a major access point into the dunes for dune buggies and sand bikes. There are also many quiet areas for hikers and photographers to enjoy the incredibly picturesque combination of vivid sands and vegetation.

From US 89, follow the signed Hancock Road for 5.5 miles to the start of the trail. An information board at the trailhead lists camping and off-road travel restrictions. Most of the Moquith Mountains are now within the boundaries of a wilderness study area, and vehicle travel is restricted to established roads. Those with sand vehicles can access the dunes themselves, but they are not suitable for 4WD vehicles, because of the extreme steepness and depth of the sand.

After 1.9 miles, you reach Sand Springs, the major camping area for the Moquith Mountains. The area is bare and open under large stands of pines. No campfires are allowed. The coral pink dunes rise abruptly on the right. Sand vehicles can use the designated access points to reach the dunes.

Some of southern Utah's unique wilderness found along the trail

From Sand Springs, the formed track follows the dunes to the Moquith Mountains. The sand is deep and the road twisty as it winds through a mixture of tall pine trees, junipers, oaks, sagebrush, and yuccas. Those with wide vehicles should exercise care to avoid scratching paintwork. The trail is used by ATVs as well as vehicles, and the sandy trail means you can expect fast-moving traffic in the opposite direction!

There are occasional patches of slickrock in the sand, but the first part of the trail is easily traveled by stock vehicles, although you may need to lower tire pressures.

After 5.2 miles, a track to the left leads to the hiking trailhead for the South Fork Indian Canyon Pictographs Trail. This narrow, twisty, 1.8-mile trail is fun to drive, but has several blind corners—watch for oncoming vehicles. At the end, hikers can follow a

trail to descend into South Fork Canyon to view the pictographs.

From the turn to the hiking trail to the turnout at the end of the mapped trail, the views get better and better. The trail runs along a ridge, with views into the deep Water Canyon to the left and toward the Moccasin Mountains and Elephant Butte to the right.

The complete Moquith Mountains Trail is a loop trail that circles around the head of Water Canyon. However, sections of the loop beyond the final turnout involve obstacles that are beyond the reach of most stock vehicles and this book. There are very loose, steep, deep sand sections that may require winching, and there is a very difficult descent to Water Canyon over some slickrock ledges nearly 24 inches high embedded in deep sand. Vehicles should turn back at the turnout indicated.

Current Road Information
BLM Kanab Field Office
318 North 100 East
Kanab, UT 84741
(435) 644-4600

Map References
BLM   Kanab
USGS 1:24,000   Yellow Jacket Canyon
      1:100,000 Kanab
Maptech CD-ROM: Escalante/Dixie
      National Forest
Utah Atlas & Gazetteer, p. 18
Utah Travel Council #4

Sand Springs and old corral at the Coral Pink Sand Dunes State Park

SW Trail #12: Moquith Mountains Trail

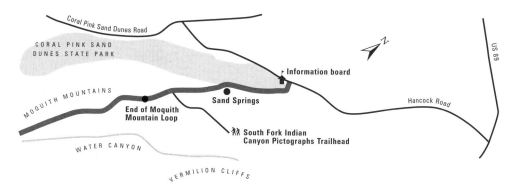

Route Directions

▼ 0.0   From Hancock Road, 5.5 miles southwest of US 89, turn southwest on graded dirt road at the information board and zero trip meter.
GPS: N 37°05.87' W 112°38.65'

▼ 0.1 SO Information board for the dunes and Moquith Mountains.

▼ 0.2 SO Track on left through gate. Sand dunes are now on right.

▼ 1.3 SO Cattle guard.

▼ 1.4 SO Faint track on left.

▼ 1.7 SO Track on left, then main trail forks and rejoins at Sand Springs.
GPS: N 37°04.70' W 112°39.75'

▼ 1.9 SO Tracks rejoin at Sand Springs. Old corral and spring on right. Many tracks lead off left to camping areas. Track on right is designated access to sand dunes for sand vehicles. Continue straight. Zero trip meter as you leave the open area on the track leading south.
GPS: N 37°04.54' W 112°39.87'

▼ 0.0   Continue south along the dunes.

▼ 3.3 SO Track on left goes 1.8 miles to South Fork Indian Canyon Pictographs Trail. Zero trip meter.
GPS: N 37°03.50' W 112°40.64'

▼ 0.0   Continue along main sandy trail.

▼ 0.7 SO Track on left is the end of the Moquith Mountains Loop.

GPS: N 37°02.93' W 112°40.88'

▼ 2.4 TL Four-way junction, with large pine tree in the middle.
GPS: N 37°01.63' W 112°41.69'

▼ 2.8 UT Views to the left into Water Canyon. Turnout on right. Main trail continues on, but becomes extremely difficult and is beyond the scope of this book. Retrace your steps to Hancock Road.
GPS: N 37°00.99' W 112°41.84'

SOUTHWEST REGION TRAIL #13

Hog Canyon Trail

STARTING POINT US 89, 1.4 miles north of Kanab
FINISHING POINT Toms Canyon Overlook
TOTAL MILEAGE 3.9 miles
UNPAVED MILEAGE 3.9 miles
DRIVING TIME 45 minutes (one-way)
ELEVATION RANGE 5,000–5,800 feet
USUALLY OPEN Year-round
DIFFICULTY RATING 6
SCENIC RATING 8
REMOTENESS RATING +0

Special Attractions

- Challenging, fun sandy climb out of Hog Canyon.
- Views into Toms Canyon.
- Short trail near to Kanab that can be completed in a couple of hours.

An alternative route bypasses the large washout in Hog Canyon

Description

The main feature of this trail is the challenging climb out of Hog Canyon—most vehicles will get a good workout.

The trail leaves US 89 just north of Kanab. The first mile or so along Hog Canyon on the roughly graded sandy track is easy going. At a four-way junction 1.6 miles into the trail, the fun starts. The trail climbs very steeply up a very loose and sandy section. The first part isn't too bad, but don't relax—the loosest and deepest sand is near the top. To add to the challenge, there are several deep holes in front of rock ledges. If you are going too fast at this stage, you risk undercarriage damage on the unexpected rocks. If you go too slowly, you will bog down and won't make it up! The best combination is a steady pace and low tire pressure.

Once you are at the top of the first climb, the worst is over, although the very loose, deep sand continues for most of the trail. There are good views over Wygaret Terrace,

the White Cliffs, and down into the red-rocked Hog Canyon. After 3 miles, the trail forks. The right-hand spur takes you 0.5 miles to the radio towers on the bluff above Kanab; this trail has some good views and very challenging sandy sections. The radio towers are gated, so there is no access to the end of the spur.

The main trail goes left at the fork and continues for another mile before ending at a viewpoint overlooking Toms Canyon. Kanab can be glimpsed between the cliffs at the end of the canyon. The promontory to the east of the overlook is Savage Point.

The trail continues at this point, but it drops steeply down to run in a narrow wash with an extremely difficult exit. This part of the trail is used mainly by ATVs and is too narrow and brushy to be a pleasant experience for those in stock vehicles.

Although the trail is normally open year-round, the summer months can be extremely hot, and the first sand climb may well be impassable due to the loose sand.

Current Road Information
BLM Kanab Field Office
318 North 100 East
Kanab, UT 84741
(435) 644-4600

Looking up the difficult, sandy climb out of Hog Canyon

KANAB WOMEN

Before national suffrage for women was ratified on August 26, 1920, there were the political endeavors of the women of Kanab. Utah was somewhat ahead of the rest of the country when it came to women's suffrage; women in the state had the right to vote since 1870. A woman voting in Utah was nothing new, but what happened in Kanab was different indeed.

In November 1912, Kane County politics were at a standstill. No one was running for mayor and the ballot for city council positions remained empty. Names of women were entered as a joke. However, no one had bothered to run against the women and on Election Day, the female candidates were a joke no more. Mary Elizabeth Wooley Chamberlain was elected as mayor of Kanab and an entire council of women backed her.

Chamberlain became the second female mayor in United States history. The Kanab city council was the first all female council. Under the women's guidance Kanab underwent many projects, including a "clean town" campaign. Laws prohibiting gambling and drinking were passed, and a new process of taxing traveling salesmen strengthened the local economy. City improvements began with new bridges, a newly platted cemetery, and a new dike that would help protect the town from floods. An unusual commission was the creation of "Stink Weed Day" (September 12, 1912). Cash prizes were given out to whoever eliminated the most stinkweed from his or her yard and sidewalk. Chamberlain and her council reinvigorated Kane County politics; but this female political reign was to be short-lived. The women didn't run for re-election in 1914, but encouraged other women to enter in their stead. However, no one stepped up to the plate and men once again made up the city council.

Map References

BLM   Kanab
USGS 1:24,000   Kanab, Thompson Point
1:100,000   Kanab
Maptech CD-ROM: Escalante/Dixie
National Forest
Utah Atlas & Gazetteer, p. 18
Utah Travel Council #4

Route Directions

▼ 0.0   From US 89, 1.4 miles north of Kanab, 0.1 miles north of mile marker 67, zero trip meter and turn northeast on roughly graded sandy trail. Trail leaves through a parking area over a rise.
GPS: N 37°04.74′ W 112°32.27′

▼ 0.1   SO Cattle guard. Entering Hog Canyon.
▼ 1.3   BL North Fork Canyon enters on left, then small dead-end track on right.
▼ 1.6   TR Four-way junction. Take second

right; this well-used trail ascends a steep, sandy hill.
GPS: N 37°05.32′ W 112°30.81′

▼ 2.2   SO Track on right. End of climb.
▼ 2.3   SO Track on right.
▼ 2.8   BL Track on right, then old, faded hiking trail sign on left and little-used hiking trail.
GPS: N 37°04.44′ W 112°30.68′

▼ 3.0   BL Track on right, then pass through fence line and bear left. The right fork goes 0.5 miles to the radio tower. Zero trip meter.
GPS: N 37°04.33′ W 112°30.55′

▼ 0.0   Continue northeast along fence line.
▼ 0.4   SO Track on left passes through fence line.
GPS: N 37°04.39′ W 112°30.08′

▼ 0.5   BR Track straight on continues along fence line.

SW Trail #13: Hog Canyon Trail

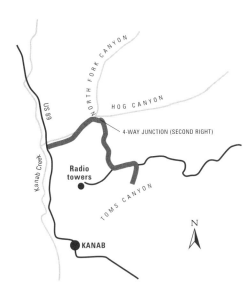

▼ 0.6   SO   Track on left goes to viewpoint.
▼ 0.7   BR   Track on left drops into Toms Canyon and continues as ATV trail.
                GPS: N 37°04.30′ W 112°29.94′

▼ 0.9   Trail ends at viewpoint over Toms Canyon and small turning circle and campsite.
                GPS: N 37°04.02′ W 112°30.04′

SOUTHWEST REGION TRAIL #14

John R Flat Trail

STARTING POINT Kanab Creek Road, 2.7 miles from Utah 89
FINISHING POINT Johnson Canyon Road, 7.4 miles north of Utah 89
TOTAL MILEAGE 9.6 miles
UNPAVED MILEAGE 9.6 miles
DRIVING TIME 1.25 hours
ELEVATION RANGE 5,200–5,800 feet
USUALLY OPEN Year-round
DIFFICULTY RATING 5 in main direction; 4 in reverse direction
SCENIC RATING 7
REMOTENESS RATING +0

Special Attractions
■ Kanab Creek Canyon.
■ Views over the White Cliffs and Cutler Point.
■ Fun, sandy trail.

History
The eastern end of this trail finishes in Johnson Canyon, a region of southwest Utah associated with tales of treasures and pioneer hardships. The canyon was settled in 1871 by the Johnson brothers, who had moved down the Virgin River to settle at the suggestion of Brigham Young. John D. Lee had become familiar with Johnson Canyon around this time, and he briefly settled in its upper reaches. He was keeping a low profile because of his association with the Mountain Meadows Massacre (in which, for reasons that are still unknown, Mormons killed more than a hundred non-Mormon pioneers), and one by one, his wives were deserting him. While there, he received word from nearby Kanab that government agents were tightening up on polygamists. As a precaution, he transferred his properties into the names of his remaining four wives. The church ordered him to move farther south, down to the confluence of the Paria and Colorado Rivers, and he initially took only one of his wives. His newest residence was to become the site of Lee's Ferry, once the only crossing point on the Colorado River in this region.

Farther down Johnson Canyon, a bit south of the end of the trail, is the ghost town of Johnson itself. Originally known as Spring Canyon Ranch, the settlement took on an air of permanence with the addition of a post office, schoolhouse, and stores. Orchards and vineyards prospered for a while before the settlers turned to ranching.

Johnson was the founding place of the United Order of Enoch in 1874. Under a socialistic ideal, all the townspeople agreed to contribute to the store and then receive dividends in return after five years of labor. However, when the time came for people to collect their rewards, there were no dividends to receive! As a result, people started

JOHN D. LEE AND THE MOUNTAIN MEADOWS MASSACRE

On September 11, 1857, Paiute Indians attacked the Fancher party, an emigrant train of about 140 men, women, and children, as it crossed through southern Utah. The migrants were able to fight off the attack and members of the local Mormon militia arrived at the scene to settle the dispute. As they escorted the travelers away from the Indians, the militiamen opened fire on the unarmed group, killing 120. The slaughter became known as the Mountain Meadows Massacre.

John D. Lee

The massacre occurred as tensions were rising between Mormon settlers and the U.S. government. President Buchanan's army was marching into Utah to suppress the possibility of a Mormon revolt, and Mormons were left fearful and angry toward the government and their gentile enemies. Utah began preparations for war and a Mormon-Indian alliance began to surface. It was into this uncertain atmosphere that the Fancher party rode in September 1857.

Animosity followed the party throughout Utah. Mormons saw the band as a part of the gentile threat, and irate Indians harassed them and accused them of poisoning their spring. The rudeness and barbarity of the party did little to sooth the tensions. When the wagon train sought provisions, they were frequently turned away. Catastrophe was nearing and a concerned town elder from Beaver warned the emigrants to arm themselves. Ten miles from Pinto, in the Mountain Meadows, the party was resting when they were surprised by the Indian attack. It's not totally clear who started the assault. Some reports blame just the Indians, whereas others say that militiamen posing as Indians accompanied the Paiute.

Regardless, the Mormons became firmly embroiled when the tribesmen turned to Iron County Indian Agent John D. Lee in order to break a deadlock in the fighting. Mormon militia from the surrounding area arrived under Lee's direction. Lee's involvement in the slaughter is still debated. In the years that followed, the Church of Latter-day Saints presented the unfortunate commander as the primary scapegoat for the massacre. In reality, he was most likely acting under orders. Local religious elders told Lee not to wait for a message from church leader Brigham Young, who indeed sent word to allow the emigrants safe passage.

Lee headed negotiations with the travelers, but the Indians would have no compromise. The Fancher party's fate was sealed. Lee presented a truce, and the wagon train agreed to be escorted out of the region. Then, as they marched, the militia and Indians annihilated the unarmed travelers. Seventeen or eighteen children were the only survivors.

Non-Mormon Americans were outraged. The church was already unpopular because of its polygamist practices and unique nature. This act served to further alienate the Mormons.

The execution of John D. Lee (he is sitting on his coffin at the left, the firing squad is at the extreme right)

Young was removed as governor of the Utah Territory the following year and federal troops occupied the area. The government also tried to punish those responsible for the massacre, but church officials pressured witnesses into silence and after two decades prosecutors could only find charges against John D. Lee. Lee was convicted and executed by a firing squad in the Mountain Meadows in 1874.

drifting away, and by 1900 the town was completely deserted.

Johnson has become famous as a ghost town because the well-preserved buildings have been used as the setting for several movies, including *Deadwood Coach,* a silent western (1924), *Buffalo Bill* (1944), *Pony Express* (1953), and *Mackenna's Gold* (1969). The people of nearby Kanab pride themselves on being a "one-stop shop" for Hollywood. Every man, woman, and child in Kanab has a photo on file, and the town offers many movie locations. Hollywood can come to Kanab and pick the needed set, extras, and locations with little effort!

Johnson Canyon is also the scene of one of the more unusual and spooky treasure tales in Utah. In the 1500s Hernando Cortés led his Spanish army across Mexico, conquering the Aztec nation. It is widely believed that Montezuma secreted away fabulous Aztec riches to protect them from the invaders. Much of his treasure was transported north, away from the marauding armies, and hidden in what is now the American Southwest.

In 1914, a man named Freddy Crystal appeared in Kanab. He had with him a map he claimed would lead to the location of Montezuma's hidden treasure. Crystal spent a long time locating the petroglyphs in Johnson Canyon that would point him to the Aztec treasure. The map led him to White Mountain. Crystal explored further and found ancient, hand-cut steps leading up the mountain to a concealed man-made shaft. The shaft was barricaded with granite blocks cemented into place. Both the blocks and the cement were of a stone unknown in the red sandstone country surrounding Johnson Canyon.

Realizing he needed help, Crystal approached the townsfolk of Kanab. Under their all-women council of the time, the townspeople flocked into Johnson Canyon, eager to find and share in the treasure. A tent city

sprung up in the canyon, as people left their homes, farms, and businesses for the more exciting business of treasure hunting.

Eventually, access was gained to the tunnel. Inside, more granite walls and cement floors blocked passageways. A maze of tunnels penetrated into the mountain, and work was slow. The treasure hunters found the tunnels booby-trapped with large boulders poised to fall when disturbed.

After two years, the people of Kanab drifted back to their homes and occupations. The search for Montezuma's treasure was abandoned, with nothing ever being recovered. Freddy Crystal, too, gave up the search and drifted away.

But in 1989, the search for the treasure was on again! A man named Grant Childs discovered what he believed was an Aztec treasure site, not in Johnson Canyon but in a pond north of Kanab on US 89. A friend of his dove in the pond, following the treasure symbol, and located what appeared to be a man-made tunnel. Childs entered the tunnel, but became disorientated and felt a heavy current of water against him. He quickly returned to the surface. He tried again, this time with a line to help him keep his bearings and find his way out, but he was concerned when the line went limp and exited quickly. Back on the surface, his friend

First part of the trail at the crossing of Kanab Creek

said the line had been taut all the time. Sonar showed that the tunnel was 100 feet long and ended in a large room.

In June, Childs returned with three professional divers, all of whom experienced disorientation and choking sensations in the tunnel. One of the divers dreamed that an Aztec warrior threw a spear at him. Every dive resulted in the same weird feelings of choking, and the divers left without ever accessing the room at the end of the tunnel.

Childs planned to drain the lake, but the lake turned out to be the only known habitat of the endangered Kanab amber snail. The property was fenced by the U.S. Fish and Wildlife Service, and all attempts to locate the treasure were halted.

Description

Like most of the trails around Kanab, the high difficulty rating for this trail is due to the extremely loose, deep sand. In this case, the most challenging section is the climb up to John R Flat from Kanab Creek.

Difficult sandy climb at the start of the John R Flat Trail

From US 89, take Kanab Creek Road, signposted for Kanab Canyon. After 2.7 miles, the trail leaves Kanab Creek Road; it's initially a graded road, but immediately crosses over the creek. After 0.4 miles, the difficult section is reached, a short, very deep sandy climb. There are two ways up, neither one easier than the other. Both routes have large deep holes in the sand and rock ledges. Traveling from Kanab Creek to Johnson Canyon, the route has a difficulty rating of 5. In the reverse direction, the difficulty rating is a 4 as you descend the hardest section.

Once on John R Flat, the ungraded trail is easier going as it winds through junipers and across open areas. There are some good views to the north over the White Cliffs, especially of the prominent Cutler Point.

The east end of the trail descends into Johnson Canyon, crossing over Johnson Wash just before it joins the paved Johnson Canyon Road. If you travel in the opposite direction, this ascent is far easier than the Kanab Creek end. However, it is still loose and sandy and may require lower tire pressures.

The trail is normally open all year, but the cooler months are the best time to travel because it is extremely hot in summer.

Current Road Information

BLM Kanab Field Office
318 North 100 East
Kanab, UT 84741
(435) 644-4600

Map References

BLM   Kanab
USGS   1:24,000   White Tower, Cutler
       Point
       1:100,000 Kanab
Maptech CD-ROM: Escalante/Dixie
       National Forest
Utah Atlas & Gazetteer, p. 18
Utah Travel Council #4

Route Directions

▼ 0.0   2.7 miles along Kanab Creek Road from US 89, turn east on unmarked, graded sandy road and zero trip meter.

SW Trail #14: John R Flat Trail

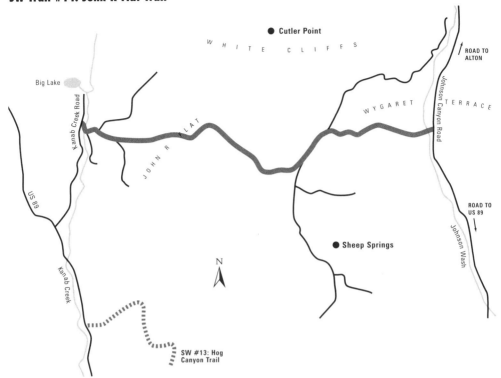

6.9 ▲   Trail ends at Kanab Creek Road. Turn left for US 89 and Kanab.
GPS: N 37°08.71′ W 112°32.41′

▼ 0.1   SO   Cross over Kanab Creek, then proceed south along the creek.

6.8 ▲   SO   Cross over Kanab Creek.

▼ 0.3   TL   Track continues straight ahead; turn left, then immediately bear left at fork.

6.6 ▲   TR   Track on left, then T-intersection. Turn right at intersection.
GPS: N 37°08.51′ W 112°32.26′

▼ 0.4   SO   Two alternate routes up very loose, steep sand and rock section.

6.5 ▲   SO   Two alternate routes down very loose, steep sand and rock section.
GPS: N 37°08.52′ W 112°32.22′

▼ 0.5   SO   Cattle guard, entering BLM land.

6.4 ▲   SO   Cattle guard, entering private land.

▼ 0.6   BR   Track on left.

6.3 ▲   SO   Track on right.
GPS: N 37°08.59′ W 112°32.09′

▼ 0.8   SO   Track on left.

6.1 ▲   BL   Track on right.

▼ 1.1   SO   Track on right.

5.8 ▲   SO   Track on left.
GPS: N 37°08.42′ W 112°31.54′

▼ 1.2   SO   Faint track on right.

5.7 ▲   SO   Faint track on left.

▼ 1.8   SO   Track on left.

5.1 ▲   SO   Track on right.
GPS: N 37°08.36′ W 112°30.81′

▼ 2.5   SO   Cattle guard, then tracks on right and left.

4.4 ▲   SO   Tracks on right and left, then cattle guard.

▼ 3.7   SO   Track on left.

3.2 ▲   SO   Track on right.
GPS: N 37°08.61′ W 112°28.91′

▼ 3.8 SO Track on left to White Cliffs viewpoint. Main trail crosses Wygaret Terrace, a long, flat, sage-covered bench.

3.1 ▲ BL Trail crosses Wygaret Terrace, a long, flat, sage-covered bench. Track on right to White Cliffs viewpoint.

▼ 4.8 SO Track on right.
2.1 ▲ SO Track on left.
　　　GPS: N 37°07.97′ W 112°28.04′

▼ 5.0 SO Track on left.
1.9 ▲ SO Track on right.

▼ 5.4 SO Track on right and track on left.
1.5 ▲ SO Track on right and track on left.
　　　GPS: N 37°07.79′ W 112°27.38′

▼ 5.6 SO Track on right and track on left, then cattle guard.
1.3 ▲ SO Cattle guard, then track on right and track on left.

▼ 5.8 SO Track on right.
1.1 ▲ SO Track on left.

▼ 5.9 SO Track on right.
1.0 ▲ SO Track on left.

▼ 6.0 SO Track on right, then track on left to two tanks, followed by track on left.
0.9 ▲ SO Track on right, then track on right to two tanks, followed by track on left.
　　　GPS: N 37°07.96′ W 112°26.84′

▼ 6.9 BR Track on left; there is a rocky section at junction. Zero trip meter.
0.0 ▲ Continue west.
　　　GPS: N 37°08.68′ W 112°26.09′

▼ 0.0 Continue southeast.
2.7 ▲ SO Track on right; there is a rocky section at junction. Zero trip meter.

▼ 0.8 SO Track on right, then cattle guard.
1.9 ▲ SO Cattle guard, then track on left.

▼ 1.5 SO Track on right and track on left.
1.2 ▲ SO Track on right and track on left.

▼ 2.1 SO Three tracks on left and track on right.
0.6 ▲ SO Three tracks on right and track on left.
　　　GPS: N 37°08.55′ W 112°23.94′

▼ 2.3 SO Bottom of descent from John R Flat. Trail divides in sandy section and rejoins almost immediately. The right fork passes a track to the right.
0.4 ▲ SO Trail divides in sandy section and rejoins almost immediately. The left fork passes a track to the left. Trail climbs to John R Flat.

▼ 2.5 SO Cattle guard.
0.2 ▲ SO Cattle guard.

▼ 2.6 SO Descend and cross Johnson Wash. Private track on left on exit.
0.1 ▲ BL Private track on right. Descend and cross Johnson Wash.

▼ 2.7 Trail ends at Johnson Canyon Road. Turn right to join US 89 and Kanab, left for Alton.
0.0 ▲ From Johnson Canyon Road, 7.4 miles north of US 89, turn west on graded road and immediately cross cattle guard. There is a mailbox at the turn but no sign.
　　　GPS: N 37°08.62′ W 112°23.55′

SOUTHWEST REGION TRAIL #15

Skutumpah Road

STARTING POINT Kodachrome Basin Road, 2.7 miles south of Cannonville
FINISHING POINT Johnson Canyon Road, 20 miles south of Alton
TOTAL MILEAGE 31.1 miles
UNPAVED MILEAGE 31.1 miles
DRIVING TIME 2.5 hours
ELEVATION RANGE 5,800–6,800 feet
USUALLY OPEN March to December
DIFFICULTY RATING 1
SCENIC RATING 9
REMOTENESS RATING +0

Special Attractions
- Historic Averett monument and grave.
- Canyon narrows of Bull Valley Gorge and Willis Canyons.
- Views of the Pink Cliffs.
- Long scenic road within the Grand Staircase–Escalante National Monument.

History
Indian Hollow and Averett Canyon along the Skutumpah Road are names reflecting the troubled times that existed between early pioneers and the Paiute Indians. In 1866, a party of Mormons from St. George was sent by Erastus Snow to Green River to assist the people there in the Black Hawk War. The party traveled up Johnson Canyon and over to what is now Cannonville. Some of the men fell sick, and a small party of six was sent back. In what is now Averett Canyon, the disabled party was attacked by Paiute Indians. Elijah Averett was killed, and the rest of the party fled. Averett was buried where he died and the grave was marked by a sandstone slab with E. A. carved on it, but the shallow grave was disturbed by coyotes and the bones scattered. Local cowboys later reburied the body in the same location. The more permanent monument you see today was put in by the Boy Scouts from Tropic in 1937.

Bull Valley Gorge got its name from the grazing of cattle that took place upstream in Bull Valley. A simple wooden bridge was erected over the gorge in the 1940s, which opened up the route between Kanab and

Heading up the ridge at the beginning of Skutumpah Road

Cannonville. In 1954, a pickup slid off the road at the old bridge and became wedged in the narrow gorge, killing all three occupants. Although the bodies were recovered with great difficulty, the pickup was left. The wooden bridge was replaced with rubble and dirt wedged into the narrow crevasse, making a more solid and permanent bridge.

The name Skutumpah originates from various Paiute words that mean "an area where rabbitbrush grows and squirrels are found." John D. Lee gave this name to one of his many settlements, this one near present-day Alton. He lived in Skutumpah for approximately a year between 1870 and 1871.

Deer Springs Ranch, at the lower end of the road, was developed by the Ford brothers toward the end of the 19th century. The ranch alternated between cattle and sheep, following the market trends, and it was later taken over by the Johnson family. Today, it has several cabins that it rents out on a timeshare basis.

Description
This trail offers the opportunity to combine a very scenic, easy drive with some short,

Averett Canyon Monument

A view of Bull Canyon where the road crosses

rewarding hikes into pretty canyon narrows. The graded road first travels along a ridge, giving good views over the Pink Cliffs in Bryce Canyon National Park, and then drops to cross several major creek drainages.

The first point of interest is Averett Canyon, where a short distance down the wash is the grave and memorial to Elijah Averett. To reach the site, park near the creek wash, and hike approximately a half mile southeast down the wash. Look for a slight bench studded with junipers that rises to the right of the creek. You can't see the memorial stone from the creek, but it is obvious once you climb up onto the bench. The GPS coordinates for the memorial are N 37°29.34' W 112°04.86'.

The next short hike is 1.4 miles farther along the main trail at Willis Creek. A hike downstream from here takes you into some spectacular canyon narrows in a very short time. The creek usually has water in it year-round.

The most exciting hike on this trail is into the Bull Valley Gorge Narrows, 1.8 miles after Willis Creek. These are the narrowest, deepest, and least accessible of the narrows on the trail. Park at the Bull Valley Gorge

HOLLYWOOD AND SOUTHWEST UTAH

Hollywood and Utah have had a unique relationship since almost the beginning of film, and that affair continues up to this day. While Wendover and the Salt Flats can brag about their roles in the desert scenes of *Independence Day* (1996), southwest Utah boasts the town Kanab, often referred to as "Utah's Little Hollywood." In the 1920s, the local scenery drew filmmakers. However it was the enthusiasm of the townspeople that persuaded them to stay. Residents supported the filming process in every way they could, including acting as extras, driving teams of horses, building sets, and providing housing for the staff. With such unique scenery and warm reception, it's no wonder why hundreds of films have been filmed in the area. *Deadwood Coach* (1922), *Buffalo Bill* (1944), *The Arabian Knights* (1942), *The Rainmaker* (1956), *Jubal* (1956), tel-

The Hollywood version of the Mormon migration to Utah as seen in *Brigham Young: Frontiersman*, 1940

evision episodes of *Gunsmoke* and *Lassie, Planet of the Apes* (1968), and the James Bond film, *Octopussy* (1985) are just a small sample of the films that have used the area.

The Paria River valley has also been used, but not to the same extent as Kanab. In the 1950s, moviemakers discovered this area and filmed several movies including *Cattle Drive* (1951), *Sergeants Three* (1963), and *Mackenna's Gold* (1969). The flooding waters of the Paria River threatened these sets, but luckily the BLM has rescued the original structures and is working on relocating them out of the reach of the Paria floodplain.

bridge and walk north through the hiker's gate on the east side of the bridge. The narrow trail runs along the rim of the gorge. After approximately one-half mile, you can scramble down into the gorge itself. To hike the full length of the narrows requires ropes and some climbing skill—the way is blocked by rubble and boulders in a couple of places. If you go as far as the Bull Valley Gorge bridge, it is just possible to see the remains of the pickup truck that became lodged in the crevasse above, although most of it is now covered by debris. Of course, do not attempt to enter any of the narrows if rain is forecast in the general region—there is little chance of escape in a flash flood.

Much of the lower part of Skutumpah Road travels through private property. Deer Springs Ranch offers seasonal cabin accommodations (bookings recommended)—possibly the only accommodations within the Grand Staircase–Escalante National Monument. It also has a very small general store.

The road is open year-round from the south as far up as Deer Springs Ranch. Above the ranch it is not maintained during the winter months, but it is often passable all year. The entire road is graded dirt or gravel and is suitable for passenger vehicles in dry weather.

The trail finishes on Johnson Canyon Road. If you turn left toward Kanab, Johnson Canyon Road passes close to the old ghost town of Johnson—a well-preserved movie set. Although privately owned, it is visible from the road. It also passes one end of Southwest #14: John R Flat Trail.

Please note that although currently no permits are required for camping within the Grand Staircase–Escalante National Monument, the management plan is still under development and this may change. Side trails mentioned in the route directions may or may not be open for vehicle travel and are included for reference purposes only. Some of the smaller trails are likely to be closed under the final management plan. Check with the Interagency Office in Escalante before planning to camp within the monument. The office is also extremely helpful with the latest information on road conditions.

Current Road Information

BLM Kanab Field Office
318 North 100 East
Kanab, UT 84741
(435) 644-4600

Grand Staircase–Escalante National
    Monument Office
190 East Center St.
Kanab, UT 84741
(435) 644-4300

Escalante Interagency Office
755 West Main
Escalante, UT 84726
(435) 826-5499

Map References

BLM   Panguitch, Kanab
USFS   Dixie National Forest: Powell
       Ranger District (incomplete)
USGS   1:24,000 Cannonville, Bull Valley
       Gorge, Rainbow Point, Deer Spring
       Point, Skutumpah Creek, Bald Knoll
       1:100,000 Panguitch, Kanab
Maptech CD-ROM: Escalante/Dixie
       National Forest
Utah Atlas & Gazetteer, pp. 18, 19
Utah Travel Council #4
Other: BLM Map of the Grand Staircase–
       Escalante National Monument

Route Directions

▼ 0.0   From Kodachrome Basin Road, 2.7 miles
           south of Cannonville, turn south on graded dirt road at sign for Bull Valley Gorge
           and Kanab and zero trip meter.

2.9 ▲   Trail ends at Kodachrome Basin Road,
           2.7 miles south of Cannonville. Turn left
           for Cannonville and Utah 12, turn right
           to visit Kodachrome Basin State Park.
           GPS: N 37°31.87′ W 112°02.95′

▼ 0.1 SO Cross through wash.
2.8 ▲ SO Cross through wash.

▼ 0.2 SO Track on left to private property, then
           enter the Grand Staircase–Escalante
           National Monument.

2.7 ▲   SO Leaving Grand Staircase–Escalante National Monument, then track on right to private property.
GPS: N 37°31.72' W 112°03.10'

▼ 0.7   SO Track on left, then main trail climbs up sandy ridge.
2.2 ▲   SO Bottom of ridge, then track on right.

▼ 1.1   SO Top of ridge, turnouts on right and left.
1.8 ▲   SO Turnouts on right and left, then trail descends sandy ridge.

▼ 1.3   SO Track on right.
1.6 ▲   SO Track on left.

▼ 1.5   SO Cattle guard, then faint track on left.
1.4 ▲   SO Faint track on right, then cattle guard.

▼ 1.6   SO Track on left, then Indian Hollow Creek runs parallel to trail on right.
1.3 ▲   SO Track on right.

▼ 2.3   SO Track on left to corral.
0.6 ▲   SO Track on right to corral.
GPS: N 37°30.20' W 112°03.90'

▼ 2.7   BR Track on left. Continue and cross over old dam wall on Sheep Creek.
0.2 ▲   BL Track on right.

▼ 2.9   SO Cross over dam overflow and zero trip meter.
0.0 ▲   Continue on main trail.
GPS: N 37°29.68' W 112°03.91'

▼ 0.0   Continue and cross over cattle guard.
8.6 ▲   SO Cattle guard, then cross over dam overflow and zero trip meter.

▼ 0.3   SO Cross through wash.
8.3 ▲   SO Cross through wash.

▼ 0.7   SO Track on left, then cattle guard, then track on right. Views ahead of the Pink Cliffs.
7.9 ▲   SO Track on left, then cattle guard, then track on right.

▼ 1.6   SO Cross through Averett Creek Wash.

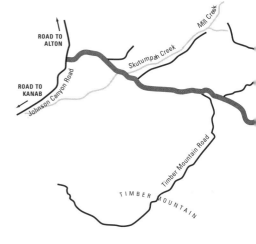

SW Trail #15: Skutumpah Road

     Park near the wash, and walk approximately 0.5 miles down the wash to the monument.
7.0 ▲   SO Cross through Averett Creek Wash. Park near the wash and walk approximately 0.5 miles down the wash to the monument.
GPS: N 37°29.47' W 112°05.24'

▼ 2.2   SO Small track on left.
6.4 ▲   SO Small track on right.

▼ 2.3   BL Major graded road on right.
6.3 ▲   SO Second entrance to graded road on left.
GPS: N 37°29.37' W 112°05.71'

▼ 2.4   SO Second entrance to graded road on right.
6.2 ▲   SO Major graded road on left.

▼ 3.0   SO Large camping area on right along Willis Creek, then cross through creek. The narrows are a short hike downstream.
5.6 ▲   SO Cross through Willis Creek, then large camping area on left along the creek. The narrows are a short hike downstream.
GPS: N 37°28.99' W 112°05.75'

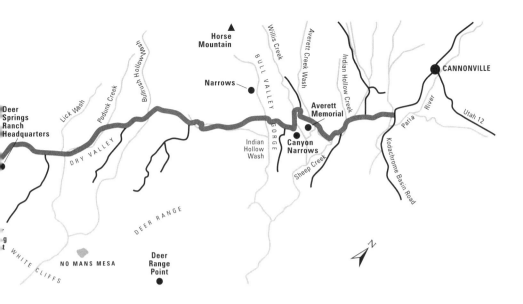

▼ 3.7	SO	Views of Powell Point on left, then track on left.
4.9 ▲	SO	Track on right. Views of the Pink Cliffs to the left and of Powell Point ahead.
		GPS: N 37°28.61' W 112°05.67'

▼ 4.2	SO	Track on right.
4.4 ▲	SO	Track on left.

▼ 4.7	SO	Cattle guard.
3.9 ▲	SO	Cattle guard.

▼ 4.8	SO	Bull Valley Gorge bridge. Park and hike through the narrow gate on east side of the bridge to access the narrows.
3.8 ▲	SO	Bull Valley Gorge bridge. Park and hike through the narrow gate on east side of the bridge to access the narrows.
		GPS: N 37°28.35' W 112°06.57'

▼ 5.7	SO	Cross through wash.
2.9 ▲	SO	Cross through wash.

▼ 5.9	SO	Track on right.
2.7 ▲	SO	Track on left.

▼ 6.7	SO	Cross through wash.
1.9 ▲	SO	Cross through wash.

▼ 6.9	SO	Cross through Indian Hollow wash.
1.7 ▲	SO	Cross through Indian Hollow wash.

▼ 7.4	SO	Cross through Indian Hollow wash.
1.2 ▲	SO	Cross through Indian Hollow wash.
		GPS: N 37°26.53' W 112°07.88'

▼ 7.6	SO	Cross through Indian Hollow wash.
1.0 ▲	SO	Cross through Indian Hollow wash.

▼ 8.0	SO	Cross through Indian Hollow wash.
0.6 ▲	SO	Cross through Indian Hollow wash.

▼ 8.5	SO	Faint track on left and campsite on left.
0.1 ▲	SO	Faint track on right and campsite on right.

▼ 8.6	BR	Cattle guard, then well-used track on left, then speed limit sign. Zero trip meter.
0.0 ▲		Continue east.
		GPS: N 37°26.04' W 112°08.67'

▼ 0.0		Continue west.
8.5 ▲	BL	Well-used track on right, then cattle guard, then speed limit sign. Zero trip meter.

▼ 1.2	SO	Faint track on left, then cattle guard.
7.3 ▲	SO	Cattle guard, then faint track on right.

▼ 1.4	SO	Track on right to private property, then track on left.

7.1 ▲ SO Track on right, then track on left to private property.

▼ 1.9 SO Cross through Bullrush Hollow wash, then track on right.
6.6 ▲ SO Track on left, then cross through Bullrush Hollow wash.
GPS: N 37°25.06′ W 112°10.25′

▼ 2.3 SO Track on right.
6.2 ▲ SO Track on left.

▼ 2.8 BR Track on left.
5.7 ▲ SO Second entrance to track on right.
GPS: N 37°24.34′ W 112°10.45′

▼ 2.9 BL Second entrance to track on left.
5.6 ▲ SO Track on right.

▼ 3.1 SO Cattle guard.
5.4 ▲ SO Cattle guard.

▼ 3.2 SO Track on left to Swallow Park Ranch (private property).
5.3 ▲ SO Track on right to Swallow Park Ranch (private property).

▼ 3.4 SO Track on right is private road.
5.1 ▲ SO Second entrance to private road on left.

▼ 3.5 SO Second entrance to private road on right.
5.0 ▲ SO Track on left is private road.

▼ 4.1 SO Track on right.
4.4 ▲ SO Track on left.

▼ 4.2 SO Track on right.
4.3 ▲ SO Track on left.

▼ 4.3 SO Corral and tank on right.
4.2 ▲ SO Corral and tank on left.
GPS: N 37°23.13′ W 112°10.95′

▼ 5.6 SO Cross through Lick Wash. Track on right at wash and track on left.
2.9 ▲ SO Track on left at wash and track on right. Cross through Lick Wash.

▼ 5.7 SO Cattle guard. Entering Deer Springs Ranch.
2.8 ▲ SO Cattle guard. Leaving Deer Springs Ranch.
GPS: N 37°21.91′ W 112°11.37′

▼ 6.6 SO Track on left to Deer Spring Point.
1.9 ▲ SO Track on right to Deer Spring Point.
GPS: N 37°21.40′ W 112°12.08′

▼ 7.2 SO Deer Springs Ranch on right.
1.3 ▲ SO Deer Springs Ranch on left.

▼ 7.3 SO Track on left.
1.2 ▲ SO Track on right.

▼ 7.5 SO Track on right.
1.0 ▲ SO Track on left.

▼ 7.8 SO Cross over wash.
0.7 ▲ SO Cross over wash.

▼ 7.9 SO Cattle guard, then tracks on right and left.
0.6 ▲ SO Tracks on left and right, then cattle guard.

▼ 8.5 SO Intersection. Water tank on left. Road on left to Deer Springs Ranch headquarters. Road on right is private. Zero trip meter.
0.0 ▲ Continue toward Cannonville.
GPS: N 37°20.18′ W 112°13.36′

▼ 0.0 Continue straight, following sign to Kanab.
5.2 ▲ SO Intersection. Water tank on right. Road on right to Deer Springs Ranch headquarters. Road on left is private. Zero trip meter.

▼ 0.2 SO Track on left to Deer Springs Ranch. Cross cattle guard.
5.0 ▲ SO Track on right to Deer Springs Ranch. Cross cattle guard.

▼ 0.3 SO Track on right is private.
4.9 ▲ SO Track on left is private.

▼ 0.7 SO Track on right.
4.5 ▲ SO Track on left.

▼ 0.8   SO Track on right, then cattle guard.
4.4 ▲   SO Cattle guard, then track on left.

▼ 0.9   SO Track on left.
4.3 ▲   SO Track on right.
            GPS: N 37°20.13′ W 112°14.35′

▼ 1.7   SO Track on right to private property.
3.5 ▲   SO Track on left to private property.

▼ 2.6   SO Track on left.
2.6 ▲   SO Track on right.
            GPS: N 37°19.07′ W 112°15.03′

▼ 3.5   SO Faint track on left.
1.7 ▲   SO Faint track on right.

▼ 3.6   SO Cattle guard, leaving Deer Springs
            Ranch.
1.6 ▲   SO Cattle guard, entering Deer Springs
            Ranch.

▼ 4.2   SO Track on right, cross over creek, then
            second track on right.
1.0 ▲   SO Track on left, cross over creek, then
            second track on left.

▼ 5.2   SO Track on left is Timber Mountain Road
            (dead end). Zero trip meter at signpost.
0.0 ▲   Continue toward Cannonville.
            GPS: N 37°18.48′ W 112°17.55′

▼ 0.0   Continue toward Kanab.
2.9 ▲   SO Track on right is Timber Mountain Road
            (dead end). Zero trip meter at signpost.

▼ 0.9   SO Track on left.
2.0 ▲   SO Track on right.

▼ 1.2   SO Track on right.
1.7 ▲   SO Track on left.

▼ 1.3   SO Cattle guard.
1.6 ▲   SO Cattle guard.

▼ 2.6   SO Track on left.
0.3 ▲   SO Track on right.

▼ 2.7   SO Cattle guard.
0.2 ▲   SO Cattle guard.

▼ 2.9   SO Track on right to Mill Creek. Zero trip
            meter.
0.0 ▲   Continue straight, following sign for
            Deer Springs Ranch.
            GPS: N 37°16.90′ W 112°20.12′

▼ 0.0   Continue toward Kanab.
3.0 ▲   SO Track on left to Mill Creek. Zero trip
            meter.

▼ 0.3   SO Cattle guard.
2.7 ▲   SO Cattle guard.

▼ 0.5   SO Cross over Skutumpah Creek.
2.5 ▲   SO Cross over Skutumpah Creek.

▼ 0.7   SO Cattle guard.
2.3 ▲   SO Cattle guard.

▼ 1.3   SO Track on right.
1.7 ▲   SO Track on left.

▼ 1.5   SO Graded road on right, and small track
            on right. Smaller, ungraded track on
            left.
1.5 ▲   SO Graded road on left and small track
            on left. Smaller, ungraded track on
            right. Follow sign for Deer Springs
            Ranch.
            GPS: N 37°16.57′ W 112°21.81′

▼ 1.8   SO Track on right.
1.2 ▲   SO Track on left.

▼ 2.4   SO Track on right, then track on left.
0.6 ▲   SO Track on right, then track on left.

▼ 2.8   SO Cattle guard.
0.2 ▲   SO Cattle guard.

▼ 3.0   Trail ends at Johnson Canyon Road.
            Turn right for Alton, turn left for
            Kanab.
0.0 ▲   On Johnson Canyon Road, 20 miles
            south of Alton, turn northeast on grad-
            ed road, following the sign for Deer
            Springs Ranch and Cannonville.
            GPS: N 37°15.55′ W 112°22.70′

Cottonwood Canyon Road

STARTING POINT Kodachrome Basin State Park
FINISHING POINT US 89, 0.7 miles west of mile
marker 17
TOTAL MILEAGE 37.1 miles
UNPAVED MILEAGE 37.1 miles
DRIVING TIME 2.5 hours
ELEVATION RANGE 4,600–6,500 feet
USUALLY OPEN Year-round
DIFFICULTY RATING 2
SCENIC RATING 10
REMOTENESS RATING +0

Special Attractions

- Kodachrome Basin State Park.
- Grosvenor Arch—a natural double arch.
- Butler Valley and Cottonwood Canyon Narrows.
- Views of the Paria River.

History

Kodachrome Basin, at the start of this trail, was originally called Thornys Pasture back in 1900, when Cannonville ranchers first used it for winter cattle grazing. In 1949, the National Geographic Society studied the area and named it after the brand of film it used. In 1962, the area was declared a state park, and for legal reasons was originally known as Chimney Rock State Park. Later, Kodak was happy to have its name associated with the area, and so the name Kodachrome Basin was reinstated.

At the southern end of the trail, the Paria River cuts a broad swath through the badlands scenery. The name comes from the Paiute word for "elk water" or "muddy water." Alongside the Paria River is Rock House Cove, the site of Peter Shirts's original settlement—he later settled the town of Paria, which was originally spelled Pahreah (located at the end of Southwest #17: Paria River Valley Trail). He moved to the Paria River region in 1865 with his family and established his small holding in Rock House Cove. He built his stone house at the back of

the cove along the cliff, using a natural cave in the cliff as the back of the dwelling. When the Black Hawk War erupted in 1866, Peter refused to leave, and he was successful in staving off the Indian attacks from his rock stronghold. However, by March 1866, he and his family decided to relocate to Toquerville, eventually returning to settle what became the townsite of Paria.

Description

Cottonwood Canyon Road is a backcountry byway, one of the dirt roads that slant down through the Grand Staircase–Escalante National Monument. Unlike most of the other roads that cross the monument on the plateaus, this one runs alongside Cottonwood Wash for most of its length, traveling through the very scenic Cottonwood Canyon.

The trail commences at the entrance to the scenic Kodachrome Basin State Park, which has many-hued rock chimneys and scenery and is well worth a visit. The graded dirt road rises to cross Slickrock Bench, giving views to the distinctive pink and white cliffs of Powell Point. It then crosses Round Valley Draw and exits by winding around a large butte on a short, narrow shelf road.

After 9.2 miles, a short detour to the left goes to Grosvenor Arch, a very distinctive, rare double arch of pale sandstone. There is

Signpost at the south end of the trail

Driving through the valley along the Cottonwood Canyon Road

a day-use picnic area, and a wheelchair-accessible path that leads to the arch's base.

About 3.4 miles after the turn to Grosvenor Arch, there is a very short, worthwhile hike into the Butler Valley Draw Narrows. Park alongside the trail near where it crosses over a side creek in a depression filled with red rock hoodoo spires. The way into the narrows is immediately west of the road. Immediately south of the drainage pipe under the road you will see a faint foot trail. Follow this west and scramble down into the main wash. Turn north (right) and immediately the canyon narrows. There is a short section of spectacular narrows, including a large tree trunk jammed in the canyon 20 feet up, washed down by flash floods. Turn south in the main wash to view the Cottonwood Canyon Narrows. Do not enter the narrows when there are any thunderstorm warnings or heavy rain in the forecast, or if there has been rain the preceding few days. To do so can be life threatening because of flash floods. In summer months, rattlesnakes like to hide in the relative coolness of the canyons, so be careful where you place hands and feet.

The main trail follows along the Cockscomb, a long, jagged ridge; the trail rises up to cross over it a couple of times. Like Comb Ridge to the east, Cockscomb is a monocline. To the west is Cottonwood Canyon, visible for most of the middle section of the trail. The lower end of the trail runs along a narrow ledge just over the Paria River, passes by Rock House Cove, and then swings up and away from the river through some badlands. It finishes at the junction with US 89, roughly midway between Kanab and Page, Arizona.

The trail is graded all the way. The section of trail that crosses over the Cockscomb travels across black shale, which gets very slippery after rain. The trail is normally open year-round, but may be temporarily impassable due to snow or heavy rain. There are many opportunities for backcountry camping along this route, especially along some of the side trails at the northern end. There are few sites within the canyon itself. Please note that although currently no permits are required for camping within the national monument, the management plan is still under development and this may change. Side trails mentioned in the route directions may or may not be open for vehicle travel and are included for reference purposes only. Some of the smaller trails are likely to be closed under the final management plan. Check with the Interagency Office in Escalante before planning to camp within the monument. The office is also extremely helpful with the latest information on road conditions.

Current Road Information

Grand Staircase–Escalante National
  Monument Office
190 East Center St.
Kanab, UT 84741
(435) 644-4300

BLM Escalante Field Office
PO Box 225
Escalante, UT 84726
(435) 826-5600

BLM Kanab Field Office
318 North 100 East
Kanab, UT 84741
(435) 644-4600

Escalante Interagency Office
755 West Main
Escalante, UT 84726
(435) 826-5499

Map References

BLM   Panguitch, Escalante, Smoky Mt.
USGS 1:24,000 Henrieville, Slickrock
      Bench, Butler Valley, Horse Flat,
      Calico Peak, Fivemile Valley, West
      Clark Bench, Bridger Point
      1:100,000 Panguitch, Escalante,
      Smoky Mt.
Maptech CD-ROM: Escalante/Dixie
      National Forest
Utah Atlas & Gazetteer, p. 19
Utah Travel Council #4
Other: BLM Map of the Grand Staircase–
      Escalante National Monument

Route Directions

▼ 0.0   At the entrance to Kodachrome Basin
         State Park, 6.5 miles south of
         Cannonville, zero trip meter and contin-
         ue east on graded dirt road; follow
         sign for Grosvenor Arch.
9.2 ▲   Trail finishes at the entrance to
         Kodachrome Basin State Park.
         Continue north for 6.5 miles on the
         paved road for Cannonville and
         Utah 12.
         GPS: N 37°30.09' W 111°59.56'

▼ 0.7   SO Track on right.
8.5 ▲   SO Track on left.

▼ 0.9   SO Track on right; views north into
             Kodachrome Basin.
8.3 ▲   SO Track on left; views north into
             Kodachrome Basin.

▼ 1.1   SO Track on left.
8.1 ▲   SO Track on right.

▼ 1.2   SO Cross over wash.
8.0 ▲   SO Cross over wash.

▼ 1.4   SO Track on left.
7.8 ▲   SO Track on right.
         GPS: N 37°29.73' W 111°58.01'

▼ 1.7   SO Track on left.
7.5 ▲   SO Track on right.

▼ 2.6   SO Two entrances to track on left, which
             goes to campsite and continues into
             Big Dry Valley.
6.6 ▲   SO Two entrances to track on right, which
             goes to campsite and continues into
             Big Dry Valley.
         GPS: N 37°29.23' W 111°56.90'

▼ 3.4   SO Track on left.
5.8 ▲   SO Track on right.

▼ 4.4   SO Track on left.
4.8 ▲   SO Track on right.

▼ 4.8   SO Track on right.
4.4 ▲   SO Track on left.

▼ 5.2   SO Faint track on left at base of short
             climb over Slickrock Bench.
4.0 ▲   SO Faint track on right at end of descent
             over Slickrock Bench.
         GPS: N 37°29.06' W 111°54.15'

▼ 5.5   SO Views from top of bench, including
             Powell Point to the north.
3.7 ▲   SO Views from top of bench, including
             Powell Point to the north.

BLACK HAWK WAR

The Black Hawk War officially took place between 1865 and 1868, though isolated raids and battles had gone on before the war and persisted after. The war started on April 9, 1865, when Ute Indians and Mormons met in Manti (in Sanpete County) to settle an argument. A Mormon insulted the band of Indians by pulling one from his horse. The Ute vowed revenge, and under the leadership of Black Hawk, they took it by stealing cattle and killing five Mormon settlers.

The incident made Black Hawk a hero in the eyes of many Ute, Paiute, and Navajo in the region, who were facing desperate times as white men pushed them out of their territory. For the next two years, Black Hawk and his loose organization of Indians raided many Mormon settlements, taking food and cattle and occasionally killing one of the settlers. The Mormons had little success in defending themselves from the Indians, so they built forts around the frontier. The Mormons even mobilized as many as 2,500 men, but they were rendered helpless because they could never find Black Hawk or his men. The Native Americans knew the land far better than the pursuing Mormons did, and they blended in among other Indians tribes who had no part in the raids.

For two years there was open warfare between the two groups. The Mormons, whose polygamist practices had alienated them from the rest of the country, received little federal aid. This allowed Black Hawk's men to continue their raids without the interference of an established federal army.

However, in the summer of 1867, Black Hawk finally made peace with the white settlers after a bullet had wounded him. Without his dynamic leadership, the loosely structured Indian resistance fell apart, and a peace treaty was signed in 1868. Fighting continued sporadically until 1872, when the federal government finally intervened by sending 200 troops to pacify the region. By this time, the Black Hawk War and its aftermath had created some of the most hostile and uncertain times ever known in Utah's frontier.

▼ 5.6 SO Cattle guard, then tracks on left and right.
3.6 ▲ SO Tracks on left and right, then cattle guard.
GPS: N 37°29.05' W 111°53.79'

▼ 6.4 SO Cross through Round Valley Draw.
2.8 ▲ SO Cross through Round Valley Draw.

▼ 6.5 BL Track on right to Rush Beds, then trail climbs around the edge of a butte.
2.7 ▲ SO Trail descends down from butte, then track on left to Rush Beds.
GPS: N 37°28.62' W 111°53.21'

▼ 7.3 SO Cattle guard, then enter Butler Valley.
1.9 ▲ SO Cattle guard, then leave Butler Valley.

▼ 8.1 SO Cross underneath power lines.
1.1 ▲ SO Cross underneath power lines.

▼ 9.2 SO Track on left to Grosvenor Arch (1 mile). Visit Grosvenor Arch, and zero trip meter on return.
0.0 ▲ Continue along Cottonwood Canyon Road toward Kodachrome Basin State Park.
GPS: N 37°27.10' W 111°50.91'

▼ 0.0 Continue along Cottonwood Canyon Road toward US 89.
7.7 ▲ SO Track on right to Grosvenor Arch (1 mile). Visit Grosvenor Arch and zero trip meter on return.

▼ 0.2 SO Two tracks on left.
7.5 ▲ SO Two tracks on right.

▼ 0.4 SO Track on right.
7.3 ▲ SO Track on left.

▼ 0.7 SO Track on left to corral.
7.0 ▲ SO Track on right to corral.

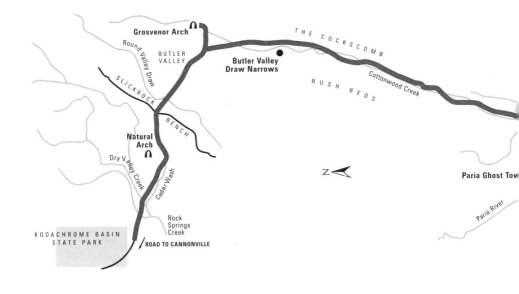

▼ 2.3   SO Cattle guard, then track on right.
5.4 ▲   SO Track on left, then cattle guard.

▼ 3.4   SO Butler Valley Draw narrows on right.
            Park where the road crosses over
            creek and hike down into the creek.
4.3 ▲   SO Butler Valley Draw narrows on left.
            Park where the road crosses over
            creek and hike down into the creek.
            GPS: N 37°24.14' W 111°50.79'

▼ 4.6   SO Track on right to campsites.
3.1 ▲   SO Track on left to campsites.

▼ 7.7   SO Track on right is signposted to Pump
            Canyon Spring. Zero trip meter.
0.0 ▲   Continue northeast.
            GPS: N 37°20.60' W 111°52.19'

▼ 0.0   Continue southwest.
8.7 ▲   SO Track on left is signposted to Pump
            Canyon Spring. Zero trip meter.

▼ 0.3   SO Cross through wash.
8.4 ▲   SO Cross through wash.

▼ 1.5   SO Track on right to parking area.
7.2 ▲   SO Track on left to parking area.

▼ 2.4   BL Track on right.
6.3 ▲   SO Track on left.

▼ 2.6   SO Cross over wash.
6.1 ▲   SO Cross over wash.

▼ 6.4   SO Cross through wash.
2.3 ▲   SO Cross through wash.
            GPS: N 37°15.42' W 111°54.49'

▼ 6.6   SO Track on left.
2.1 ▲   SO Track on right.
            GPS: N 37°15.25' W 111°54.56'

▼ 6.7   SO Cattle guard.
2.0 ▲   SO Cattle guard.

▼ 7.8   SO Cattle guard.
0.9 ▲   SO Cattle guard.

▼ 8.7   SO Track on right to confluence of Paria
            River and Cottonwood Creek. Main
            trail now follows the Paria River. Zero
            trip meter.
0.0 ▲   Continue north along Cottonwood
            Canyon.
            GPS: N 37°13.66' W 111°55.52'

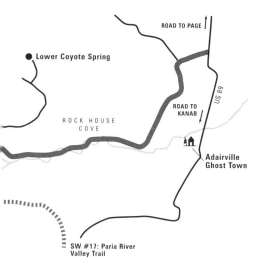

ROAD TO PAGE

Lower Coyote Spring

US 89

ROAD TO
KANAB

ROCK HOUSE
COVE

Adairville
Ghost Town

SW #17: Paria River
Valley Trail

SW Trail #16: Cottonwood Canyon Road

▼ 0.0   Continue south along the Paria River.

11.5 ▲   SO   Track on left to confluence of Paria River and Cottonwood Creek. Main trail now follows Cottonwood Creek. Zero trip meter.

▼ 0.2   SO   Track on right.
11.3 ▲   SO   Track on left.

▼ 2.7   SO   Track on left to campsite.
8.8 ▲   SO   Track on right to campsite.

▼ 3.4   SO   Cross through wash. Rock House Cove is on the left.
8.1 ▲   SO   Cross through wash. Rock House Cove is on the right.

▼ 4.5   SO   Cross through wash.
7.0 ▲   SO   Cross through wash.

▼ 5.0   SO   Track on right to campsite. Main trail leaves Paria River.
6.5 ▲   SO   Track on left to campsite. Main trail now follows Paria River.

▼ 6.4   SO   Track on left, and track on right goes to viewpoint over Paria River.
5.1 ▲   SO   Track on right, and track on left goes

to viewpoint over Paria River.

▼ 6.5   SO   Cattle guard.
5.0 ▲   SO   Cattle guard.
      GPS: N 37°08.44' W 111°54.45'

▼ 6.8   SO   Cross through wash.
4.7 ▲   SO   Cross through wash.

▼ 7.6   SO   Cross through wash.
3.9 ▲   SO   Cross through wash.

▼ 10.0   SO   Track on left and track on right.
1.5 ▲   SO   Track on right and track on left.
      GPS: N 37°07.45' W 111°51.25'

▼ 10.2   SO   Leaving Grand Staircase–Escalante National Monument.
1.3 ▲   SO   Entering Grand Staircase–Escalante National Monument.

▼ 10.4   SO   Track on left.
1.1 ▲   SO   Track on right.

▼ 10.6   SO   Track on right, then cattle guard.
0.9 ▲   SO   Cattle guard, then track on left.

▼ 11.0   SO   Track on left.
0.5 ▲   SO   Track on right.

▼ 11.3   SO   Track on right.
0.2 ▲   SO   Track on left.

▼ 11.4   SO   Cattle guard.
0.1 ▲   SO   Cattle guard.

▼ 11.5   Trail ends at US 89, just west of the Grand Staircase–Escalante National Monument boundary. Turn left for Page, Arizona; turn right for Kanab.
0.0 ▲   On US 89, just west of the Grand Staircase–Escalante National Monument boundary, 0.7 miles west of mile marker 17, turn north on graded dirt road at the sign for Cottonwood Canyon and Cannonville and zero trip meter.
      GPS: N 37°06.32' W 111°50.77'

Paria River Valley Trail

STARTING POINT US 89, 0.7 miles west of mile marker 30
FINISHING POINT Ghost town of Paria
TOTAL MILEAGE 5.5 miles
UNPAVED MILEAGE 5.5 miles
DRIVING TIME 30 minutes (one-way)
ELEVATION RANGE 4,800–5,300 feet
USUALLY OPEN Year-round
DIFFICULTY RATING 2
SCENIC RATING 8
REMOTENESS RATING +0

Special Attractions

- Old Paria movie set.
- Paria ghost town and cemetery.
- Views of the Paria River valley.

History

Paria (originally Pahreah) was founded in 1870 by Peter Shirts and his family after their original settlement at Rock House Cove (on Southwest #16: Cottonwood Canyon Road) was abandoned. The small settlement grew to

Tucked away in the Paria River valley, the remains of an old cabin slowly fall victim to the elements

include a general store, a post office, and some prosperous farmland. Like many pioneer settlements in the area, Paria suffered repeated flooding of the Paria River, which regularly wiped out both crops and housing. Disheartened by the cyclical struggle, the settlers abandoned their town.

As many people were leaving, the promise of gold attracted others, and some new buildings and a sluice gate were built. The gold rush, too, was short-lived, and by 1910 most miners had moved on to better pickings. One old miner's light lingered until 1929, but the floods and droughts won in the end and the settlement became a ghost town.

In the 1950s, moviemakers discovered the Paria River valley and filmed several movies here—including *Cattle Drive* (1951), *Sergeants Three* (1963), and *Mackenna's Gold* (1969). The movie set for which the town is now best known was built for *Sergeants Three.*

However, history keeps repeating in Paria. In November 1999, a group of BLM employees and 85 volunteers dismantled the movie set from its original location next to the picnic ground. Frequent flooding from the creek was making the buildings unstable and unsafe. The original timbers were saved, and the BLM intends to reconstruct two of the buildings farther away from the creek, elsewhere on the backway, where they will be out of reach of floodwaters. Interpretive information will be added, and the project is to be completed in 2000.

Today, you can see remains of stone cabins and an old sluice from the mining operations on the far bank of the river, slightly downstream from where the road ends. The town site was upstream from the trail end, but little remains.

Description

This is one of the designated scenic backways in this area; it's a short spur trail allowing vehicle access to the Paria River and to the ghost town of Paria. The trail is a well-maintained graded dirt road that, in dry weather, is suitable for passenger vehicles as far as the picnic ground. The sandy wash below the picnic area is more suited for high-clearance vehicles.

It is a pretty drive to the town site. The trail drops abruptly to the creek giving views into the Paria River valley and the red rock surroundings. The picnic area, set at the base of a red rock bluff on a slight rise, is a pleasant place for lunch. There is limited shade, however, and summers are very hot!

The trail passes the old Paria cemetery. It has only a solitary marker that lists the names of the 13 people buried in the cemetery. At the trail's end on the banks of the Paria River, you can walk across the river to view the remains of the town and the mining operations.

Current Road Information

BLM Kanab Field Office
318 North 100 East
Kanab, UT 84741
(435) 644-4600

Escalante Interagency Office
755 West Main
Escalante, UT 84726
(435) 826-5499

Map References

BLM Smoky Mt.
USGS 1:24,000 Five Mile Valley, Calico Peak
1:100,000 Smoky Mt.
Maptech CD-ROM: Escalante/Dixie National Forest
Utah Atlas & Gazetteer, p. 19
Utah Travel Council #4
Other: BLM Map of the Grand Staircase–Escalante National Monument

Route Directions

▼ 0.0   From US 89, 0.7 miles west of mile marker 30, zero trip meter and turn northeast on graded dirt road. The road is unmarked, but there is a historical marker at the turn. Immediately cross cattle guard.
GPS: N 37°11.12' W 111°59.71'

SW Trail #17: Paria River Valley Trail

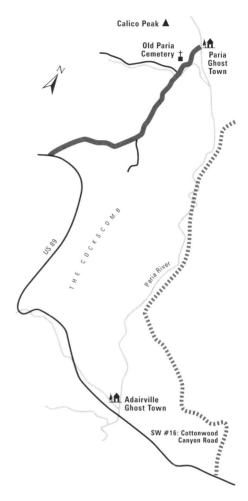

▼ 0.7   SO Track on right.
▼ 0.8   SO Entering Grand Staircase–Escalante National Monument, then track on right.
GPS: N 37°11.75' W 111°59.14'

▼ 1.1   SO Cross through wash.
▼ 2.4   SO Track on right, then cattle guard.
▼ 4.4   SO Cross through wash.
▼ 4.5   SO Picnic area and pit toilet on right, then cross through wash. This was the original location of the Paria movie set.
GPS: N 37°14.25' W 111°57.42'

▼ 4.6   SO Cross through wash.
▼ 4.7   SO Track on right.

▼ 4.8	BR	Cross through wash, then bear right after wash.
▼ 4.9	SO	Track on left goes to Paria cemetery; fork rejoins almost immediately.
		GPS: N 37°14.56′ W 111°57.39′

▼ 5.3	BR	Track on left.
▼ 5.4	SO	Cross through wash.
▼ 5.5		Trail ends on the bank of the Paria River. To find the remains of Paria, walk a short distance south. The remains of one rock cabin and the sluice are on the far bank.
		GPS: N 37°15.04′ W 111°57.29′

SOUTHWEST REGION TRAIL #18

Smoky Mountain Road

STARTING POINT US 89 at Big Water
FINISHING POINT Escalante
TOTAL MILEAGE 74.4 miles
UNPAVED MILEAGE 71.8 miles
DRIVING TIME 5 hours
ELEVATION RANGE 3,900–7,000 feet
USUALLY OPEN March to December
DIFFICULTY RATING 2
SCENIC RATING 8
REMOTENESS RATING +1

Special Attractions

- Grand Staircase–Escalante National Monument and Glen Canyon National Recreation Area.
- The switchbacks of Kelly Grade.
- Underground smoldering coal deposits.
- Long trail with varied scenery over the Kaiparowits Plateau.

History

When the pioneers and stockmen settled this region, they must have been intrigued by the wisps of smoke rising up from Smoky Mountain. Much of the mountain and the surrounding Kaiparowits Plateau have large deposits of underground coal, which are slowly smoldering and which give the mountain its name. As the coal underneath the topsoil burns, the topsoil collapses in on itself, causing slight depressions in the ground. On two occasions in the 1960s, the Bureau of Mines attempted to extinguish the fires by bulldozing vast tracts of land. Although the fires were put out wherever they were bulldozed, the burning ran underground to emerge elsewhere. For the most part now, they are left alone.

Early pioneers lent their names to many features along this trail. Alvey Wash and the Left Hand and Right Hand Collets are named after settlers who ran cattle and horses in the area.

The name for Wahweap Creek, at the southern end of the trail, comes from a Paiute Indian word that refers to the creek's brackish water. For a time the creek was known as Sentinel Creek. The bentonite clay hills at the south end of Smoky Mountain Road have been used as movie locations. They are featured in *Planet of the Apes* (1968) and *The Greatest Story Ever Told* (1965).

Description

The Smoky Mountain Road is the longest of the backcountry byways that cross through the Grand Staircase–Escalante National Monument. For the most part it crosses the Kaiparowits Plateau, providing good views of diverse scenery. Near Big Water, the trail runs across the steep Kelly Grade, an exciting drive of narrow switchbacks.

The trail commences in Big Water on US 89 (at the same starting point as Southwest #20: Nipple Creek and Tibbet Canyon Trail. The entrance from the highway is not marked except the sign for Ethan Allen Street, but the route is well signed from the first intersection in town. The road turns to graded gravel when it enters the Glen Canyon National Recreation Area, and it maintains a good standard as it winds along the face of Nipple Bench, underneath tall cliffs, and through a mix of badlands scenery.

Side roads lead farther into the Glen Canyon National Recreation Area; one such road is Recreation Road 230, which leads 4.1 miles to Southwest #19: Alstrom Point Trail and 27 miles to Grand Bench. Southwest

Spectacular views from Kelly Grade

#21: Smoky Hollow Trail then enters on the left, just as the main trail enters the Grand Staircase–Escalante National Monument.

As you drive toward Kelly Grade, it is difficult to envisage how you will manage to climb up the sheer cliff face. The first mile along a narrow shelf road is very steep, with one particularly tight switchback. As you climb, the views spread out to the south and west. Although the trail is narrow, it is well graded and two vehicles will be able to squeeze past each other at several places. The grader has created an earth barrier on the outside edge, but this is very soft and there is a sheer drop of 600 feet near the saddle. From the first saddle, the grade starts to level out, but the shelf road continues as it winds around the north side before climbing steeply again to the top. This north section can make Kelly Grade impassable in winter months, as snow and ice remain on the north face well after the snow has melted elsewhere. However, in a mild winter, Smoky Mountain Road can remain open all year. Heavy rainfall can also close Kelly Grade temporarily, as it is carved through mostly black Tropic shale, which quickly becomes impassable when wet.

Southwest #21: Smoky Hollow Trail provides an alternate route around Kelly Grade that may be passable in wet conditions.

Once on top of Kelly Grade, Smoky Mountain Road starts its long run across the Kaiparowits Plateau to Escalante. The vegetation is mainly sagebrush with scattered junipers and pinyon pines, which contrast well with the many-colored rocks along the plateau. As you travel across Smoky Mountain, look for wisps of smoke; these mark the naturally burning coal deposits that give the mountain its name. You can feel the heat of the smoldering coal by holding your hand above the earth. On the cliffs, look for the black charcoal that marks previously burnt areas.

On top of the plateau, the trail undulates, dropping slowly as it crosses several deep canyons—at Drip Tank Canyon, Last Chance Creek, and Dry Wash. Some of the climbs out of these, although not steep, can be a bit rougher and looser than the rest of the trail. The northern end of the trail travels through Alvey Wash Valley, a long, wide, flat-bottomed, sagebrush-covered valley, which gradually gets narrower until it

Approaching Kelly Grade

becomes a high-walled rocky canyon. The trail crosses Alvey Wash many times; the wash has water in it most of the year.

The trail finishes in the center of Escalante.

There are many opportunities for back-country camping along this route, especially along some of the side trails. Please note that although currently no permits are required for camping in the national monument, the management plan is still under development and this may change. Side trails mentioned in the route directions may or may not be open for vehicle travel and are included for reference purposes only. Some of the smaller trails are likely to be closed under the final management plan. Check with the Interagency Office in Escalante before planning to camp within the monument. The office is also extremely helpful with the latest information on road conditions.

Current Road Information

Grand Staircase–Escalante National
   Monument Office
190 East Center St.
Kanab, UT 84741
(435) 644-4300

BLM Escalante Field Office
PO Box 225
Escalante, UT 84726
(435) 826-5600

Escalante Interagency Office
755 West Main
Escalante, UT 84726
(435) 826-5499

Map References

BLM   Smoky Mt., Escalante
USFS   Dixie National Forest: Escalante
      Ranger District
USGS 1:24,000 Escalante, Dave Canyon,
      Death Ridge, Carcass Canyon, Petes
      Cove, Ship Mt. Point, Needle Eye
      Point, Smoky Hollow, Warm Creek
      Bay, Lone Rock, Glen Canyon City
      1:100,000 Smoky Mt., Escalante
Maptech CD-ROM: Escalante/Dixie
      National Forest
Trails Illustrated, #213; #710 (incomplete)
Utah Atlas & Gazetteer, p. 19
Utah Travel Council #4
Other: BLM Map of the Grand Staircase–
      Escalante National Monument

Route Directions

▼ 0.0   On US 89 at Big Water, 0.3 miles west of mile marker 7, turn east on paved Ethan Allen Street at sign for the Lake Powell Village Resort Motel. Zero trip meter.

2.0 ▲   Trail finishes on US 89 at Big Water. Turn right for Kanab; turn left for Page, Arizona.
        GPS: N 37°04.66' W 111°39.69'

▼ 0.3 TR Intersection. Turn right, following sign for the Glen Canyon National Recreation Area and Utah 12. Ahead is Southwest #20: Nipple Creek and Tibbet Canyon Trail. Another road junction follows immediately; continue straight, following signs for Glen Canyon.

1.7 ▲ TL Continue straight at first road junction, then at intersection at the RV park,

turn left and proceed through Big Water toward US 89. Road on right at the RV park is Southwest #20: Nipple Creek and Tibbet Canyon Trail.
GPS: N 37°04.90′ W 111°39.66′

▼ 0.9   SO   Cross through Wahweap Creek on a gravel ford, then track on right.
1.1 ▲   SO   Track on left, then cross through Wahweap Creek on a gravel ford.

▼ 2.0   SO   Entering Glen Canyon National Recreation Area. Road is now graded gravel. Zero trip meter.
0.0 ▲   Continue toward Big Water.
GPS: N 37°04.58′ W 111°37.87′

▼ 0.0   Continue into Glen Canyon National Recreation Area.
6.8 ▲   SO   Leaving Glen Canyon National Recreation Area. Road is now paved. Zero trip meter.

▼ 0.9   SO   Cross over wash and pass around the end of Mustard Point.
5.9 ▲   SO   Pass around the end of Mustard Point and cross over wash.

▼ 2.7   SO   Cross through Wiregrass Canyon Wash.
4.1 ▲   SO   Cross through Wiregrass Canyon Wash.

▼ 4.8   SO   Pass around the head of Lone Rock Canyon.
2.0 ▲   SO   Pass around the head of Lone Rock Canyon.
GPS: N 37°04.56′ W 111°33.15′

▼ 6.8   SO   Track on right to Warm Creek Bay via Crosby Canyon Road. Zero trip meter at signpost.
0.0 ▲   Continue toward Big Water.
GPS: N 37°05.40′ W 111°31.31′

▼ 0.0   Continue through Crosby Canyon Wash.
3.5 ▲   SO   Track on left to Warm Creek Bay via Crosby Canyon Road. Zero trip meter at signpost.

▼ 2.4   SO   Track on right.
1.1 ▲   SO   Track on left.
GPS: N 37°06.82′ W 111°29.50′

▼ 3.5   BR   Track to the left is Southwest #21: Smoky Hollow Trail. Bear right, following sign for Smoky Mountain Road and Grand Bench. Zero trip meter.
0.0 ▲   Proceed toward Big Water.
GPS: N 37°07.80′ W 111°29.66′

▼ 0.0   Proceed toward Smoky Mountain.
1.0 ▲   SO   Track to the right is Southwest #21: Smoky Hollow Trail. Zero trip meter.

▼ 0.2   SO   Corral on left.
0.8 ▲   SO   Corral on right.

▼ 0.4   SO   Cross through wash.
0.6 ▲   SO   Cross through wash.

▼ 0.5   SO   Track on right.
0.5 ▲   SO   Track on left.

▼ 1.0   SO   Track on right is Recreation Road 230 and goes to Southwest #19: Alstrom Point Trail (4.1 miles) and Grand Bench (27 miles). Smoky Mountain Road continues straight ahead; entering the Grand Staircase–Escalante National Monument. Zero trip meter.
0.0 ▲   Continue into Glen Canyon National Recreation Area.
GPS: N 37°08.13′ W 111°28.89′

▼ 0.0   Continue into Grand Staircase–Escalante National Monument.
12.6 ▲   SO   Track on left (Recreation Road 230) goes to Southwest #19: Alstrom Point Trail (4.1 miles) and Grand Bench (27 miles). Smoky Mountain Road continues straight ahead; entering Glen Canyon National Recreation Area. Zero trip meter.

▼ 0.1   SO   Track on left.
12.5 ▲   SO   Track on right.

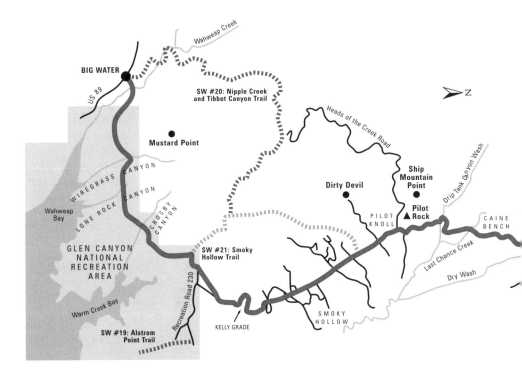

▼ 2.3	SO	Cross through wash.
10.3 ▲	SO	Cross through wash.

▼ 2.6	SO	Cross through wash. Bottom of Kelly Grade.
10.0 ▲	SO	Cross through wash. Bottom of Kelly Grade.
		GPS: N 37°09.68' W 111°27.00'

▼ 3.6	SO	Saddle at top of first steep climb. Trail levels out but continues along narrow shelf road.
9.0 ▲	SO	Saddle, then descend steepest section.

▼ 7.2	SO	Top of Kelly Grade. Track on left to Lookout Point.
5.4 ▲	SO	Track on right to Lookout Point. Top of Kelly Grade.
		GPS: N 37°11.29' W 111°27.03'

▼ 7.4	SO	Campsite on left, track on right.
5.2 ▲	SO	Campsite on right, track on left.

▼ 8.5	SO	Track on left, then track on right.
4.1 ▲	SO	Track on left, then track on right.

▼ 8.7	SO	Track on left.
3.9 ▲	SO	Track on right.

▼ 9.5	SO	Track on right.
3.1 ▲	SO	Track on left.

▼ 9.8	SO	Faint track on left.
2.8 ▲	SO	Faint track on right.

▼ 10.1	SO	Faint track on right.
2.5 ▲	SO	Faint track on left.

▼ 10.2	SO	Faint track on left.
2.4 ▲	SO	Faint track on right.

▼ 11.3	SO	Track on left, then track on right.
1.3 ▲	SO	Track on left, then track on right.

▼ 11.4	BR	Graded track on left.
1.2 ▲	SO	Graded track on right.
		GPS: N 37°14.62' W 111°29.25'

▼ 11.9	SO	Graded track on right.
0.7 ▲	BL	Graded track on left.

▼ 12.3	SO	Track on left.

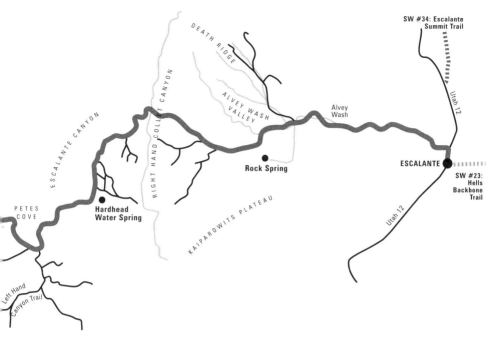

SW Trail #18: Smoky Mountain Road

0.3 ▲   SO   Track on right.

▼ 12.5   SO   Track on right.
0.1 ▲   SO   Track on left.

▼ 12.6   SO   Graded track on left is Southwest #21: Smoky Hollow Trail. Signpost is just past the junction. Zero trip meter.
0.0 ▲   Continue along Smoky Mountain Road.
GPS: N 37°15.43′ W 111°29.80′

▼ 0.0   Continue along Smoky Mountain Road.
2.5 ▲   SO   Graded track on right is Southwest #21: Smoky Hollow Trail. Zero trip meter.

▼ 1.5   SO   Track on left, then faint track on right.
1.0 ▲   SO   Faint track on left, then track on right.

▼ 1.9   SO   Pilot Knoll is left of the trail.
0.6 ▲   SO   Pilot Knoll is right of the trail.
GPS: N 37°16.82′ W 111°31.13′

▼ 2.5   SO   Track to left is Heads of the Creek Road, which joins Southwest #20: Nipple Creek and Tibbet Canyon

Trail. Faint track on right. Zero trip meter. Signpost: "Escalante, 42 miles."
0.0 ▲   Continue toward Big Water.
GPS: N 37°17.32′ W 111°31.39′

▼ 0.0   Continue toward Escalante.
15.5 ▲   SO   Track on right is Heads of the Creek Road, which joins Southwest #20: Nipple Creek and Tibbet Canyon Trail. Faint track on left. Zero trip meter. Signpost: "Big Water, 30 miles."

▼ 0.3   SO   Cross through wash, then round the bottom of Pilot Rock at the end of Ship Mountain Point.
15.2 ▲   SO   Round the bottom of Pilot Rock at the end of Ship Mountain Point, then cross through wash.

▼ 0.7   SO   Track on left to campsite.
14.8 ▲   SO   Track on right to campsite.

▼ 1.1   SO   Cross through wash.
14.4 ▲   SO   Cross through wash.

▼ 1.4　SO　Cattle guard.
14.1 ▲　SO　Cattle guard.
　　　　GPS: N 37°18.38' W 111°31.61'

▼ 2.0　SO　Cross through wash.
13.5 ▲　SO　Cross through wash.

▼ 2.7　SO　Cross through wash.
12.8 ▲　SO　Cross through wash.

▼ 2.9　SO　Track on right.
12.6 ▲　SO　Track on left.
　　　　GPS: N 37°19.37' W 111°31.95'

▼ 3.1　SO　Cross through Drip Tank Canyon wash.
12.4 ▲　SO　Cross through Drip Tank Canyon wash.
　　　　GPS: N 37°19.41' W 111°32.12'

▼ 4.6　SO　Cross through wash.
10.9 ▲　SO　Cross through wash.

▼ 5.7　SO　Faint track on right, then cattle guard.
9.8 ▲　SO　Cattle guard, then faint track on left.

▼ 5.8　SO　Cross through Last Chance Creek.
9.7 ▲　SO　Cross through Last Chance Creek.
　　　　GPS: N 37°20.79' W 111°31.54'

▼ 6.0　SO　Cross through wash; trail crosses Caine Bench.
9.5 ▲　SO　Cross through wash; trail crosses Caine Bench.

▼ 7.3　SO　Cross through wash.
8.2 ▲　SO　Cross through wash.

▼ 7.6　SO　Cross through rocky wash.
7.9 ▲　SO　Cross through rocky wash.

▼ 8.6　SO　Two faint tracks on right.
6.9 ▲　SO　Two faint tracks on left.

▼ 9.0　SO　Track on left, then cattle guard, then views on right into Dry Wash.
6.5 ▲　SO　Views on left into Dry Wash. Cattle guard, then track on right.
　　　　GPS: N 37°23.25' W 111°30.85'

▼ 10.1　SO　Track on right.
5.4 ▲　SO　Track on left.

▼ 12.2　SO　Cross through wash.
3.3 ▲　SO　Cross through wash.

▼ 13.0　SO　Cattle guard.
2.5 ▲　SO　Cattle guard.
　　　　GPS: N 37°26.13' W 111°31.83'

▼ 13.1　SO　Cross through wash.
2.4 ▲　SO　Cross through wash.

▼ 13.7　SO　Faint tracks on left and right.
1.8 ▲　SO　Faint tracks on left and right.

▼ 15.0　SO　Track on right.
0.5 ▲　SO　Track on left.
　　　　GPS: N 37°26.99' W 111°30.47'

▼ 15.5　TL　Track on right is Left Hand Collet Canyon Trail. Large corral directly ahead. Zero trip meter.
0.0 ▲　　　Continue toward Big Water.
　　　　GPS: N 37°27.38' W 111°30.32'

▼ 0.0　　　Continue toward Escalante.
21.7 ▲　TR　Track on left is Left Hand Collet Canyon Trail. Large corral on left. Zero trip meter.

▼ 0.1　SO　Two tracks on right.
21.6 ▲　SO　Two tracks on left.

▼ 0.8　SO　Cross over wash, then pass through fence line.
20.9 ▲　SO　Pass through fence line, then cross over wash.

▼ 2.8　SO　Cattle guard.
18.9 ▲　SO　Cattle guard.
　　　　GPS: N 37°28.25' W 111°32.52'

▼ 2.9　SO　Cross through Left Hand Collet Canyon wash.
18.8 ▲　SO　Cross through Left Hand Collet Canyon wash.

▼ 3.5　SO　Faint track on left.
18.2 ▲　SO　Faint track on right.

▼ 3.6　SO　Track on right.

18.1 ▲ SO Track on left.

▼ 4.3 SO Two tracks on right.
17.4 ▲ SO Two tracks on left.

▼ 4.6 SO Cattle guard.
17.1 ▲ SO Cattle guard.

▼ 5.6 SO Track on right.
16.1 ▲ SO Track on left.
GPS: N 37°29.95' W 111°34.03'

▼ 6.1 SO Track on right.
15.6 ▲ SO Track on left.

▼ 6.2 SO Cattle guard.
15.5 ▲ SO Cattle guard.

▼ 8.1 SO Cross through wash.
13.6 ▲ SO Cross through wash.

▼ 9.3 BL Track on right, on top of ridge in clearing.
12.4 ▲ BR Track on left, on top of ridge in clearing.
GPS: N 37°31.37' W 111°36.88'

▼ 9.7 SO Cattle guard.
12.0 ▲ SO Cattle guard.

▼ 10.8 SO Cross through wash.
10.9 ▲ SO Cross through wash.

▼ 12.0 BL Track on right. Bear left, then cross through Right Hand Collet Creek.
9.7 ▲ BR Cross through Right Hand Collet Creek, then track on left.
GPS: N 37°32.51' W 111°38.38'

▼ 12.1 BR Track on left.
9.6 ▲ BL Track on right.

▼ 12.7 SO Track on right.
9.0 ▲ SO Track on left.

▼ 13.4 SO Cross over creek, then track on left.
8.3 ▲ SO Track on right, then cross over creek.

▼ 14.1 SO Cross through wash.
7.6 ▲ SO Cross through wash.

▼ 15.5 SO Cattle guard.

6.2 ▲ SO Cattle guard.
GPS: N 37°34.69' W 111°36.95'

▼ 16.0 SO Track on right. Main trail crosses Camp Flat.
5.7 ▲ SO Track on left. Main trail crosses Camp Flat.

▼ 16.2 SO Track on right.
5.5 ▲ SO Track on left.

▼ 16.6 SO Track on left.
5.1 ▲ SO Track on right.

▼ 16.8 SO Track on right.
4.9 ▲ SO Track on left.

▼ 17.4 SO Nice campsite in a stand of pines on right. Track on right and track on left.
4.3 ▲ SO Nice campsite in a stand of pines on left. Track on right and track on left.
GPS: N 37°36.11' W 111°36.18'

▼ 19.0 SO Track on right. Trail enters Alvey Wash Valley.
2.7 ▲ SO Track on left. Trail leaves Alvey Wash Valley.

▼ 20.5 SO Cattle guard.
1.2 ▲ SO Cattle guard.

▼ 21.3 SO Track on right.
0.4 ▲ SO Track on left.

▼ 21.7 SO Two entrances to track on left go to Death Ridge (6 miles). Signpost: "Escalante, 8 miles." Zero trip meter.
0.0 ▲ Continue straight, following sign to Big Sage Junction.
GPS: N 37°39.38' W 111°37.94'

▼ 0.0 Continue toward Escalante.
6.8 ▲ SO Two entrances to track on right go to Death Ridge (6 miles). Signpost to Big Sage Junction. Zero trip meter.

▼ 0.6 SO Cross through Alvey Wash.
6.2 ▲ SO Cross through Alvey Wash.

▼ 1.0 SO Track on left.

5.8 ▲   SO   Track on right.

▼ 1.2   SO   Cross through Alvey Wash.
5.6 ▲   SO   Cross through Alvey Wash.

▼ 1.6   SO   Faint track on left.
5.2 ▲   SO   Faint track on right.

▼ 2.0   SO   Faint track on right. Trail crosses
             through Alvey Wash often in the next
             4.8 miles.
4.8 ▲   SO   Faint track on left.

▼ 4.4   SO   Track on right.
2.4 ▲   SO   Track on left.
             GPS: N 37°42.88′ W 111°37.78′

▼ 5.6   SO   Cattle guard.
1.2 ▲   SO   Cattle guard.

▼ 6.1   SO   Track on right.
0.7 ▲   SO   Track on left.

▼ 6.7   SO   Faint track on left.
0.1 ▲   SO   Faint track on right.

▼ 6.8   SO   Track on left. Leaving Grand Staircase–
             Escalante National Monument; cross
             over cattle guard into private land. Zero
             trip meter.
0.0 ▲   Continue into Grand Staircase–
             Escalante National Monument. Trail
             crosses through Alvey Wash often in
             the next 4.8 miles.
             GPS: N 37°44.76′ W 111°37.47′

▼ 0.0   Continue into Escalante.
2.0 ▲   SO   Leave private land over cattle guard
             and enter the Grand Staircase–
             Escalante National Monument, then
             track on right. Zero trip meter.

▼ 0.3   SO   Track on left.
1.7 ▲   SO   Track on right.

▼ 0.6   SO   Escalante County Landfill on left.
1.4 ▲   SO   Escalante County Landfill on right.

▼ 0.7   SO   Track on left.
1.3 ▲   SO   Track on right.

▼ 1.0   SO   Two tracks on left, then cattle guard.
1.0 ▲   SO   Cattle guard, then two tracks on right.

▼ 1.1   BR   Entering edge of Escalante. Remain on
             main road.
0.9 ▲   SO   Leaving Escalante.

▼ 1.4   SO   Road is now paved.
0.6 ▲   SO   Road is now graded gravel.

▼ 1.7   SO   Old County Fairgrounds on right.
0.3 ▲   SO   Old County Fairgrounds on left.

▼ 2.0   Road ends at Utah 12 in Escalante.
0.0 ▲   On Utah 12 in Escalante, turn south
             onto 500 West Street next to the
             Broken Bow RV Camp and zero trip
             meter.
             GPS: N 37°46.23′ W 111°36.54′

Alstrom Point Trail

STARTING POINT Recreation Road 230, 4.1
miles east of Southwest #18: Smoky
Mountain Road in Glen Canyon
National Recreation Area

FINISHING POINT Alstrom Point

TOTAL MILEAGE 6.5 miles

UNPAVED MILEAGE 6.5 miles

DRIVING TIME 45 minutes (one-way)

ELEVATION RANGE 4,300–4,600 feet

USUALLY OPEN Year-round

DIFFICULTY RATING 3

SCENIC RATING 10

REMOTENESS RATING +0

Special Attractions

■ Views of Gunsight Butte and Padre Bay
and a high viewpoint over Lake Powell.
■ Excellent photography point.
■ Backcountry campsites.

Description

If you only have time to take in one trail
with a view over Lake Powell, this is the one!

Vehicle parked at the end of Alstrom Point Trail

The short spur in the Glen Canyon National Recreation Area travels on a sandy ungraded trail onto Alstrom Point, a mesa about 500 feet above Lake Powell. The sand can be soft, but it is not extremely deep and it is unlikely you will need to drop tire pressures. The trail is often slightly washed out at the start, but as it travels along the point it becomes rockier and lumpier. There are a few tracks leading off the main trail—most of them lead quickly to viewpoints, though staying on the main trail leads past several great views.

The first viewpoint is 4.6 miles from the start; this spot is also popular for camping. It looks west over red Gunsight Butte rising out of the clear blue waters of Lake Powell. The notch in the rock immediately to the north of the butte is Gunsight Pass. In front of the butte is Gunsight Bay, and behind it is Padre Bay, which takes its name from the now flooded Padre Creek. It was at the mouth of this creek that the Domínguez-Escalante expedition managed to cross the Colorado River in 1776.

Low-clearance vehicles often turn back here, but high-clearance vehicles can continue along a rocky section of trail. A track to the right 1.5 miles later leads out for 0.4 miles onto the extremely narrow neck of land that connects Romana Mesa to Alstrom Point. There are no vehicle trails on Romana Mesa.

The main trail ends at a higher viewpoint that allows you to see Tower Butte and Wild Horse Mesa in the Navajo Nation to the south, Navajo Mountain, Gooseneck Point, and the pillar of Cookie Jar Butte behind Padre Bay, as well as the features in Gunsight Bay.

There is no shade along this trail, and it is extremely hot in summer.

Current Road Information
Glen Canyon National Recreation Area
PO Box 1507
Page, AZ 86040
(928) 608-6404

Map References
BLM   Smoky Mt.
USGS 1:24,000   Smoky Hollow, Warm
         Creek Bay
         1:100,000 Smoky Mt.
Maptech CD-ROM: Escalante/Dixie
         National Forest
Trails Illustrated, #213
Utah Atlas & Gazetteer, p. 20
Utah Travel Council #5
Other: Glen Canyon National Recreation
         Area map

Route Directions

▼ 0.0   From Recreation Road 230, 4.1 miles
         east of Southwest #18: Smoky
         Mountain Road, on top of a small
         ridge, turn south on unmarked roughly

SW Trail #19: Alstrom Point Trail

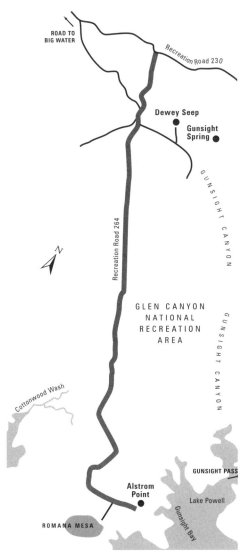

ROAD TO BIG WATER

Recreation Road 230

Dewey Seep

Gunsight Spring

GUNSIGHT CANYON

Recreation Road 264

N

GLEN CANYON NATIONAL RECREATION AREA

GUNSIGHT CANYON

Cottonwood Wash

GUNSIGHT PASS

Alstrom Point

Lake Powell

ROMANA MESA

Gunsight Bay

graded small trail and zero trip meter.
GPS: N 37°07.84' W 111°24.80'

▼ 0.6 SO Track on right rejoins Recreation Road 230.
GPS: N 37°07.33' W 111°24.71'

▼ 0.8 SO Track on right, then track on left.
▼ 2.9 SO Faint track on right goes short distance to drill hole.
▼ 4.0 SO Well-used track on right goes 0.3 miles

to a tank and viewpoint over Lake Powell. Zero trip meter.
GPS: N 37°04.59' W 111°23.06'

▼ 0.0 Continue toward Alstrom Point.
▼ 0.6 SO Viewpoint and campsite on left over Gunsight Bay, Gunsight Pass, and Gunsight Butte, with Padre Bay behind.
GPS: N 37°04.15' W 111°22.84'

▼ 0.7 SO Two alternate routes up small ridge.
▼ 1.6 BL Track on right.
GPS: N 37°03.51' W 111°22.67'

▼ 2.1 BL Track on right goes 0.4 miles out on the neck of Romana Mesa.
GPS: N 37°03.47' W 111°22.21'

▼ 2.2 SO Faint track on right.
▼ 2.3 SO Viewpoint on right looks over the lake to the Navajo Nation.
▼ 2.4 BR Track on left goes 0.1 miles to slightly lower viewpoint and continues on.
GPS: N 37°03.56' W 111°21.84'

▼ 2.5 Trail ends at panoramic viewpoint over Lake Powell.
GPS: N 37°03.54' W 111°21.80'

SOUTHWEST REGION TRAIL #20

Nipple Creek and Tibbet Canyon Trail

STARTING POINT Big Water on US 89
FINISHING POINT Southwest #21: Smoky Hollow Trail, 3.4 miles from Southwest #18: Smoky Mountain Road
TOTAL MILEAGE 22.2 miles
UNPAVED MILEAGE 21.9 miles
DRIVING TIME 2 hours
ELEVATION RANGE 4,000–5,000 feet
USUALLY OPEN Year-round
DIFFICULTY RATING 3
SCENIC RATING 8
REMOTENESS RATING +1

Special Attractions
- Varied scenery within the Grand Staircase–Escalante National Monument.
- Winding creek canyons of Nipple Creek and Tibbet Canyon.
- Nipple Butte.

Description
Most of this trail is contained within the Grand Staircase–Escalante National Monument. The winding trail runs up narrow Nipple Canyon, leaves it briefly to run through a very scenic area of badlands, and then climbs out the head of Nipple Canyon. It passes prominent Nipple Butte before descending back down wider Tibbet Canyon. There are a couple of backcountry campsites, but those looking to camp for the night will find better spots along Smoky Mountain Road.

The entire trail is graded dirt, but there are several rough spots that make it preferable to have a 4WD vehicle. One in particular is a short, low-traction, steep climb as the trail leaves Nipple Creek Canyon and ascends onto a bench. From the top of the bench, the trail passes through blue-gray shale before climbing around a narrow shelf road. This type of soil is extremely susceptible to damage, and vehicle tires can leave a visible scar on the landscape for a very long time. Please be extra careful to remain on the designated trail.

Back in Nipple Creek, the trail passes close to Nipple Spring and then exits to run

Nipple Butte

alongside Nipple Butte. The cattle in the region often use the creek bed as their trail, churning it up and making it looser and sandier for vehicles.

The trail passes the start of the Heads of the Creek Road, which eventually joins Southwest #18: Smoky Mountain Road and then descends into Tibbet Canyon, where you can see some fair examples of the naturally occurring burnt coal deposits that are characteristic of Smoky Mountain.

The trail finishes at Southwest #21: Smoky Hollow Trail, 3.4 miles from its southern junction with Southwest #18: Smoky Mountain Road.

Current Road Information
BLM Kanab Field Office
318 North 100 East
Kanab, UT 84741
(435) 644-4600

Grand Staircase–Escalante National
    Monument Office
190 East Center St.
Kanab, UT 84741
(435) 644-4300

Nipple Spring

Sandy section of the trail along Wahweap Creek

Map References

BLM Smoky Mt.
USGS 1:24,000 Glen Canyon City,
        Nipple Butte, Tibbet Bench
        1:100,000 Smoky Mt.
Maptech CD-ROM: Escalante/Dixie
        National Forest
Utah Atlas & Gazetteer, p. 19
Utah Travel Council #5

Route Directions

▼ 0.0   Begin on US 89, 15 miles west of
           Page, Arizona, at Big Water, 0.3 miles
           west of mile marker 7. Turn east on
           paved Ethan Allen Street (at the sign
           for the Lake Powell Village Resort
           Motel) and zero trip meter.
2.2 ▲   Trail finishes on US 89 at Big Water.
           Turn right for Kanab, turn left for Page,
           Arizona.
           GPS: N 37°04.66′ W 111°39.69′

▼ 0.3 SO Intersection. Southwest #18: Smoky
           Mountain Road is on right. Continue
           straight to the edge of town.
1.9 ▲ SO Intersection. Southwest #18: Smoky
           Mountain Road is on left. Continue
           straight through Big Water to US 89.

▼ 0.6 TL T-intersection. Right goes to a gravel
           pit. Turn left and continue past the
           northern edge of Big Water. Road is
           now graded gravel.
1.6 ▲ TR Straight on goes to a gravel pit.
           Turn right onto paved road and contin-
           ue through Big Water.

GPS: N 37°05.16′ W 111°39.65′

▼ 0.9 SO Track on left. Gravel road on right to
           gravel pit.
1.3 ▲ SO Track on right. Gravel road on left to
           gravel pit.

▼ 1.3 SO Gravel road on right to gravel pit.
0.9 ▲ SO Gravel road on left to gravel pit.

▼ 1.5 SO Gravel road on right to gravel pit.
0.7 ▲ SO Gravel road on left to gravel pit.

▼ 2.2 BL Fish hatchery (no sign) is directly
           ahead. Zero trip meter.
0.0 ▲   Continue away from the fish hatchery.
           GPS: N 37°06.00′ W 111°40.41′

▼ 0.0   Continue with the fish hatchery on
           your right.
10.0 ▲ BR Fish hatchery is on the left. Zero trip
           meter.

▼ 0.2 BL Two tracks on right into fish hatchery.
9.8 ▲ BR Two tracks on left into fish hatchery.

▼ 0.6 TL Intersection. Old water tank on right.
           Turn left onto sandy track and immedi-
           ately bear right and follow along
           Wahweap Creek.
9.4 ▲ TR Bear left at faint track to the right, then
           intersection. Old water tank is ahead.
           Turn right onto larger track, then pass
           a fish hatchery (no sign) on left.
           GPS: N 37°06.35′ W 111°40.97′

▼ 0.9 SO Cross through the wide, sandy
           Wahweap Creek, then follow along
           creek to the northwest on the far side.
9.1 ▲ SO Cross through the wide, sandy
           Wahweap Creek, then follow along the
           creek to the southeast on the far side.

▼ 1.0 SO Cross through small wash.
9.0 ▲ SO Cross through small wash.

▼ 1.6 BR Enter Nipple Creek Wash and bear
           right up wash. Trail crosses the wash
           often for the next 1.2 miles. Track on
           left crosses wash and continues.

8.4 ▲   BL   Bear left and exit Nipple Creek Wash. Track to the right leaves wash and continues.
GPS: N 37°06.85' W 111°41.07'

▼ 2.0   SO   Cross through wire gate. Entering the Grand Staircase–Escalante National Monument.

8.0 ▲   SO   Cross through wire gate. Leaving the Grand Staircase–Escalante National Monument.
GPS: N 37°07.01' W 111°40.78'

▼ 2.5   SO   Faint track on right. Remain in main creek wash.

7.5 ▲   SO   Faint track on left. Remain in main creek wash.

▼ 2.8   BL   Bear left out of creek wash.

7.2 ▲   BR   Enter Nipple Creek Wash and bear right down wash. Trail crosses wash often for the next 1.2 miles.

▼ 2.9   SO   Cross through wire gate; entering an area of blue-gray shale. Swing left and climb to top of bench.

7.1 ▲   SO   Bottom of descent from bench. Swing

right and cross through wire gate.
GPS: N 37°07.57' W 111°40.44'

▼ 3.1   BR   Top of climb. Track on left.

6.9 ▲   BL   Track on right, then descend down from bench.

▼ 4.2   SO   Pass through wire gate.

5.8 ▲   SO   Pass through wire gate.
GPS: N 37°08.32' W 111°40.45'

▼ 4.6   SO   Cross through wash.

5.4 ▲   SO   Cross through wash.

▼ 5.0   SO   Cross through wash, then trail swings down to rejoin Nipple Creek Wash.

5.0 ▲   SO   Cross through wash.

▼ 5.7   SO   Enter Nipple Creek Wash. Area of naturally occurring burnt coal on left. Trail now follows alongside Nipple Creek Wash for the next 3.4 miles, crossing it frequently.

4.3 ▲   SO   Trail leaves Nipple Creek Wash. Area of naturally occurring burnt coal on right.
GPS: N 37°09.01' W 111°39.82'

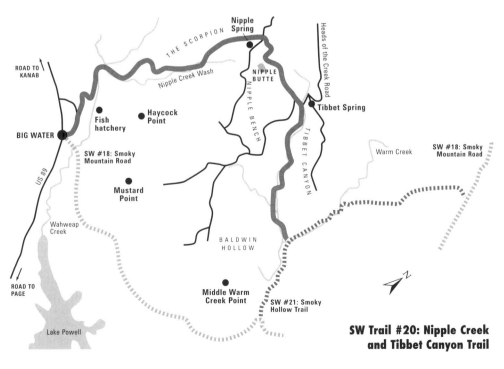

SW Trail #20: Nipple Creek and Tibbet Canyon Trail

| ▼ 6.6 | SO | Track on right. |
| 3.4 ▲ | SO | Track on left. |

| ▼ 7.1 | SO | Mushroom-shaped rock in the wash on left. |
| 2.9 ▲ | SO | Mushroom-shaped rock in the wash on right. |

▼ 9.1	SO	Trail leaves Nipple Creek Wash.
0.9 ▲	SO	Trail enters Nipple Creek Wash, crossing it often for the next 3.4 miles.
		GPS: N 37°11.25' W 111°39.84'

▼ 9.6	TL	T-intersection. Turn left and pass through tall posts marking the fence line in the thick scrub. Track on right to Nipple Spring.
0.4 ▲	TR	Turn right just after two tall posts marking the fence line in the thick scrub, just before a large cottonwood. Follow alongside Nipple Creek Wash. Track ahead to Nipple Spring.
		GPS: N 37°11.52' W 111°39.68'

▼ 10.0	BR	Track on left at the base of a large butte. Zero trip meter.
0.0 ▲		Descend toward Nipple Creek Wash.
		GPS: N 37°11.85' W 111°39.64'

| ▼ 0.0 | | Continue toward Nipple Butte. |
| 3.3 ▲ | BL | Track on right at the base of a large butte. Zero trip meter. |

| ▼ 0.1 | SO | Track on right. |
| 3.2 ▲ | SO | Track on left. |

| ▼ 0.2 | SO | Cross through wash, then large, fat pillar of rock immediately on the right. |
| 3.1 ▲ | SO | Large, fat pillar of rock immediately on the left, then cross through wash. |

| ▼ 0.3 | SO | Enter wash. |
| 3.0 ▲ | SO | Exit wash. |

| ▼ 0.4 | SO | Exit wash. |
| 2.9 ▲ | SO | Enter wash. |

| ▼ 0.8 | BR | Faint track on left. Bear right up the rise. Nipple Butte is directly ahead. |
| 2.5 ▲ | BL | Descend rise, then faint track on right. |

GPS: N 37°11.79' W 111°38.86'

| ▼ 1.5 | SO | Pass through wire gate. |
| 1.8 ▲ | SO | Pass through wire gate. Nipple Butte is ahead. |

| ▼ 2.2 | SO | Cross through wash. |
| 1.1 ▲ | SO | Cross through wash. |

| ▼ 2.3 | SO | Cross through wash. |
| 1.0 ▲ | SO | Cross through wash. |

| ▼ 2.4 | SO | Cross through wash. |
| 0.9 ▲ | SO | Cross through wash. |

| ▼ 2.5 | SO | Enter wash. |
| 0.8 ▲ | SO | Exit wash. |

| ▼ 2.7 | SO | Exit wash. |
| 0.6 ▲ | SO | Enter wash. |

| ▼ 2.8 | SO | Cross through wash. |
| 0.5 ▲ | SO | Cross through wash. |

▼ 2.9	BL	Graded track on right goes out on Nipple Bench.
0.4 ▲	BR	Graded track on left goes out on Nipple Bench.
		GPS: N 37°11.88' W 111°37.10'

| ▼ 3.0 | SO | Enter wash. |
| 0.3 ▲ | SO | Exit wash. |

| ▼ 3.2 | SO | Pass through fence line. |
| 0.1 ▲ | SO | Pass through fence line. |

▼ 3.3	BR	Exit wash, then graded track on left is Heads of the Creek Road, which goes to Southwest #18: Smoky Mountain Road. Zero trip meter.
0.0 ▲		Leave Tibbet Canyon, then enter wash and continue toward Nipple Butte.
		GPS: N 37°11.99' W 111°36.73'

| ▼ 0.0 | | Continue into Tibbet Canyon. |
| 6.7 ▲ | SO | Graded track on right is Heads of the Creek Road, which goes to Southwest #18: Smoky Mountain Road. Zero trip meter. |

▼ 0.1	SO	Track on left joins Heads of the Creek Road.
6.6 ▲	BL	Track on right joins Heads of the Creek Road.

▼ 0.2	SO	Cross through Tibbet Canyon Wash. Trail crosses wash and enters it often for the next 6.2 miles.
6.5 ▲	SO	Cross through Tibbet Canyon Wash for the last time.

▼ 0.3	SO	Cross through fence line.
6.4 ▲	SO	Cross through fence line.

▼ 2.6	SO	Area of naturally occurring burnt coal on left of trail.
4.1 ▲	SO	Area of naturally occurring burnt coal on right of trail.
		GPS: N 37°10.94' W 111°34.70'

▼ 5.1	SO	Cattle guard, rock pour-off on left.
1.6 ▲	SO	Cattle guard, rock pour-off on right.
		GPS: N 37°09.84' W 111°33.23'

▼ 6.4	SO	Exit Tibbet Canyon Wash.
0.3 ▲	SO	Enter Tibbet Canyon Wash. Trail crosses wash and enters it often for the next 6.2 miles.

▼ 6.5	SO	Cross through wash at the confluence of Tibbet Canyon Wash and Warm Creek.
0.2 ▲	SO	Cross through wash at the confluence of Tibbet Canyon Wash and Warm Creek.
		GPS: N 37°09.71' W 111°32.17'

▼ 6.7		Trail ends at Southwest #21: Smoky Hollow Trail. Turn right to exit along Southwest #18: Smoky Mountain Road to US 89, turn left to ascend Smoky Hollow Trail.
0.0 ▲		On Southwest #21: Smoky Hollow Trail, 3.4 miles from the southern junction with Southwest #18: Smoky Mountain Road, zero trip meter and turn west on sandy, graded trail. Junction is unmarked.
		GPS: N 37°09.69' W 111°32.00'

Smoky Hollow Trail

STARTING POINT Southwest #18: Smoky Mountain Road, 5.4 miles from the top of Kelly Grade

FINISHING POINT Southwest #18: Smoky Mountain Road, 12.3 miles west of Big Water

TOTAL MILEAGE 13.3 miles

UNPAVED MILEAGE 13.3 miles

DRIVING TIME 1 hour

ELEVATION RANGE 4,000–5,400 feet

USUALLY OPEN Year-round

DIFFICULTY RATING 2

SCENIC RATING 7

REMOTENESS RATING +0

Special Attractions

- Easy, scenic trail winding through a pleasant canyon.
- Naturally occurring slow-burning coal deposits.
- Can be driven as a loop trail with the Kelly Grade portion of Southwest #18: Smoky Mountain Road.

Description

Smoky Hollow is a narrow canyon that is a tributary of the main Wesses Canyon, and the easy trail through it is accessed from

Middle part of Smoky Hollow

Trail in the wash traveling along the eroded cliff

Southwest #18: Smoky Mountain Road. In the canyon, the trail passes some good examples of the naturally occurring slow-burning coal deposits that characterize the Smoky Mountain region. For the most part, the trail winds along in the wash, so sections can be slightly loose and sandy. The canyon is pretty, and at the lower end there are some good views down the larger Tibbet Canyon out into the Glen Canyon National Recreation Area.

This route is often passable in winter when there is snow on the Kelly Grade at the lower end of the Smoky Mountain Road, making the steep, narrow switchbacks on that route inadvisable for travel.

Current Road Information
BLM Kanab Field Office
318 North 100 East
Kanab, UT 84741
(435) 644-4600

Escalante Interagency Office
755 West Main
Escalante, UT 84726
(435) 826-5499

Map References
BLM   Smoky Mt.
USGS 1:24,000   Smoky Hollow, Tibbet
Bench, Ship Mt. Point, Needle Eye
Point

1:100,000 Smoky Mt.
Maptech CD ROM: Escalante/Dixie
National Forest
Utah Atlas & Gazetteer, p. 19
Utah Travel Council # 5
Other: Glen Canyon National Recreation
Area map
BLM Map of the Grand Staircase–
Escalante National Monument

Route Directions

▼ 0.0   From Southwest #18: Smoky
           Mountain Road, 5.4 miles north of the
           top of Kelly Grade, turn west on the
           graded dirt road, following BLM sign
           for Smoky Hollow, and zero trip meter.
           Don't confuse the turn with the large
           graded road 1.2 miles south of it that
           goes to an airstrip.
9.9 ▲   Trail ends at Southwest #18: Smoky
           Mountain Road, north of the Kelly
           Grade. Turn right to descend the Kelly
           Grade to US 89, turn left to continue
           along Smoky Mountain Road to
           Escalante.
           GPS: N 37°15.43' W 111°29.80'

▼ 0.3   SO Track on right, trail drops into Smoky
           Hollow.
9.6 ▲   SO Track on left.

▼ 0.5   SO Cattle guard.
9.4 ▲   SO Cattle guard.

▼ 1.0   SO Cross through wash.
8.9 ▲   SO Cross through wash.

▼ 1.4   SO Cross through wash, then Smoky
           Hollow Wash comes in from the right.
           Trail crosses the wash many times in
           the next 9 miles.
8.5 ▲   SO Cross through wash, trail leaves
           Smoky Hollow Wash.

▼ 3.1   SO Good example of naturally burnt coal
           deposits under the ledge to left of trail.
6.8 ▲   SO Good example of naturally burnt coal
           deposits under the ledge to right of
           trail.

SW Trail #21: Smoky Hollow Trail

GPS: N 37°13.90' W 111°31.37'

▼ 3.4   SO   Burnt coal deposits under ledges to right of trail.

6.5 ▲   SO   Burnt coal deposits under ledges to left of trail.

▼ 3.6   SO   Large tailings piles of old mine right on trail.

6.3 ▲   SO   Large tailings piles of old mine on left of trail.

     GPS: N 37°13.47' W 111°31.39'

▼ 3.8   SO   Track on right to mine.

6.1 ▲   SO   Track on left to mine.

▼ 6.6   SO   Small campsite and turnout on right. Smoky Hollow joins the main Wesses Canyon.

3.3 ▲   SO   Small campsite and turnout on left. Smoky Hollow joins the main Wesses Canyon.

     GPS: N 37°11.67' W 111°32.27'

▼ 7.3   SO   Cattle guard.

2.6 ▲   SO   Cattle guard.

     GPS: N 37°11.55' W 111°32.03'

▼ 9.9   SO   Graded road on right is Southwest #20: Nipple Creek and Tibbet Canyon Trail. Zero trip meter.

0.0 ▲   Continue along to rejoin Smoky Mountain Road.

GPS: N 37°09.69' W 111°32.00'

▼ 0.0   Continue along to rejoin Smoky Mountain Road.

3.4 ▲   SO   Graded road on left is Southwest #20: Nipple Creek and Tibbet Canyon Trail. Zero trip meter.

▼ 0.5   SO   Exit wash for final time.

2.9 ▲   SO   Enter wash. Trail crosses the wash many times in the next 9 miles.

▼ 2.2   SO   Cross through wash.

1.2 ▲   SO   Cross through wash.

▼ 2.4   SO   Faint track on left.

1.0 ▲   SO   Faint track on right.

▼ 2.7   SO   Cross through wash.

0.7 ▲   SO   Cross through wash.

▼ 3.4   Trail ends at Southwest #18: Smoky Mountain Road. Turn west to exit to US 89. Turn east to ascend the Kelly Grade and continue along Smoky Mountain Road.

0.0 ▲   On Southwest #18: Smoky Mountain Road, 12.3 miles from Big Water, turn northwest on the graded dirt road at sign for Smoky Hollow and zero trip meter.

GPS: N 37°07.79' W 111°29.68'

Hole-in-the-Rock Trail

STARTING POINT Utah 12, 3.6 miles east of
Escalante
FINISHING POINT Hole-in-the-Rock
TOTAL MILEAGE 53.1 miles
UNPAVED MILEAGE 53.1 miles
DRIVING TIME 3 hours (one-way)
ELEVATION RANGE 4,200–5,800 feet
USUALLY OPEN Year-round
DIFFICULTY RATING 1 for most of trail; 4 for last
5.3 miles
SCENIC RATING 10
REMOTENESS RATING +1

Special Attractions

■ Historic Mormon Pioneer Trail.
■ The Hole-in-the-Rock and Dance Hall
Rock historic sites.
■ Long interesting trail within the Grand
Staircase–Escalante National Monument.
■ Devils Garden, an outstanding natural
feature.

History

The Hole-in-the-Rock, a remarkable
achievement by a few hardy Mormon pioneers, enabled them to succeed in their quest
to form the San Juan Mission in the southeast corner of Utah. Throughout the 1870s,
the Mormon Church, under the direction of
Brigham Young, was expanding into its new
territory, and many families were sent to pioneer new regions in Utah. Most of the new

settlements were west of the Colorado River,
which was a major barrier to travel. In order
to establish a footing for the church in the
southeast, a scouting party was sent in 1879
to select a suitable site for the new colony. A
site on the San Juan River at the mouth of
Montezuma Creek was considered the best
place, but there was no direct route to the
proposed new San Juan Mission. The scouts
had traveled a route of nearly 500 miles from
Paragonah.

Two hundred men and women and 50
children traveling in 83 wagons, along with
200 horses and over a thousand head of cattle, gathered in Escalante in November 1879
and headed southeast. At first they made
rapid progress, building a wagon road south
toward the chosen shortcut, a narrow opening in the canyon rim, just downstream from
the mouth of the Escalante River. The party
moved to its new base camp at Forty-Mile
Spring, and a group camped at the Hole-in-
the-Rock to work at enlarging the opening.

The party at the base camp was in good
spirits, and regular square dances were held
at a large slickrock dome with a natural
amphitheater on one side, which became
known as Dance Hall Rock.

The work at the opening in the rim
proved far harder than anyone had envisaged.
The pioneers used mostly picks and shovels,
and what little blasting powder they had was
carefully used to the best effect. Men were
lowered in barrels down the steep crack to
manually hack away at the rocky sides of the
passage. The drop to the river was nearly
2,000 feet, and the resulting grade was very
steep, in some places as much as
45 degrees. In what seems an
incredibly short time for the
amount of work they had to do,
the rough and steep passage was
ready, and on January 26, 1880,
the party made its way through.
Wagons were lowered with the
rear wheels tied, full brakes, and
still a dozen men strained on
ropes to stop them from plum-
meting to the river below.

Once down at the Colorado

An old cabin and corral still remain along Hurricane Wash at Willow Tank

One of the more challenging 4WD sections of the Hole-in-the-Rock Trail

River, the expedition crossed on a ferry built by Charles Hall, at what is now called Halls Crossing.

The Mormons found the trail on the far side of the Colorado very difficult, and it wasn't until May 1880 that the travelers established their new settlement in what is now Bluff, Utah. Bluff is a few miles away from the original site chosen by Silas S. Smith and his scouting party. The journey, originally estimated to take six weeks, took the expedition six months.

The Hole-in-the-Rock Road remained the primary link between the new San Juan Mission and the established settlements in the west for many years before it was abandoned.

Today, almost a third of the Hole-in-the-Rock is under the waters of Lake Powell. Many large boulders have fallen into the passageway, making it difficult to access Lake Powell through the gap. The original trail dropped 1,800 feet in less than a mile. Photographs of the Hole-in-the-Rock do not do it justice. It is difficult to imagine the enormity of the task the Mormon pioneers faced without seeing the difficult passage for yourself. If you plan on hiking down to the lake, allow at least an hour for the round trip. The Hole-in-the-Rock is listed on the National Register of Historic Places.

Description

This very long trail is mainly contained within the Grand Staircase–Escalante National Monument, with the final few

miles traveling through the Glen Canyon National Recreation Area. The trail gently slopes down for most of its 53 miles, passing across several benches and flats. The graded dirt or gravel road can be very washboardy—it depends on how recently the last grader went down. There are a couple of sandy wash crossings and some slightly uneven road surfaces, particularly as you climb out of the wash crossings, but in dry weather all but the last 5.3 miles is suitable for a passenger vehicle. These last miles are for high-clearance 4WDs only—don't even think about attempting it in anything else!

The trail leaves Utah 12, 0.1 miles west of mile marker 65, 3.6 miles east of Escalante. The start of the trail is clearly marked to Hole-in-the-Rock. This modern-day route closely follows the original pioneer trail—wooden posts marked with a wagon symbol show the original route—and much of the original trail can still be seen. The trail descends across a series of flats interspersed

The Colorado River flows past a cutting from the Mormon Hole-in-the-Rock Expedition of 1879–80

THE HOLE-IN-THE-ROCK TRAIL

In 1879 Mormons in southwest Utah were called upon to blaze a trail across the southern portion of the state to the unexplored region to the east. Mormon leaders wanted to colonize this area and develop strong relations with the local Indians. The route was scouted, and it was decided that, although it would be extremely difficult, they would take a direct line from Escalante to Montezuma Creek.

Hole-in-the-Rock

Under the leadership of Silas Stanford Smith, 236 people headed out; this route saved the pioneers over 250 miles, and at first travel went smoothly and they were in good spirits. Then they reached their most difficult obstacle, what would come to be known as the Hole-in-the-Rock Pass: a steep, 1,200-foot gorge down to the Colorado River. They arrived at the gorge in November 1879 and were faced with negotiating it in the freezing winter temperatures.

With no feasible way around it, Smith decided that the gorge had to be crossed. The plan was to build a series of roads along the cliff edges that the settlers could descend to the river. Blasting away boulders, widening crevice walls, and grading the path smoothed the first drop-off. Toward the bottom, other steep drops made passage impossible. Through an amazing feat of engineering, the men of the expedition tacked a road on to the face of the gorge. They chiseled holes into the rock and inserted log supports, creating a 50-foot wooden road. The roads were still very steep, and many of the horses balked at the prospect of descent. Braking systems using ropes were designed to keep the wagons from rolling away out of control.

After the long and arduous road construction, the expedition had to then ferry across the 300-foot-wide river. When they were done, most of the pioneers were exhausted, without strength or will to carry on. However, they kept moving east, and eventually settled at the foot of the cliffs overlooking the San Juan River, calling the town Bluff City. Others pushed on for another hundred or so miles across extremely rugged terrain. Once arriving in southeast Utah, they were forced to tame the land, make peace with local Indians, and survive in whatever way they could. The journey, originally thought to take six weeks, had taken over six months. However, the successful expedition opened a crucial link across southern Utah.

with wash crossings. The gently sloping flats are covered with sagebrush and scattered with juniper trees. To the west, Fiftymile Bench rises up above the flats. The trail crosses over the wide, sandy Tenmile Wash, then crosses Tenmile Flat and Seep Flat.

The first major track to the left goes 7 miles to the Harris Wash Trail, which offers several hiking opportunities in Upper Harris Wash, including some spectacular slot canyons in some of the side canyons. Another 1.5 miles along the main trail is the Devils Garden Picnic Area. This day-use area has pit toilets and several picnic tables set among extremely beautiful multicolored rock pillars and shapes. It makes a lovely place for a break and photo opportunity.

The main trail then passes the turnoffs for the Left Hand Collet Canyon Trail, a Jeep trail that climbs steeply onto Fiftymile Bench, and for the graded road that goes to Egypt, an area of sand dunes and interesting rock features. The trail then passes the well and corral at Cat Pasture, still used for cattle, and the left turn for the Dry Fork Trail, which provides access to several slot canyons off Dry Fork Wash.

After 35 miles, you reach Dance Hall Rock. You can clearly see the large bowl in the rock used for the early square dances. After another 2.5 miles, the trail dips to cross Carcass Wash. This is one of the lumpier, steeper exits—drivers of passenger vehicles may need to take extra care. A memorial in the wash marks the site of a truck accident in 1963 in which seven people died.

The trail is slightly rougher here as it winds through the picturesque slickrock domes of Sooner Rocks. Just before leaving the Grand Staircase–Escalante National Monument, the trail passes alongside Cave Point, which has many large cavelike hollows in the base of the rock. The trail then enters the Glen Canyon National Recreation Area.

Almost 4 miles after entering the recreation area, the road becomes rougher. A grid marks this point. Passenger vehicles and low-clearance 4WDs will not be able to go much farther, and the flat area around the grid has the easiest parking that does not block the trail for other users. Low-clearance vehicles should definitely stop before the first rocky slickrock section to avoid vehicle damage. From this point, the trail crosses several rough and ledgy sections of slickrock as it passes through a very scenic area of colorful slickrock domes. There are some short, steep climbs, and careful wheel placement is needed in some sections to avoid underbody damage. Those driving vehicles with side steps or long front or rear overhangs will need to be extra careful—vehicles bend easier than slickrock does!

The trail ends at the Hole-in-the-Rock. A short scramble down to the hole soon shows the immensity of the work undertaken by the early pioneers. It is still possible to see scrapes from the wagons on the sides of the passage.

There are many opportunities for backcountry camping along this route, especially along some of the side trails. Please note that although currently no permits are required for camping in the national monument, the management plan is still under development and this may change. Side trails mentioned in the route directions may or may not be open for vehicle travel and are included for reference purposes only. Some of the smaller trails are likely to be closed under the final management plan. Check with the Interagency Office in Escalante before planning to camp within the monument. The office is also extremely helpful with the latest information on road conditions.

Current Road Information

Grand Staircase–Escalante National
    Monument Office
190 East Center St.
Kanab, UT 84741
(435) 644-4300

BLM Escalante Field Office
PO Box 225
Escalante, UT 84726
(435) 826-5600

Escalante Interagency Office
755 West Main
Escalante, UT 84726
(435) 826-5499

Map References

BLM   Escalante, Smoky Mt.
USGS 1:24,000   Escalante, Dave Canyon,
    Tenmile Flat, Seep Flat, Sunset Flat,
    Basin Canyon, Big Hollow Wash,
    Blackburn Canyon, Sooner Bench,
    Davis Gulch
    1:100,000 Escalante, Smoky Mt.
Maptech CD-ROM: Escalante/Dixie
    National Forest
Trails Illustrated, #213; #710 (incomplete)
Utah Atlas & Gazetteer, pp. 19, 20
Utah Travel Council #5
Other: BLM Map of the Grand Staircase–
    Escalante National Monument

Route Directions

▼ 0.0   From Utah 12, 0.1 miles west of mile marker 65, 3.6 miles east of Escalante, turn southeast on the graded gravel road at the sign for Hole-in-the-Rock and zero trip meter.
    GPS: N 37°43.65' W 111°31.84'

▼ 0.2   SO Track on right.
▼ 0.4   SO Information board and mileage chart for the route.
▼ 1.0   SO Track on right.

SW Trail #22: Hole-in-the-Rock Trail

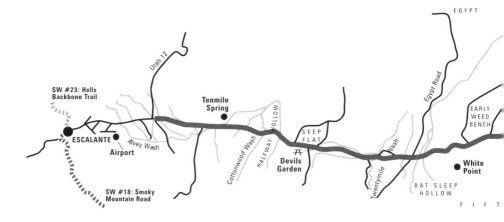

▼ 1.2 SO Track on left.

▼ 2.1 SO Track on right.

▼ 2.8 SO Track on left.

▼ 3.2 SO Track on right.

▼ 3.6 SO Cattle guard.

▼ 4.0 SO Cross over the wide channel of Tenmile Wash.

GPS: N 37°40.83' W 111°29.08'

▼ 4.1 SO Corral on right.

▼ 5.6 SO Track on right.

▼ 7.0 SO Track on right.

▼ 7.5 SO Cattle guard.

▼ 7.7 SO Track on right.

▼ 7.9 SO Cross over Halfway Hollow wash.

▼ 8.5 SO Track on right.

▼ 9.6 SO Track on right.

▼ 10.0 SO Track on left is signposted to Harris Wash (7 miles). Zero trip meter.

GPS: N 37°36.39' W 111°25.63'

▼ 0.0 Continue southeast, crossing Seep Flat.

▼ 1.5 SO Track on right goes 0.25 miles to Devils Garden Picnic Area.

GPS: N 37°35.28' W 111°24.57'

▼ 2.7 SO Cross over wash.

▼ 3.0 SO Track on right is Left Hand Collet Canyon Trail, signposted to Collet Top (11 miles).

GPS: N 37°34.15' W 111°23.69'

▼ 3.2 SO Corral on left.

▼ 3.5 SO Cross over Twentymile Wash, then cross

cattle guard, then track on left to corral.

▼ 3.8 SO Track on right.

▼ 5.6 SO Track on left is Egypt Road and is sign-posted to Egypt (10 miles). Zero trip meter.

GPS: N 37°32.46' W 111°21.65'

▼ 0.0 Continue southeast, crossing Sunset Flat.

▼ 0.1 SO Track on left joins Egypt Road, also track on right. Main trail now enters Kane County.

▼ 0.4 SO Track on right.

▼ 0.6 SO Cross through wash.

▼ 0.7 SO Track on left and track on right.

▼ 1.0 SO Track on left.

▼ 2.2 SO Track on right. White Point is on the right.

▼ 2.7 SO Track on right.

▼ 3.2 SO Track on left and faint track on right.

▼ 4.7 SO Track on left.

▼ 5.4 SO Track on left.

▼ 5.9 SO Track on left.

▼ 6.7 SO Cross through wash. Trail enters Cat Pasture.

GPS: N 37°29.29' W 111°15.32'

▼ 6.8 SO Track on left is signposted to Early Weed Bench (6 miles). Zero trip meter.

GPS: N 37°29.22' W 111°15.22'

▼ 0.0 Continue southeast.

▼ 0.1 SO Corral on right, then cattle guard.

▼ 0.3 SO Cattle guard.

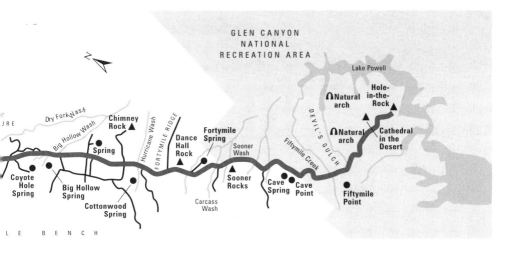

▼ 1.2　SO　Track on right, views to the left into Dry Fork Wash.

▼ 2.2　SO　Track on right is dead-end road, then track on left is signposted to Dry Fork Trail (1.7 miles).
　　　　　GPS: N 37°28.00′ W 111°13.42′

▼ 2.3　SO　Track on right to Coyote Hole Spring.
▼ 4.2　SO　Track on right.
▼ 4.3　SO　Cattle guard.
▼ 4.9　SO　Cross through Big Hollow Wash.
　　　　　GPS: N 37°26.33′ W 111°11.13′

▼ 5.9　SO　Cross through small wash.
▼ 6.3　SO　Track on left.
▼ 6.7　SO　Track on left is signposted to Red Well Trail (1.5 miles). Also track on right.
　　　　　GPS: N 37°25.27′ W 111°09.69′

▼ 7.0　SO　Cattle guard, then track on left goes to private property.
▼ 8.8　SO　Track on left goes to Chimney Rock.
　　　　　GPS: N 37°23.60′ W 111°08.55′

▼ 9.4　SO　Cattle guard, then Willow Tank on the left, with old corral and cabin.
▼ 9.6　SO　Hurricane Wash 4WD Trail on the left, then cross over Hurricane Wash.
　　　　　GPS: N 37°23.16′ W 111°07.89′

▼ 9.9　SO　Track on right is signposted to Fiftymile Bench.
　　　　　GPS: N 37°22.85′ W 111°07.80′

▼ 10.6　SO　Cross through tributary of Hurricane Wash.

▼ 11.8　SO　Track on left is signposted to Fortymile Ridge Trail and runs out along the Fortymile Ridge. Dance Hall Rock can be seen immediately ahead.
　　　　　GPS: N 37°21.73′ W 111°06.84′

▼ 12.2　SO　Track on right.
▼ 12.5　SO　Dance Hall Rock on the left. Zero trip meter.
　　　　　GPS: N 37°21.40′ W 111°06.12′

▼ 0.0　　　Continue southeast.
▼ 0.2　SO　Track on left, then cattle guard.
▼ 0.6　SO　Cross through wash, then track on left to Fortymile Spring.
　　　　　GPS: N 37°20.87′ W 111°06.01′

▼ 1.6　SO　Cross through wash.
▼ 2.5　SO　Descend to cross Carcass Wash. Memorial marker on right at exit. Climb out of wash can be lumpy for passenger vehicles.
　　　　　GPS: N 37°20.17′ W 111°04.27′

▼ 2.7　SO　Track on right.
▼ 3.2　SO　Cross through wash.
▼ 3.5　SO　Faint track on right, then cross through Sooner Wash, followed by track on right after wash. The trail passes through the Sooner Rocks.
　　　　　GPS: N 37°19.79′ W 111°03.51′

▼ 3.7	SO	Track on right.
▼ 3.8	SO	Track on right.
▼ 3.9	SO	Track on right.
▼ 4.5	SO	Track on left.
▼ 5.0	SO	Cattle guard, then track on right and corral on right.
▼ 5.4	SO	Cross through wash.
▼ 5.9	SO	Cross through wash.
▼ 6.3	SO	Track on right is signposted to Fiftymile Bench. Zero trip meter.
		GPS: N 37°18.25' W 111°02.28'

▼ 0.0		Continue southeast.
▼ 0.8	SO	Cross through Willow Gulch Wash.
▼ 1.8	SO	Cattle guard.
▼ 2.1	SO	Track on right, then cross through wash. Cave Point is to the right.
▼ 2.3	SO	Cross through wash.
▼ 2.7	SO	Entering Glen Canyon National Recreation Area.
		GPS: N 37°16.94' W 111°01.07'

▼ 3.5	SO	Cross through wash.
▼ 3.8	SO	Track on left.
▼ 3.9	SO	Soda Spring on the right, then cross through wash.
		GPS: N 37°16.32' W 111°00.29'

▼ 4.3	SO	Cross through wash.
▼ 4.5	SO	Track on right.
▼ 5.4	SO	Cross through wash.
▼ 6.1	SO	Track on right.
▼ 6.2	SO	Track on right.
▼ 6.6	SO	Cattle guard. Passenger vehicles and low-clearance vehicles should stop here. Difficulty rating is now a 4.
		GPS: N 37°15.16' W 110°58.58'

▼ 7.7	SO	Track on right.
▼ 7.9	SO	Plaque on the rock on the right for Hole-in-the-Rock Arch.
		GPS: N 37°15.46' W 110°57.54'

▼ 11.4	SO	Cross through wash.
▼ 11.9		Trail ends at the Hole-in-the-Rock. There is a small information board. The Hole-in-the-Rock is a short scramble over the slickrock.
		GPS: N 37°15.41' W 110°54.02'

Hells Backbone Trail

STARTING POINT Utah 12 in Escalante
FINISHING POINT Utah 12, 2.8 miles south of Boulder Town
TOTAL MILEAGE 36.6 miles
UNPAVED MILEAGE 33.3 miles
DRIVING TIME 2 hours
ELEVATION RANGE 5,700–9,200 feet
USUALLY OPEN June to November
DIFFICULTY RATING 1
SCENIC RATING 8
REMOTENESS RATING +0

Special Attractions

- Historic Hells Backbone Bridge.
- Panoramic views over the Box–Death Hollow Wilderness.
- Aspen viewing in the fall.

History

The Hells Backbone Trail connects the towns of Escalante and Boulder Town. Escalante was first settled in 1876. The town was officially named on July 4 of that year, when with no American flag available, a Navajo blanket was raised on the flagpole. The town was named after Father Silvestre Vélez de Escalante, a Spanish priest who traversed this region with Father Francisco Domínguez in the late 1700s looking for a route from Santa Fe to California. Their expedition was the first to survey Utah.

Escalante was also the starting point for the Mormon Hole-in-the-Rock Expedition, which left there in 1879. For more on that incredible journey, see Southwest #22: Hole-in-the-Rock Trail. If you want to blend in with the locals, pronounce the name ES-ca-lant.

Boulder Town, at the northeastern end of this trail, was first settled in 1889 as a cattle and farming community. Prior to 1935, it had no automobile access, and it was the last town in the United States to receive its mail via mule. In winter, the mail was transported via the Old Boulder Road, but in the warmer summer months, the more intrepid mail carriers used the Boulder Mail Trail, which traversed Death Hollow. This route was shorter but much more dangerous—one origin of the name "Death Hollow" refers to a mule that fell to its death in the deep gorge.

The U.S. Forest Service connected the citizens of Boulder Town to the outside world in 1910. They strung galvanized wire from Escalante along the Boulder Mail Trail route, thus bringing telephone service to the isolated town. This line served the town as late as 1955.

During the Depression, the Civilian Conservation Corps constructed the bridge across the narrow chasm at Hells Backbone, which was one of their many projects in southern Utah. The narrow, single-lane, precarious timber bridge made it possible to drive from Escalante to Boulder Town, but only in dry weather.

Panoramic view over the rock pillars of Hells Backbone

Today, Escalante and Boulder Town are established small towns offering services and recreation opportunities for the traveler.

Description

This easy trail provides a wonderful, relaxing drive through some incredibly scenic country, which culminates at the spectacular Hells Backbone Bridge. The long and winding trail is graded gravel for its entire length, making it passable for passenger cars in good weather. It leaves from the edge of Escalante and steadily climbs into the Dixie National Forest, winding around the edge of the Box–Death Hollow Wilderness area. The two main access points for hikers to enter the wilderness area depart from this route. The trail also connects to Southwest #26: Posey Lake Road.

After 10 miles, the focal point of the route is reached: Hells Backbone Bridge. Though now a sturdy concrete bridge, it is still only a single track, and it briefly crosses a dizzying gap in the ridge before reaching solid ground again. There are panoramic views from the bridge—to the north over

Sand Creek and beyond to Burr Top and the Aquarius Plateau, and to the south over the Box–Death Hollow Wilderness area, with its sheer cliffs and deep chasms.

From the bridge, the trail descends gradually to Boulder Town. It passes Southwest #24: McGath Lake Trail and then winds past some private property to finish on Utah 12 just south of Boulder Town.

Current Road Information

Dixie National Forest
Escalante Ranger District
PO Box 246
Escalante, UT 84726
(435) 826-5400

BLM Escalante Field Office
PO Box 225
Escalante, UT 84726
(435) 826-5600

Escalante Interagency Office
755 West Main
Escalante, UT 84726
(435) 826-5499

DOMINGUEZ-ESCALANTE EXPEDITION

In the summer of 1776, Spanish Franciscan missionaries Francisco Atanasio Domínguez and Silvestre Vélez de Escalante set out with cartographer Bernardo Miera y Pacheco to travel from Santa Fe, New Mexico, to Monterey, California.

Interestingly enough, if not for a delay in the original date of departure, the expedition would have begun on July 4, 1776. The men traveled, charted, and kept a precise journal of the different landforms, Indian tribes, plants, and animals they encountered. They entered Utah from northwestern Colorado near Dinosaur National Monument and went west through Spanish Fork Canyon to Utah Lake, never quite making it to the Great Salt Lake. The expedition then headed south to the area just north of present-day Cedar City. By this time it was late September, and the early mountain snows had become too great a threat to allow further travel west. Disappointed, the expedition decided to turn around and head back toward Santa Fe. They left Utah, crossing south into Arizona. While they didn't reach their final destination, their five-month, almost 2,000-mile journey provided the first glimpse of the Utah region to European settlers.

They disproved many common myths of the day, such as that there were cities of gold and countries of giants. However, they also set a few new ones in circulation, the greatest of which described the Utah and Great Salt Lakes as one big lake and part of a westward drainage basin. This mapping error would affect maps of the region for the better part of a century. Despite some inaccurate information, the exploration and its records blazed a trail for the many later expeditions and for the westward expansion of European settlers in general.

Map References

BLM Escalante
USFS Dixie National Forest: Escalante Ranger District
USGS 1:24,000 Escalante, Wide Hollow Reservoir, Posey Lake, Roger Peak, Boulder Town
1:100,000 Escalante
Maptech CD-ROM: Escalante/Dixie National Forest
Trails Illustrated, #710
Utah Atlas & Gazetteer, pp. 19, 27, 28
Utah Travel Council #4
Other: BLM Map of the Grand Staircase–Escalante National Monument

Route Directions

▼ 0.0   From Utah 12 on the eastern edge of Escalante, turn north on 300E Road at the sign for Hells Backbone. Zero trip meter.

6.7 ▲   Trail finishes at Utah 12 on the eastern edge of Escalante.
GPS: N 37°46.17′ W 111°35.61′

▼ 0.5   SO   Cross over Escalante River on bridge.
6.2 ▲   SO   Cross over Escalante River on bridge.

▼ 0.6   TR   T-intersection.
6.1 ▲   TL   Turn south toward Escalante.
GPS: N 37°46.73′ W 111°35.51′

▼ 2.0   SO   Cattle guard.
4.7 ▲   SO   Cattle guard.

▼ 2.7   SO   Track on left.
4.0 ▲   SO   Track on right.

▼ 3.1   SO   Cattle guard.
3.6 ▲   SO   Cattle guard.

▼ 3.3   SO   Road surface turns to graded gravel.
3.4 ▲   SO   Road surface turns to pavement.

▼ 3.4   SO   Track on left.
3.3 ▲   SO   Track on right.

▼ 6.7   SO   Cattle guard, then enter Dixie National Forest, followed by Roundy hiking trail on right. Trail becomes FR 153. Zero trip meter at cattle guard.

0.0 ▲   Continue toward Escalante.
GPS: N 37°51.37' W 111°38.02'

▼ 0.0   Continue along FR 153.
6.2 ▲ SO Roundy hiking trail on left. Leave Dixie National Forest over cattle guard, and zero trip meter.

▼ 0.3 SO Track on right is lower access to Box–Death Hollow Wilderness.
5.9 ▲ SO Track on left is lower access to Box–Death Hollow Wilderness.

▼ 0.9 SO Cross through creek on concrete ford.
5.3 ▲ SO Cross through creek on concrete ford.

▼ 1.5 SO Track on left.
4.7 ▲ SO Track on right.

▼ 3.0 SO Track on left to shed.
3.2 ▲ SO Track on right to shed.

▼ 4.3 SO Track on left.
1.9 ▲ SO Track on right.

▼ 6.2 TR T-intersection. Track on left is Southwest #26: Posey Lake Road (FR 154) to Posey Lake and Bicknell. Zero trip meter.
0.0 ▲   Continue south toward Escalante.
GPS: N 37°55.53' W 111°40.30'

▼ 0.0   Continue toward Hells Backbone.
4.3 ▲ TL Track on right is Southwest #26: Posey Lake Road (FR 154) to Posey Lake and Bicknell. Zero trip meter.

▼ 0.4 SO Cattle guard, then track on left.
3.9 ▲ SO Track on right, then cattle guard.

▼ 0.5 SO Cross over Hungry Creek on culvert.
3.8 ▲ SO Cross over Hungry Creek on culvert.

▼ 1.1 SO Cross over Deep Creek on culvert.
3.2 ▲ SO Cross over Deep Creek on culvert.

▼ 2.1 SO Track on left.
2.2 ▲ SO Track on right.

GPS: N 37°56.74' W 111°39.50'

▼ 2.5 BL Five-way junction, stay on main gravel track.
1.8 ▲ BR Five-way junction, stay on main gravel track.

▼ 3.8 SO Hiking trail on left on left-hand bend at Blue Spring Creek.
0.5 ▲ SO Hiking trail on right on right-hand bend at Blue Spring Creek.
GPS: N 37°57.70' W 111°39.25'

▼ 4.1 SO Box–Death Hollow Wilderness, upper Box access hiking trail on right.
0.2 ▲ SO Box–Death Hollow Wilderness, upper Box access hiking trail on left.

▼ 4.3 BR Cross over Pine Creek on culvert, followed by track on left (FR 145) to Blue Spruce Campground. Zero trip meter.
0.0 ▲   Continue on graded gravel road.
GPS: N 37°58.00' W 111°39.10'

▼ 0.0   Continue toward Hells Backbone.
6.0 ▲ BL Track on right is FR 145 to Blue Spruce Campground, then cross over Pine Creek on culvert.

▼ 1.4 SO Track on left is FR 745. Views right over Pine Creek in the Box.
4.6 ▲ SO Track on right is FR 745. Views left over Pine Creek in the Box.

▼ 2.7 SO Track on right, followed by track on left.
3.3 ▲ SO Track on right, followed by track on left.
GPS: N 37°57.55' W 111°37.41'

▼ 3.1 SO Track on right.
2.9 ▲ SO Track on left.

▼ 4.2 SO Box–Death Hollow Wilderness, Death Hollow access on right.
1.8 ▲ SO Box–Death Hollow Wilderness, Death Hollow access on left.
GPS: N 37°58.34' W 111°37.01'

▼ 5.1 SO Track on left to Sand Creek hiking trail.

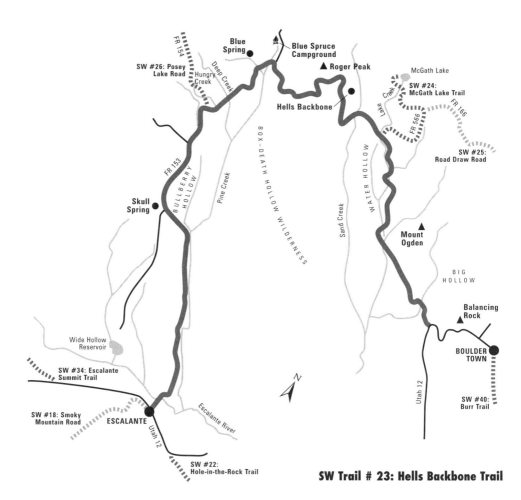

SW Trail # 23: Hells Backbone Trail

Track dead-ends at an oil drill hole and spectacular campsite.

0.9 ▲   SO   Track on right to Sand Creek hiking trail. Track dead-ends at an oil drill hole and spectacular campsite.
      GPS: N 37°58.79' W 111°36.20'

▼ 5.2   SO   Cattle guard.
0.8 ▲   SO   Cattle guard.

▼ 6.0   SO   Cross over single-track Hells Backbone Bridge, then over a narrow ridge with views on both sides: Sand Creek to the left, Box–Death Hollow Wilderness to the right. Zero trip meter just after bridge.
0.0 ▲   Continue to climb.
      GPS: N 37°58.22' W 111°35.91'

▼ 0.0   Descend from ridge.
4.7 ▲   SO   Trail runs over a narrow ridge with views on both sides: Sand Creek to the right, Box–Death Hollow Wilderness to the left. Then cross over single-track Hells Backbone Bridge. Zero trip meter just before bridge.

▼ 2.6   SO   Cross over Sand Creek on culvert, then track on left. Campsite on right.
2.1 ▲   SO   Track on right, campsite on left, then cross over Sand Creek on culvert.
      GPS: N 37°58.27' W 111°34.88'

▼ 4.5   SO   Track on right to campsites.
0.2 ▲   SO   Track on left to campsites.

▼ 4.7   SO   Cross over Lake Creek on culvert, then Southwest #24: McGath Lake Trail

	(FR 566) on left. Zero trip meter.
0.0 ▲	Continue toward Hells Backbone. **GPS: N 37°57.86' W 111°33.19'**

▼ 0.0	Continue toward Boulder Town.
8.7 ▲	SO Track on right is Southwest #24: McGath Lake Trail (FR 566). Cross over Lake Creek on culvert, then zero trip meter.

▼ 0.1	SO Track on right.
8.6 ▲	SO Track on left.

▼ 0.5	SO Track on right.
8.2 ▲	SO Track on left.

▼ 0.7	SO Track on right.
8.0 ▲	SO Track on left.

▼ 1.1	SO Track on left.
7.6 ▲	SO Track on right.

▼ 1.8	SO Track on right.
6.9 ▲	SO Track on left.

▼ 3.7	SO Entering private property on right and left.
5.0 ▲	SO Leaving private property.

▼ 5.1	SO Leaving private property.
3.6 ▲	SO Entering private property on right and left.

▼ 5.7	SO Track on left.
3.0 ▲	SO Track on right.

▼ 6.0	SO Track on right.
2.7 ▲	SO Track on left.

▼ 6.2	SO Track on right.
2.5 ▲	SO Track on left.

▼ 8.0	SO Track on right.
0.7 ▲	SO Track on left.

▼ 8.3	SO Track on left.
0.4 ▲	SO Track on right.

▼ 8.4	SO Leaving Dixie National Forest.
0.3 ▲	SO Entering Dixie National Forest.

▼ 8.6	SO Track on right.
0.1 ▲	SO Track on left.

▼ 8.7	Trail finishes at Utah 12. Turn right for Escalante, left for Boulder Town.
0.0 ▲	On Utah 12, 2.8 miles south of Boulder Town, turn at sign for Hells Backbone and proceed northwest along graded gravel road. **GPS: N 37°53.31' W 111°27.45'**

SOUTHWEST REGION TRAIL #24

McGath Lake Trail

STARTING POINT Southwest #23: Hells Backbone Trail (FR 153)
FINISHING POINT McGath Lake
TOTAL MILEAGE 5.5 miles
UNPAVED MILEAGE 5.5 miles
DRIVING TIME 1.5 hours (one-way)
ELEVATION RANGE 8,300–9,400 feet
USUALLY OPEN June to October
DIFFICULTY RATING 6
SCENIC RATING 8
REMOTENESS RATING +0

Special Attractions

■ Challenging 4WD trail through spectacular scenery.
■ Backcountry camping and fishing at McGath Lake.
■ Aspen viewing in fall.

Description

This challenging trail has something for everyone: a technically difficult drive, panoramic views, and a secluded lake at the end.

The trail leaves Southwest #23: Hells Backbone Trail 8.7 miles from its eastern end, near Boulder Town. The first 2.6 miles are easy graded gravel as the trail winds along a wide shelf road. The trail then forks: the right-hand fork is Southwest #25: Road Draw Road, and the left-hand fork takes you to McGath Lake. The difficulty of the trail increases immediately. The next 1.5 miles

View of McGath Lake from a creek overflow

portion of the trail, which is still to come, are advised to park here and hike the remaining distance to the lake.

After Grimes Creek, the trail climbs a rocky section interspersed with loose shale, on which you can quickly lose traction. Drivers in wide or tall vehicles will need to watch their roofline on the trees in off-camber sections.

After 2.6 miles from the junction, you reach the most difficult section of the trail—a very steep, very loose climb with several large rock steps that need careful wheel placement. The difficulty is increased by the looseness of the surface, making it almost impossible to avoid spinning your wheels. At 2.8 miles, the track levels off, and apart from a couple of rocky sections, the worst is over. The final portion of the trail descends a hill to McGath Lake. This portion will cause no problems for an SUV unless it is wet. McGath Lake has a couple of beautiful campsites tucked into the trees at the water's edge. The lake provides good trout fishing, and it's a wonderful place to relax for a couple of hours before tackling the drive back.

alternates between slow crawls over large boulders and long drives across meadows that can be very muddy. There are many excellent backcountry campsites along the route, mainly tucked into the aspens at the edge of the meadows.

After 1.5 miles from the junction, the trail crosses Grimes Creek. This can be a difficult crossing, especially after rain. There are two alternatives, both potentially difficult. The left-hand crossing traverses an area of boggy patches and then a large drainage pipe that the creek flows through. The right-hand crossing has less boggy spots, but fords the creek at a spot with a steep and greasy entrance and exit, both potentially difficult. Those not wanting to tackle the most difficult

Current Road Information

Dixie National Forest
Escalante Ranger District
PO Box 246
Escalante, UT 84726
(435) 826-5400

Map References

BLM   Escalante
USFS   Dixie National Forest: Escalante
       Ranger District
USGS   1:24,000   Roger Peak
       1:100,000   Escalante
Maptech CD-ROM: Escalante/Dixie
       National Forest
Trails Illustrated, #710 (incomplete)
Utah Atlas & Gazetteer, p. 27

Climbing one of the more difficult rocky sections of the trail

Route Directions

▼ 0.0　　On Southwest #23: Hells Backbone Trail, 8.7 miles from Boulder Town end, turn north on graded gravel FR 566, cross cattle guard, and zero trip meter.

2.6 ▲　　Trail ends on Southwest #23: Hells Backbone Trail. Turn left for Boulder Town. Turn right for Escalante.
　　　　GPS: N 37°57.85′ W 111°33.19′

▼ 0.2　SO　Large camping area on left.
2.4 ▲　SO　Large camping area on right.

▼ 0.8　SO　Wide shelf road with views to the southeast.
1.8 ▲　SO　Wide shelf road with views to the southeast.

▼ 1.2　SO　End of shelf road.
1.4 ▲　SO　Start of shelf road.

▼ 1.6　SO　Campsite with good views on right.
1.0 ▲　SO　Campsite with good views on left.

▼ 2.1　BR　Track on left along fence line.
0.5 ▲　BL　Track on right along fence line.
　　　　GPS: N 37°58.51′ W 111°32.41′

▼ 2.4　SO　Campsite on left.
0.2 ▲　SO　Campsite on right.

▼ 2.6　BL　Bear left, following sign to McGath Lake. Right is Southwest #25: Road Draw Road (signed to Boulder Swale ATV trail). Trail standard drops to rough, ungraded dirt. Zero trip meter.

0.0 ▲　　Intersection of Southwest #24: McGath Lake Trail and Southwest #25: Road Draw Road. Proceed south toward Southwest #23: Hells Backbone Trail.
　　　　GPS: N 37°58.90′ W 111°32.20′

▼ 0.0　　Continue over ungraded track.
▼ 0.8　SO　Track on right.
　　　　GPS: N 37°59.09′ W 111°33.00′

SW Trail #24: McGath Lake Trail

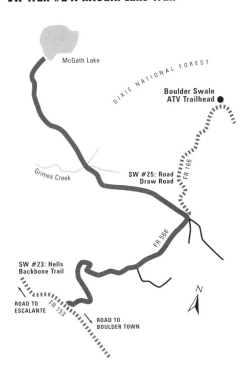

▼ 1.2　SO　Faint track on right.
▼ 1.4　SO　Cattle guard.
▼ 1.5　BL　Cross Grimes Creek over pipe; crossing can be very muddy. Right fork fords through creek, but entry and exit can be difficult.
▼ 2.2　SO　Short, steep, rocky creek crossing.
　　　　GPS: N 37°59.45′ W 111°34.12′

▼ 2.5　BL　Bear left at fork; right is mainly ATV use.
　　　　GPS: N 37°59.56′ W 111°34.24′

▼ 2.6　SO　Loose, steep, washed-out climb.
▼ 2.8　BR　Slightly rutted descent to McGath Lake.
　　　　GPS: N 37°59.79′ W 111°34.27′

▼ 2.9　　McGath Lake, end of trail. Campsite on left on lakeshore; trail on right continues over dam wall to second campsite.
　　　　GPS: N 37°59.86′ W 111°34.18′

Road Draw Road

STARTING POINT Southwest #24: McGath Lake Trail

FINISHING POINT Utah 12, 4.5 miles north of Boulder Town

TOTAL MILEAGE 10 miles

UNPAVED MILEAGE 10 miles

DRIVING TIME 1.5 hours

ELEVATION RANGE 7,700–9,500 feet

USUALLY OPEN June to October

DIFFICULTY RATING 4

SCENIC RATING 8

REMOTENESS RATING +0

Special Attractions

- Moderately challenging 4WD trail.
- Access to ATV trails and backcountry campsites.
- Aspen viewing in the fall.

Description

This moderately challenging trail is easily handled by a high-clearance SUV in dry weather. The trail begins along Southwest

A lumpy section of the trail just after its intersection with the ATV trailhead

#24: McGath Lake Trail, 2.6 miles from Southwest #23: Hells Backbone Trail and continues as a graded gravel road until the ATV unloading point for the Boulder Swale ATV trailhead. The routes over the divide are limited to ATVs from this point by a width restriction; there is ample parking at the trailhead. Just before the ATV trail, Road Draw Road heads east, becoming an ungraded, defined 4WD trail. The lumpy route descends through stands of aspens, twisting and turning as it crosses open meadows before reaching the graded road at Haws Pasture. The driving is not difficult; there are some moderately steep descents and rocky sections interspersed with long smooth sections across open meadow. However, use extra care when the road is wet because those smooth meadow runs can become slow mud wallows. The trail is easiest downhill, from McGath Lake to Utah 12. Some of the climbs have a loose rocky surface that may cause loss of traction going uphill. There are several good backcountry campsites en route as well as large stands of aspens, whose colors are splendid in fall.

Current Road Information

Dixie National Forest
Escalante Ranger District
PO Box 246
Escalante, UT 84726
(435) 826-5400

Map References

BLM   Escalante
USFS   Dixie National Forest: Escalante
       Ranger District
USGS   1:24,000   Roger Peak, Boulder Town
       1:100,000 Escalante
Maptech CD-ROM: Escalante/Dixie
       National Forest
Utah Atlas & Gazetteer, pp. 27, 28

Route Directions

▼ 0.0   Begin from Southwest #24: McGath
         Lake Trail (FR 566), 2.6 miles from
         Southwest #23: Hells Backbone Trail.
         Zero trip meter and turn north onto FR

166, following signs to Boulder Swale ATV trailhead.

1.6 ▲ Trail ends at Southwest #24: McGath Lake Trail (FR 566). Turn left to join Southwest #23: Hells Backbone Trail, right to McGath Lake.

GPS: N 37°58.89′ W 111°32.19′

▼ 0.2 SO Track on right.
1.4 ▲ SO Track on left.

▼ 0.6 SO Gravel road turns to graded dirt.
1.0 ▲ SO Graded dirt road turns to gravel.

▼ 1.6 TR T-intersection. Follow sign right to Haws Pasture. Ahead goes to the Boulder Swale ATV trailhead. Zero trip meter.
0.0 ▲ Continue on graded dirt road.

GPS: N 38°00.03′ W 111°31.68′

▼ 0.0 Continue on lesser standard 4WD track.
2.8 ▲ TL Follow sign left to Hells Backbone. Right goes to the Boulder Swale ATV trailhead. Zero trip meter.

▼ 0.2 SO Small waterhole on right.
2.6 ▲ SO Small waterhole on left.

▼ 0.7 SO Faint track on left.
2.1 ▲ SO Faint track on right.

▼ 0.8 SO Track on left, then cattle guard.
2.0 ▲ SO Cattle guard, then track on right.

GPS: N 37°59.57′ W 111°31.13′

▼ 0.9 BL Left turn is fainter.
1.9 ▲ TR T-intersection.

▼ 1.5 BL Right track to campsite with great view.
1.3 ▲ TR T-intersection. Left track to campsite with great view.

GPS: N 37°59.39′ W 111°30.56′

▼ 1.7 BR Cross through small creek; faint track on left. Cross small creek a second time.
1.1 ▲ BL Cross through small creek; faint track on right. Cross small creek a second time.

SW Trail #25: Road Draw Road

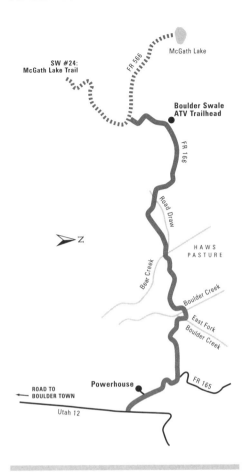

▼ 1.9 SO Views left toward Boulder Mountain.
0.9 ▲ SO Views right toward Boulder Mountain.

▼ 2.0 BL Fork.
0.8 ▲ TR T-intersection.

GPS: N 37°59.26′ W 111°30.14′

▼ 2.7 SO Track on right.
0.1 ▲ SO Track on left.

GPS: N 37°59.64′ W 111°29.69′

▼ 2.8 TR Cross through small creek, then turn right at T-intersection. Zero trip meter.
0.0 ▲ Continue on lesser standard trail and cross through small creek.

GPS: N 37°59.66′ W 111°29.67′

▼ 0.0 Continue on graded gravel road.

5.6 ▲	TL	At junction, follow sign left to Boulder Swale ATV trailhead. Zero trip meter.

▼ 0.2	SO	Cattle guard, then cross over Bear Creek on culvert.
5.4 ▲	SO	Cross over Bear Creek on culvert, then cattle guard.

▼ 0.7	SO	Track on left.
4.9 ▲	SO	Track on right.

▼ 1.2	SO	Track on left.
4.4 ▲	SO	Track on right.

GPS: N 37°59.81′ W 111°28.61′

▼ 2.2	SO	Cross over Boulder Creek on culvert, then track on left.
3.4 ▲	SO	Track on right, then cross over Boulder Creek on culvert.

▼ 2.4	SO	Cross over East Fork Boulder Creek on culvert.
3.2 ▲	SO	Cross over East Fork Boulder Creek on culvert.

▼ 2.9	SO	Pass through gate.
2.7 ▲	SO	Pass through gate.

▼ 3.0	SO	Track on right.
2.6 ▲	SO	Track on left.

▼ 3.1	SO	Track on left.
2.5 ▲	SO	Track on right.

▼ 3.9	BR	Track on left is FR 165 to Kings Pasture. Bear right, remaining on FR 166.
1.7 ▲	BL	Track on right is FR 165 to Kings Pasture. Remain on FR 166.

GPS: N 37°59.97′ W 111°26.69′

▼ 4.7	SO	Cattle guard.
0.9 ▲	SO	Cattle guard.

▼ 4.8	SO	Track on left (private).
0.8 ▲	SO	Track on right (private).

▼ 5.2	SO	Track on right to powerhouse.
0.4 ▲	SO	Track on left to powerhouse.

▼ 5.6		Cross cattle guard; trail ends at Utah 12, 4.5 miles north of Boulder Town.
0.0 ▲		On Utah 12, 4.5 miles north of Boulder Town, turn west on FR 166, cross cattle guard, and zero trip meter.

GPS: N 37°58.94′ W 111°25.78′

Posey Lake Road

STARTING POINT Utah 24 in Bicknell
FINISHING POINT Southwest #23: Hells Backbone Trail (FR 153)
TOTAL MILEAGE 34.1 miles
UNPAVED MILEAGE 32.4 miles
DRIVING TIME 2 hours
ELEVATION RANGE 7,000–9,900 feet
USUALLY OPEN May to November
DIFFICULTY RATING 1
SCENIC RATING 8
REMOTENESS RATING +0

Special Attractions

- Long and scenic road for easy touring.
- Fishing and camping opportunities at Posey Lake, Cyclone Lake, and others.
- Access to a network of 4WD trails.

Description

This long, extremely scenic route crosses the Aquarius Plateau from north to south. The Aquarius Plateau is the highest timbered plateau in North America; it contains stands of spruces, pines, and aspens interspersed with large, natural grassy meadows. In the 1920s the plateau suffered an attack of spruce bark beetle, which decimated the mature trees. Affected trees were harvested and the trees on the plateau now mainly date from after the infestation. Currently, there are no logging operations on the plateau.

The drive is suitable for a passenger car in dry weather; the entire trail is wide, graded gravel or dirt. From Bicknell, it climbs through BLM lands, crossing undulating plains of sagebrush where pronghorn antelope are frequently seen. After 8.2 miles, you pass Southwest #27: Boulder Tops Road.

After 16 miles, you enter the Dixie National Forest. The road meanders across open meadows, through stands of trees, and past many small lakes and reservoirs. Mule deer and elk live on the plateau in great numbers and are often seen. One likely area is around Big Lake, which is a wildlife area (established in 1957) where ponds and nesting islands have been constructed to improve the habitat for waterfowl. There are small numbers of black bear on the plateau; they can be a definite concern in the developed campgrounds in the summer months. On the plateau, this trail connects with Southwest #31: Dark Valley Trail and Southwest #33: Griffin Road.

Near the end of the trail is Posey Lake, which has a developed national forest campground and offers good fishing opportunities. There is a small boat launching area. The campground is popular in summer and has some pretty sites set back from the lake. From Posey Lake, the trail descends to join the spectacular Southwest #23: Hells Backbone Trail. The road is a popular snowmobile route in winter, though it is not groomed for such use.

Current Road Information

Dixie National Forest
Escalante Ranger District
PO Box 246
Escalante, UT 84726
(435) 826-5400

BLM Escalante Field Office
PO Box 225
Escalante, UT 84726
(435) 826-5600

Escalante Interagency Office
755 West Main
Escalante, UT 84726
(435) 826-5499

Map References

BLM Loa, Escalante
USFS Dixie National Forest: Teasdale and Ecalante Ranger Districts (incomplete)

Posey Lake

USGS 1:24,000   Bicknell, Smooth Knoll, Big Lake, Posey Lake
    1:100,000 Escalante
Maptech CD-ROM: Escalante/Dixie National Forest
Trails Illustrated, #213; #710 (incomplete)
Utah Atlas & Gazetteer, p. 27
Utah Travel Council #4
Other: BLM Map of the Grand Staircase–Escalante National Monument (incomplete)

Route Directions

▼ 0.0   From Utah 24, on the western edge of Bicknell, turn south on paved 400 West Street at the scenic byway sign, and zero trip meter.
1.8 ▲   Trail ends at Utah 24, on the western edge of Bicknell.
    GPS: N 38°20.46′ W 111°33.02′

▼ 0.8   BR Road swings right. Track on left.
1.0 ▲   TL Track on right.

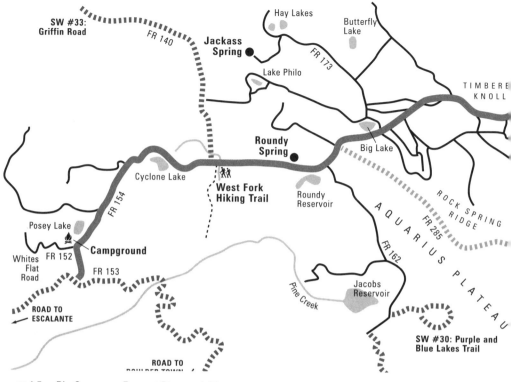

▼ 1.5	BL	Cross over Fremont River on bridge; swing left on the pavement road. Track on right.	
0.3 ▲	BR	Track on left, then cross over Fremont River on bridge.	

▼ 1.7	SO	Road turns to graded gravel.
0.1 ▲	SO	Road turns to pavement.
		GPS: N 38°19.65′ W 111°34.03′

▼ 1.8	BL	Unsigned fork, road on right. Zero trip meter.
0.0 ▲		Continue along graded gravel road.
		GPS: N 38°19.58′ W 111°34.11′

▼ 0.0		Continue along graded gravel road.
6.4 ▲	SO	Unsigned road on left. Zero trip meter.

▼ 0.2	BR	Fork. Bear right, following sign to Dixie National Forest.
6.2 ▲	SO	Continue toward Bicknell.
		GPS: N 38°19.45′ W 111°34.18′

▼ 3.4	TL	Turn left at intersection. Track ahead to the Flat Tops.
3.0 ▲	BR	Bear right at intersection. Track

		on left to the Flat Tops.
		GPS: N 38°17.89′ W 111°36.98′

▼ 4.1	SO	Bicknell Reservoir on left.
2.3 ▲	SO	Bicknell Reservoir on right.

▼ 5.0	SO	Track on left.
1.4 ▲	SO	Track on right.

▼ 5.2	SO	Gravel road on left.
1.2 ▲	BL	Fork; gravel road on right.
		GPS: N 38°16.23′ W 111°36.97′

▼ 5.7	BL	Fork. Road on right to Antelope Spring and Pollywog Lake.
0.7 ▲	SO	Road on left to Antelope Spring and Pollywog Lake.
		GPS: N 38°15.78′ W 111°37.03′

▼ 6.4	BR	Fork. Left is Southwest #27: Boulder Tops Road (FR 178), immediately followed by track on right and second entrance to Boulder Tops Road. Zero trip meter.
0.0 ▲		Continue toward Bicknell.
		GPS: N 38°15.19′ W 111°37.32′

WILDCAT HOLLOW

OOTH OLL

GILES HOLLOW

son Grove

SW #27:
Boulder Tops Ro

FR 178

1:
alley Trail

SW #28:
ns Point Trail

N

▼ 0.0   Continue toward Escalante.
7.9 ▲ SO Two entrances to Southwest #27: Boulder Tops Road on the right, and track on left. Zero trip meter.

▼ 0.6 SO Track on right.
7.3 ▲ SO Track on left.

▼ 1.4 SO Track on left.
6.5 ▲ SO Track on right.

▼ 2.1 SO Cattle guard. Views north over Thousand Lake Mountain.
5.8 ▲ SO Cattle guard. Views north over Thousand Lake Mountain.

▼ 2.9 SO Track on left.
5.0 ▲ SO Track on right.

▼ 3.3 SO Track on left.
4.6 ▲ SO Track on right.

▼ 3.6 SO Track on right.
4.3 ▲ SO Track on left.

▼ 3.8 SO Track on right, followed by track on left.
4.1 ▲ SO Track on right, followed by track on left.

▼ 6.0 SO Tracks on right and left.
1.9 ▲ SO Tracks on left and right.

▼ 6.7 SO Track on right.
1.2 ▲ SO Track on left.

▼ 7.9 SO Enter Dixie National Forest over cattle guard. Road is now FR 154. Zero trip meter.
0.0 ▲   Continue on graded gravel road.
    GPS: N 38°08.56' W 111°40.21'

▼ 0.0   Continue on graded dirt road.
6.6 ▲ SO Leaving Dixie National Forest over cattle guard; enter BLM land. Zero trip meter.

▼ 0.1 SO Track on right.
6.5 ▲ SO Track on left.

▼ 1.0 SO Track on left to Peterson Grove.
5.6 ▲ SO Track on right to Peterson Grove.
    GPS: N 38°07.73' W 111°40.57'

▼ 1.8 BL Track on right to Antelope Spring and Pollywog Lake. Dog Lake (dry) at intersection.
4.8 ▲ SO Track on left to Antelope Spring and Pollywog Lake. Dog Lake (dry) at intersection.
    GPS: N 38°07.33' W 111°41.34'

▼ 2.2 SO Track on left.
4.4 ▲ SO Track on right.

▼ 2.4 SO Track on right.
4.2 ▲ SO Track on left.

▼ 2.6 SO Track on left.
4.0 ▲ SO Track on right.

▼ 2.8 SO Track on right.
3.8 ▲ SO Track on left.

▼ 3.2 SO Cattle guard.
3.4 ▲ SO Cattle guard.

▼ 3.6   SO   Track on left, then Big Lake Environmental Enclosure on right.

3.0 ▲   SO   Big Lake Environmental Enclosure on left, then track on right.

GPS: N 38°05.79′ W 111°41.48′

▼ 4.5   SO   FR 173 on right to Hay Lakes and Lake Philo. Small track on left.

2.1 ▲   SO   FR 173 on left to Hay Lakes and Lake Philo. Small track on right.

GPS: N 38°05.07′ W 111°41.37′

▼ 4.6   SO   Big Lake Wildlife Area on right.

2.0 ▲   SO   Big Lake Wildlife Area on left.

GPS: N 38°04.92′ W 111°41.28′

▼ 5.7   SO   FR 285 on left is Southwest #31: Dark Valley Trail.

0.9 ▲   SO   FR 285 on right is Southwest #31: Dark Valley Trail.

GPS: N 38°03.94′ W 111°41.45′

▼ 5.9   SO   Track on right.

0.7 ▲   SO   Track on left.

▼ 6.2   SO   Cattle guard.

0.4 ▲   SO   Cattle guard.

▼ 6.6   SO   Track on left is FR 162 and leads to Southwest #30: Purple and Blue Lakes Trail, Southwest #29: Spectacle Lake Trail, and to Jacobs Valley. Zero trip meter.

0.0 ▲   Continue toward Bicknell.

GPS: N 38°03.29′ W 111°40.79′

▼ 0.0   Continue toward Escalante.

3.8 ▲   SO   Track on right is FR 162 and leads to Southwest #30: Purple and Blue Lakes Trail, Southwest #29: Spectacle Lake Trail, and to Jacobs Valley. Zero trip meter.

▼ 0.6   SO   Track on right.

3.2 ▲   SO   Track on left.

▼ 0.7   SO   Roundy Reservoir on left.

3.1 ▲   SO   Roundy Reservoir on right.

▼ 1.0   SO   Track on left.

2.8 ▲   SO   Track on right.

GPS: N 38°02.44 W 111°41.10′

▼ 1.5   SO   Great Western Trail, hiking access on left to Auger Hole Lake.

2.3 ▲   SO   Great Western Trail, hiking access on right to Auger Hole Lake.

▼ 1.6   SO   Track on left.

2.2 ▲   SO   Track on right.

▼ 2.1   SO   Campsite on left and track on right.

1.7 ▲   SO   Track on left and campsite on right.

▼ 2.7   SO   Track on left.

1.1 ▲   SO   Track on right.

▼ 3.1   SO   Track on right.

0.7 ▲   SO   Track on left.

▼ 3.4   SO   West Fork hiking trail to Pine Creek on left.

0.4 ▲   SO   West Fork hiking trail to Pine Creek on right.

▼ 3.8   SO   Track on right is Southwest #33: Griffin Road (FR 140) to Escalante Summit. Zero trip meter.

0.0 ▲   Continue north.

GPS: N 38°00.20′ W 111°42.40′

▼ 0.0   Continue south.

7.6 ▲   SO   Track on left is Southwest #33: Griffin Road (FR 140) to Escalante Summit. Zero trip meter.

▼ 0.9   SO   Track on right is FR 763.

6.7 ▲   SO   Track on left is FR 763.

▼ 1.4   SO   Track on left to corral.

6.2 ▲   SO   Track on right to corral.

▼ 1.6   SO   Track on right, trail runs alongside Cyclone Lake.

6.0 ▲   SO   Track on left, main trail leaves Cyclone Lake.

▼ 1.8   SO   Track on right.

5.8 ▲   SO   Track on left.

▼ 2.2　SO　Trail leaves Cyclone Lake.
5.4 ▲　SO　Cyclone Lake on right.

▼ 2.9　SO　Track on right.
4.7 ▲　SO　Track on left.

▼ 3.0　SO　Track on right to Velvet Lake.
4.6 ▲　SO　Track on left to Velvet Lake.
　　　　　GPS: N 37°58.10′ W 111°43.34′

▼ 4.0　SO　Cattle guard.
3.6 ▲　SO　Cattle guard.

▼ 4.9　SO　Great Western Trail on right and left;
　　　　　right provides vehicle access to Barker
　　　　　Reservoir.
2.7 ▲　SO　Great Western Trail on left and right;
　　　　　left provides vehicle access to Barker
　　　　　Reservoir.

▼ 5.8　SO　Posey Lake on right.
1.8 ▲　SO　Posey Lake on left.

▼ 5.9　SO　Posey Lake National Forest
　　　　　Campground on right (fee area).
1.7 ▲　SO　Posey Lake National Forest
　　　　　Campground on left (fee area).
　　　　　GPS: N 37°56.20′ W 111°41.58′

▼ 6.4　SO　Gravel road on right is Whites Flat
　　　　　Road (FR 152).
1.2 ▲　SO　Gravel road on left is Whites Flat Road
　　　　　(FR 152).
　　　　　GPS: N 37°55.86′ W 111°41.47′

▼ 6.7　SO　Small track on left.
0.9 ▲　SO　Small track on right.

▼ 6.9　SO　Track on right over cattle guard and
　　　　　track on left.
0.7 ▲　SO　Track on left over cattle guard and
　　　　　track on right.
　　　　　GPS: N 37°55.79′ W 111°40.93′

▼ 7.4　SO　Track on right.
0.2 ▲　SO　Track on left.

▼ 7.5　SO　Cattle guard.
0.1 ▲　SO　Cattle guard.

▼ 7.6　　　Trail ends at Southwest #23: Hells
　　　　　Backbone Trail (FR 153). Turn left to
　　　　　continue over Hells Backbone to
　　　　　Boulder Town, turn right for Escalante.
0.0 ▲　　　On Southwest #23: Hells Backbone
　　　　　Trail (FR 153), 13 miles from Escalante,
　　　　　turn northwest on FR 154 and zero trip
　　　　　meter.
　　　　　GPS: N 37°55.53′ W 111°40.32′

Boulder Tops Road

STARTING POINT Southwest #26: Posey Lake
Road (FR 154)
FINISHING POINT Southwest #28: Bowns Point
Trail
TOTAL MILEAGE 12.5 miles
UNPAVED MILEAGE 12.5 miles
DRIVING TIME 1 hour
ELEVATION RANGE 9,000–10,800 feet
USUALLY OPEN May to October
DIFFICULTY RATING 1
SCENIC RATING 7
REMOTENESS RATING +0

Special Attractions
■ Provides access to a network of more-dif-
ficult 4WD trails on Boulder Tops.
■ Access to three different lakes.
■ Scenic drive across undulating country in
the Dixie National Forest.

History
This trail crosses the main part of the
Aquarius Plateau, which was named by the
Spanish explorer Silvestre Escalante. The
plateau has many natural bodies of water, so
he named it after the zodiac sign Aquarius,
the water bearer. This plateau, with an elevation of over 10,000 feet, is the highest
timbered plateau in the United States. Portions of Boulder Tops reach 11,300 feet.
The area of Boulder Tops refers to the east-
ernmost edge of the Aquarius Plateau as it
abuts Boulder Mountain. This entire region

forms part of the northwestern edge of the massive Colorado Plateau, a vast area spanning the Four Corners region of Colorado, Utah, New Mexico, and Arizona. Boulder Mountain is composed of sedimentary rocks topped with a cap of lava. The harder lava has protected the underlying formations from erosion. When this hard cap is eventually worn away, Boulder Mountain will become like the eroded buttes and canyons of the surrounding desert areas, such as Capitol Reef National Park. The height and spread of Boulder Mountain, and its northern neighbor Thousand Lake Mountain, support an alpine environment of spruce forests, wildflowers, aspens, and small natural lakes. As you travel on either of these mountains, you progress through a number of life zones, from the desert floor up to the alpine settings.

The names of these mountains are the result of an interesting blunder. When this region was mapped by the government survey team, it surveyed and named both Boulder and Thousand Lake Mountains, the area's two major mountains. The names were self-descriptive: Boulder Mountain has a proliferation of rocks on its summit, and Thousand Lake Mountain has many small natural lakes. However, somehow in the process from survey team to mapmakers to transcriber, the names of the mountains were switched. Boulder Mountain is really Thousand Lake Mountain, and vice versa.

Historically, the water rights to the small lakes on top of the plateau are owned by many of the ranchers who live miles away down in the valley. This fact does not affect fishing or recreation rights, however, and the Boulder Mountain lakes provide some of the best brook trout fishing in Utah!

The Great Western Trail passes along or crosses many of the roads in this area. The designation refers to a continuous recreation trail linking local trails in many regions to form a continuous trail from Mexico to Canada. Standards and permitted uses along the trail vary widely, from sedan car to hiking and horseback use only.

Description

This drive within the Dixie National Forest links Southwest #26: Posey Lake Road (FR 154) with the network of more difficult 4WD trails on Boulder Mountain. It is a beautiful drive in its own right, and it provides vehicle access to three small natural lakes. As you ascend Aquarius Plateau, you pass from the sagebrush and juniper of the lower benches up to the higher elevation alpine settings. There are few trees on the plateau itself, which is mainly open meadow with scattered stands of aspens, but as you ascend the western side, you pass through a mix of spruce and aspen forest.

The entire trail is graded dirt road, and it finishes at the 4WD/ATV trailhead on Boulder Tops, which includes Southwest #28: Bowns Point Trail. From here the standard immediately drops and recreationalists can choose from a variety of tracks with an equally diverse variety of standards.

After 2 miles, you reach the turn for Pine

Looking back toward Dark Valley from Boulder Tops Road

Creek Reservoir, just north of the Aquarius Ranger Station. This three-acre lake contains some large brook trout.

After 6.8 miles, you reach Southwest #31: Dark Valley Trail. A sign warns that the trails ahead on Boulder Tops are closed annually from November 1 to June 15 to protect wildlife and control erosion on the plateau. The second lake, Cook Lake, is another 3.8 miles farther on, and it's reached by a short, mile-long vehicle spur. This is also a popular trout fishing spot. About a mile farther on the main trail brings you to the vehicle access for Miller Lake, which can be seen down the valley to the south. Just after this turn is the closure gate to restrict vehicle access to Boulder Tops. The road then climbs for half a mile to the end of the trail, which is marked by an information board and motorized travel map for the Boulder Tops area.

Current Road Information

Dixie National Forest
Fremont River Ranger District
PO Box 129; 138 South Main St.
Loa, UT 84747
(435) 425-3702

Map References

BLM   Loa
USFS   Dixie National Forest: Teasdale
    Ranger District
USGS   1:24,000   Bicknell, Government
    Point
    1:100,000 Loa
Maptech CD-ROM: Escalante/Dixie
    National Forest
Trails Illustrated, #707
Utah Atlas & Gazetteer, p. 27
Utah Travel Council #4

Route Directions

▼ 0.0   On Southwest #26: Posey Lake Road (FR 154), 8.2 miles from Bicknell, zero trip meter and turn southeast on FR 178; follow sign to Aquarius Ranger Station.

5.2 ▲   Trail ends at Southwest #26: Posey Lake Road (FR 154). Turn right for

Bicknell, left to continue along Posey Lake Road toward Escalante.
    GPS: N 38°15.21' W 111°37.33'

▼ 0.3 SO Track on left.
4.9 ▲ SO Track on right.

▼ 0.6 SO Track on right.
4.6 ▲ SO Track on left.

▼ 1.0 SO Track on left.
4.2 ▲ SO Track on right.

▼ 1.5 SO Entering Dixie National Forest over cattle guard.
3.7 ▲ SO Leaving Dixie National Forest over cattle guard.
    GPS: N 38°14.22' W 111°36.36'

▼ 1.8 SO Giles Hollow Exclosure on right.
3.4 ▲ SO Giles Hollow Exclosure on left.

▼ 2.0 SO Cross over Giles Hollow on culvert, then track on left.
3.2 ▲ SO Track on right, then cross over Giles Hollow on culvert.

▼ 2.1 SO FR 1288 on right, followed by track on left through a wire gate, signed to Pine Creek.
3.1 ▲ SO Track on right through a wire gate to Pine Creek, followed by FR 1288 on left.
    GPS: N 38°14.05' W 111°35.78'

▼ 2.8 SO Cross over Dark Valley Draw on culvert.
2.4 ▲ SO Cross over Dark Valley Draw on culvert.

▼ 2.9 SO Track on right.
2.3 ▲ SO Track on left.

▼ 4.4 SO Track on left.
0.8 ▲ SO Track on right.

▼ 5.0 SO Track on left to Pine Creek Reservoir. Trail crosses Allans Flat.
0.2 ▲ SO Track on right to Pine Creek Reservoir. Trail crosses Allans Flat.
    GPS: N 38°11.86' W 111°35.03'

SW Trail #27: Boulder Tops Road

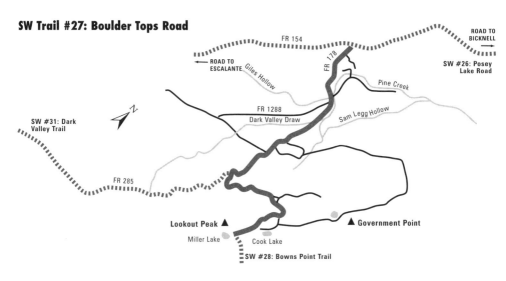

▼ 5.1	SO	Track on right.
0.2 ▲	SO	Track on left.

▼ 5.2	BR	Bear right at fork; left goes to Aquarius Field Station. Zero trip meter.
0.0 ▲		Continue along FR 178.
		GPS: N 38°11.63' W 111°34.90'

▼ 0.0		Continue toward Boulder Tops.
1.6 ▲	SO	Track on right to Aquarius Field Station. Zero trip meter.

▼ 0.8	BR	Two tracks on left; first is Great Western Trail.
0.8 ▲	BL	Two tracks on right; second is Great Western Trail.
		GPS: N 38°10.96' W 111°34.72'

▼ 1.4	SO	Potholes Exclosure, a protected wildlife area established in 1958, on left.
0.2 ▲	SO	Potholes Exclosure, a protected wildlife area established in 1958, on right.

▼ 1.6	BL	Track on right is Southwest #31: Dark Valley Trail (FR 285/Great Western Trail). Zero trip meter.
0.0 ▲		Continue across sagebrush benches.
		GPS: N 38°10.39' W 111°34.86'

▼ 0.0		Climb toward Boulder Tops.
5.7 ▲	TR	Track on left is Southwest #31: Dark Valley Trail (FR 285/Great Western Trail). Zero trip meter.

▼ 0.1	SO	Track on left.
5.6 ▲	SO	Track on right.

▼ 0.3	SO	Views south over the Potholes.
5.4 ▲	SO	Views south over the Potholes.

▼ 1.0	SO	Track on left.
4.7 ▲	SO	Track on right.

▼ 1.1	SO	Track on right.
4.6 ▲	SO	Track on left.

▼ 2.7	SO	Track on right, followed by track on left.
3.0 ▲	SO	Track on right, followed by track on left.

▼ 2.9	SO	Track on left.
2.8 ▲	SO	Track on right.

▼ 3.1	SO	Track on left.
2.6 ▲	SO	Track on right.

▼ 3.8	SO	Track on right, followed by track on left to Cook Lake.
1.9 ▲	SO	Track on right to Cook Lake, followed by track on left.
		GPS: N 38°11.02' W 111°32.77'

▼ 4.2	SO	Track on right.
1.5 ▲	SO	Track on left.

| ▼ 4.5 | SO | Track on right. |
| 1.2 ▲ | SO | Track on left. |

| ▼ 4.6 | SO | Track on left. |
| 1.1 ▲ | SO | Track on right. |

| ▼ 5.0 | SO | Track on right to Miller Lake, followed by cattle guard. |
| 0.7 ▲ | SO | Cattle guard, followed by track on left to Miller Lake. |

GPS: N 38°10.08' W 111°32.59'

| ▼ 5.2 | SO | Closure gate, followed by section of wide shelf road. |
| 0.5 ▲ | SO | End of shelf road at closure gate. |

| ▼ 5.7 | | Trail ends at information board at the start of Southwest #28: Bowns Point Trail. |
| 0.0 ▲ | | At information board for ATV/4WD trail-head, at endpoint of Southwest #28: Bowns Point Trail, zero trip meter and proceed on wide graded shelf road. |

GPS: N 38°09.75' W 111°32.48'

SOUTHWEST REGION TRAIL #28

Bowns Point Trail

STARTING POINT End of Southwest #27: Boulder Tops Road (FR 178)
FINISHING POINT Bowns Point
TOTAL MILEAGE 14.5 miles
UNPAVED MILEAGE 14.5 miles
DRIVING TIME 2 hours (one-way)
ELEVATION RANGE 10,700–11,100 feet
USUALLY OPEN June 16 to October 31
DIFFICULTY RATING 4
SCENIC RATING 10
REMOTENESS RATING +0

Special Attractions

■ Panoramic viewpoint from Bowns Point.
■ Moderately challenging trail for a stock SUV.
■ Many small, natural lakes on the Boulder Tops that offer fishing and secluded camping.

History

Bowns Point takes its name from a local rancher who used to farm the Sandy Ranch, east of Boulder Tops. Sandy Ranch owned the water rights for Lower Bowns Reservoir and Upper Bowns Reservoir, now called Oak Creek Reservoir, and cattle from the ranch would spend the summer grazing on Boulder Tops. The quickest way up and down from the plateau was via what is now the Bowns Point Stock Driveway, which continues in a dizzying descent off the edge of the plateau from Bowns Point. The wide trail was originally put in by lumbermen in the 1950s, but is now used predominantly by cattle. Vehicle use is prohibited on the stock driveway.

Description

This meandering trail provides a moderately challenging drive, some beautiful scenery, the opportunity to relax by some tranquil mountain lakes, and finally a panoramic view east from Bowns Point.

The trail starts where the graded dirt Southwest #27: Boulder Tops Road ends, at the ATV/4WD trailhead on the western edge of Boulder Tops. There is a useful forest service information board that shows motorized travel routes. However, when surveyed, it was no longer strictly accurate; some routes had closed, and others had different uses to those shown.

The first few miles of the trail have been roughly graded, as they provide access to a number of ATV and 4WD trails off to both sides. Navigation is easy along this stretch, since most trails have clearly posted forest route numbers. After 3.4 miles, you reach Elbow Lake and the connection with Southwest #29: Spectacle Lake Trail, and the trail becomes rougher.

Almost 3 miles past Elbow Lake is Southwest #32: Chokecherry Point Trail, a very rough and technically difficult 4WD trail. Continue on to Bowns Point, passing the very pretty Noon Lake on the right. The small lake is cradled in a scenic half circle of rock. Other tracks lead off from this trail to other Boulder Tops lakes, including Bess Lake, Skillet Lake, Raft Lake, and Big Lake; all have short trails leading to them, and most provide good trout fishing opportunities.

On the right of the trail, 5.5 miles past the turnoff for Chokecherry Point, is an old mill site. All that remains now is a well-constructed timber cabin and a large pile of sawdust. Loggers were responsible for many of the tracks on Boulder Tops. Once past the cabin, the trail standard drops again, and it traverses a large meadow as a faint two-track—take care not to become confused by the many faint tracks leading off from the main trail. If in doubt, take the one that's been most used. Deer Lakes are passed on the right, then the trail is indistinct again as it crosses the meadow. Follow in a southeasterly direction toward the trees.

The trail becomes lumpier, with many large boulders making for slow progress. Care is needed with wheel placement to avoid undercarriage damage, but the trail is suitable for most high-clearance SUVs with a careful driver. A mile past Deer Lakes, the trail finishes at Bowns Point. The Bowns Point Stock Driveway leads on from here, descending over the escarpment to Oak Creek Reservoir. This trail is for hiking and horse use only.

The view from Bowns Point is unparalleled: Capitol Reef National Park is northwest, and the Waterpocket Fold runs north to south parallel to the ridge. Directly below are Oak Creek Reservoir, Scout Lake, and Long Lake. Farther away is Lower Bowns Reservoir with the conical Wildcat Hill immediately to its south. On a clear day, you can see the Henry Mountains.

Current Road Information

Dixie National Forest
Fremont River Ranger District
PO Box 129; 138 South Main St.
Loa, UT 84747
(435) 425-3702

Dixie National Forest
Escalante Ranger District
PO Box 246
Escalante, UT 84726
(435) 826-5400

Map References

BLM   Loa
USFS   Dixie National Forest: Teasdale
       Ranger District
USGS   1:24,000   Government Point,
       Blind Lake, Deer Creek Lake,
       Lower Bowns Reservoir
       1:100,000 Loa
Maptech CD-ROM: Escalante/Dixie
       National Forest
Trails Illustrated, #707
Utah Atlas & Gazetteer, pp. 27, 28
Utah Travel Council #4

A view of Bowns Point Trail

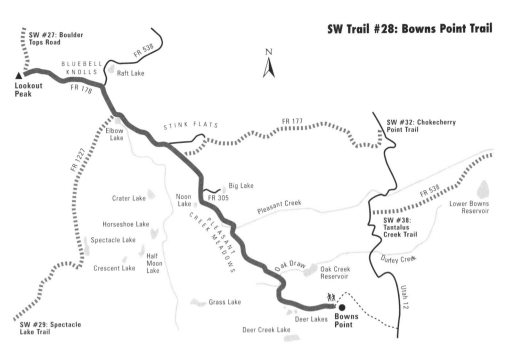

Route Directions

GPS: N 38°09.38' W 111°29.83'

▼ 0.0   From the information board at the southern end of Southwest #27: Boulder Tops Road, zero trip meter and proceed east on FR 178.

3.4 ▲   Trail ends at information board at the southern end of Southwest #27: Boulder Tops Road.
GPS: N 38°09.75' W 111°32.48'

▼ 0.2   SO   Closed road to the left now gives hiking access to Government Point.

3.2 ▲   SO   Closed road to the right now gives hiking access to Government Point.

▼ 0.8   SO   FR 541 on right to Chuck Lake and Surveyors Lake.

2.6 ▲   SO   FR 541 on left to Chuck Lake and Surveyors Lake.
GPS: N 38°09.60' W 111°31.59'

▼ 1.8   SO   Track on left.

1.6 ▲   SO   Track on right.

▼ 2.5   BR   FR 538 on left to Raft Lake.

0.9 ▲   BL   FR 538 on right to Raft Lake.

▼ 3.4   SO   Elbow Lake. FR 1277 on right is Southwest #29: Spectacle Lake Trail. Zero trip meter.

0.0 ▲   Proceed northwest on FR 178.
GPS: N 38°08.61' W 111°29.40'

▼ 0.0   Proceed southeast on FR 178. Trail is rougher.

2.8 ▲   SO   Elbow Lake. FR 1277 on left is Southwest #29: Spectacle Lake Trail. Zero trip meter.

▼ 1.4   BL   FR 522 on right to Crater Lake, Horseshoe Lake, and Crescent Lake.

1.4 ▲   BR   FR 522 on left to Crater Lake, Horseshoe Lake, and Crescent Lake.
GPS: N 38°07.91' W 111°28.21'

▼ 2.1   BR   FR 424 on left to Bess Lake.

0.7 ▲   BL   FR 424 on right to Bess Lake.
GPS: N 38°07.73' W 111°27.52'

▼ 2.8   SO   Track on left is Southwest #32: Chokecherry Point Trail. Zero trip meter.

0.0 ▲		Intersection of Southwest #28: Bowns Point Trail and Southwest #32: Chokecherry Point Trail. Proceed northwest toward Southwest #27: Boulder Tops Road (FR 178).
		GPS: N 38°07.42′ W 111°26.88′

▼ 0.0		Continue to Bowns Point.
▼ 1.8	SO	FR 305 on left to Big Lake.
		GPS: N 38°06.11′ W 111°26.07′

▼ 2.1	SO	Noon Lake on right.
		GPS: N 38°05.98′ W 111°25.88′

▼ 2.8	SO	Descend into Pleasant Creek Meadows.
▼ 3.1	SO	Cross over Pleasant Creek.
▼ 5.5	SO	Old cabin and sawdust pile from old mill on right.
		GPS: N 38°04.13′ W 111°23.70′

▼ 5.9	BR	Track on left, cross through Oak Draw.
▼ 6.1	SO	Cross through Oak Draw a second time, then track on left. Trail crosses meadow and is hard to follow. Watch carefully, and follow most-used track.
		GPS: N 38°03.94′ W 111°23.33′

▼ 7.0	SO	Deer Lakes on right.
		GPS: N 38°03.41′ W 111°22.96′

▼ 7.1	SO	Trail is again indistinct; head in a southeasterly direction to the trees.
▼ 7.5	SO	Trail enters trees.
		GPS: N 38°03.22′ W 111°22.34′

▼ 8.1	BL	Bear left in clearing; correct exit is hard to follow.
		GPS: N 38°03.21′ W 111°21.73′

▼ 8.3		Trail ends at Bowns Point. Gap in fence line is entrance to Bowns Point Stock Driveway (no vehicles). Great Western Trail goes left from this point to Behunin Point and Meeks Lake.
		GPS: N 38°03.36′ W 111°21.54′

Spectacle Lake Trail

STARTING POINT Southwest #28: Bowns Point Trail (FR 178) at Elbow Lake
FINISHING POINT Junction of FR 162 and FR 1277
TOTAL MILEAGE 11.4 miles
UNPAVED MILEAGE 11.4 miles
DRIVING TIME 1.5 hours
ELEVATION RANGE 10,400–11,100 feet
USUALLY OPEN June 16 to October 31
DIFFICULTY RATING 3
SCENIC RATING 8
REMOTENESS RATING +0

Special Attractions
- Bakeskillet and Spectacle Lakes.
- Scenic trail traversing the open Boulder Tops.

Description
This trail traverses the length of the Boulder Tops region, passing by two small lakes and providing access to several more. The trail is ungraded dirt and is suitable for any high-clearance SUV. Most of the surface across the tops is fairly smooth and easygoing, although it may be impassable after rain. The descent after Spectacle Lake is rocky and the road surface is lumpy, but there are no difficult sections that might cause any problems.

A log cabin overlooks the south end of Spectacle Lake

The trail begins at Elbow Lake from Southwest #28: Bowns Point Trail and heads southwest across the plateau. It undulates down to cross West Boulder Draw and then climbs to Spectacle Lake. The lake is a reservoir that is dammed at the south end. In summer, when it is partially dry, the lake separates into two ovals joined by a small channel of water—resembling spectacles. The water level in this lake is often low as it is used for irrigation storage. The lake provides some trout fishing opportunities, and there are some pleasant campsites around it, mainly at the southern end.

From the lake, the trail descends to join FR 162. It passes the small, natural depressions of Five Lakes, and 1.5 miles from the end of the trail you pass the seasonal closure sign—motorized travel is prohibited on the Boulder Tops between November 1 and June 15. However, when there is sufficient snow, snowmobiles can use the trail. FR 162 is about 6 miles from Spectacle Lake.

Current Road Information
Dixie National Forest
Fremont River Ranger District
PO Box 129; 138 South Main St.
Loa, UT 84747
(435) 425-3702

Dixie National Forest
Escalante Ranger District
PO Box 246
Escalante, UT 84726
(435) 826-5400

Map References
BLM   Loa
USFS   Dixie National Forest: Teasdale and
       Escalante Ranger Districts
USGS   1:24,000   Blind Lake, Government
       Point, Jacobs Reservoir
       1:100,000 Loa
Maptech CD-ROM: Escalante/Dixie
       National Forest
Trails Illustrated, #707
Utah Atlas & Gazetteer, pp. 27, 28
Utah Travel Council #4 (incomplete)

Route Directions

▼ 0.0   From Southwest #28: Bowns Point
           Trail (FR 178) at Elbow Lake, zero trip
           meter and turn southwest on
           Spectacle Lake Trail (FR 1277).
5.6 ▲   Trail finishes at Southwest #28:
           Bowns Point Trail (FR 178) at Elbow
           Lake. Turn right to continue to Bowns
           Point, left to exit the national forest via
           Southwest #27: Boulder Tops Road.
           GPS: N 38°08.60' W 111°29.40'

▼ 0.2   SO Gravel pit on right.
5.4 ▲   SO Gravel pit on left.

▼ 1.0   SO Track on left to Rain Lake.
4.6 ▲   SO Track on right to Rain Lake.
           GPS: N 38°07.93' W 111°30.07'

▼ 1.7   SO Bakeskillet Lake on left.
3.9 ▲   SO Bakeskillet Lake on right.
           GPS: N 38°07.35' W 111°30.36'

▼ 1.9   SO Oil drilling marker post on right.
3.7 ▲   SO Oil drilling marker post on left.
           GPS: N 38°07.27' W 111°30.44'

▼ 2.0   SO FR 541 on right to Surveyors Lake and
              Chuck Lake.
3.6 ▲   SO FR 541 on left to Surveyors Lake and
              Chuck Lake.
           GPS: N 38°07.19' W 111°30.54'

▼ 2.2   SO Boulder Draw Exclosure on right.
3.4 ▲   SO Boulder Draw Exclosure on left.

▼ 2.3   SO Cross through West Boulder Draw
              wash.
3.3 ▲   SO Cross through West Boulder Draw
              wash.

▼ 3.6   SO Small lake in hollow on right.
2.0 ▲   SO Small lake in hollow on left.
           GPS: N 38°05.96' W 111°30.94'

▼ 4.0   SO Cross through small wash.
1.6 ▲   SO Cross through small wash.

▼ 4.6   BL Faint track on right.

SW Trail #29: Spectacle Lake Trail

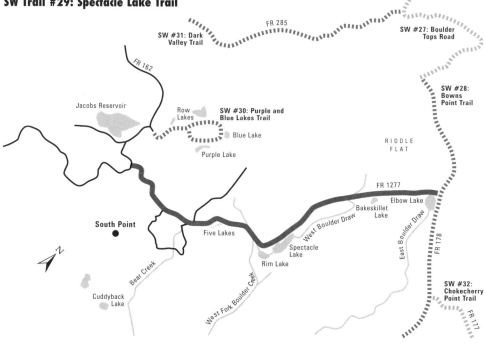

1.0 ▲	SO	Faint track on left.

▼ 5.1	SO	Spectacle Lake; trail winds around the west side.
0.5 ▲	SO	Trail leaves Spectacle Lake.

▼ 5.6	TR	South end of Spectacle Lake. Small cabin directly ahead. Track on left goes across dam wall to an exposed but pretty campsite and continues as a foot/pack trail. Zero trip meter.
0.0 ▲		Continue along west side of Spectacle Lake.
		GPS: N 38°04.68' W 111°30.45'

▼ 0.0		Leave Spectacle Lake.
5.8 ▲	TL	South end of Spectacle Lake. Small cabin on right. Track on right goes across dam wall to an exposed but pretty campsite and continues as a foot/pack trail. Zero trip meter.

▼ 0.2	SO	Track on right.
5.6 ▲	BR	Track on left.

▼ 0.3	SO	Track on left to Rim Lake.

5.5 ▲	BL	Track on right to Rim Lake.
		GPS: N 38°04.44' W 111°30.65'

▼ 0.9	SO	Cross through rocky wash.
4.9 ▲	SO	Cross through rocky wash.

▼ 1.8	SO	Faint track on left.
4.0 ▲	BL	Faint track on right.

▼ 2.1	SO	Trail passes alongside Five Lakes.
3.7 ▲	SO	Trail leaves Five Lakes.
		GPS: N 38°03.85' W 111°32.08'

▼ 2.4	SO	Trail leaves Five Lakes.
3.4 ▲	SO	Trail passes alongside Five Lakes.

▼ 3.5	SO	Trail splits; both forks run parallel to each other.
2.3 ▲	SO	Trails rejoin.

▼ 3.9	SO	Trails rejoin.
1.9 ▲	SO	Trail splits; both forks run parallel to each other.

▼ 4.1	SO	Cattle guard.
1.7 ▲	SO	Cattle guard.

▼ 4.2	SO	Leaving seasonal closure area on Boulder Tops.
1.6 ▲	SO	Entering seasonal closure area for Boulder Tops.
▼ 5.4	SO	Track on left.
0.4 ▲	BL	Track on right.
▼ 5.5	SO	Track on right.
0.3 ▲	BR	Track on left.
		GPS: N 38°02.96′ W 111°34.33′
▼ 5.8		Trail finishes at FR 162. Turn right for Southwest #30: Purple and Blue Lakes Trail and also Southwest #26: Posey Lake Road which provides access to Escalante and Bicknell.
0.0 ▲		At intersection of FR 162 and FR 1277 (Spectacle Lake Road), zero trip meter and proceed northeast.
		GPS: N 38°02.77′ W 111°34.62′

SOUTHWEST REGION TRAIL #30

Purple and Blue Lakes Trail

STARTING POINT FR 162, 5.8 miles east of Southwest #26: Posey Lake Road
FINISHING POINT Blue Lake
TOTAL MILEAGE 4.1 miles
UNPAVED MILEAGE 4.1 miles
DRIVING TIME 1 hour
ELEVATION RANGE 10,200–10,500 feet
USUALLY OPEN May to October
DIFFICULTY RATING 5
SCENIC RATING 8
REMOTENESS RATING +0

Special Attractions

- Short, scenic trail that passes four small lakes.
- Challenging 4WD trail in beautiful scenery.
- Fishing opportunities at Row, Blue, and Purple Lakes.

Description

This beautiful, scenic trail is a challenging drive for a high-clearance SUV. The trail leaves from FR 162, a graded gravel road that leads east from Southwest #26: Posey Lake Road. The trail standard is immediately rough, ungraded dirt; it winds around, crossing many boulder fields, to the first of the two major Row Lakes. These are some of the many small natural lakes scattered around the lava cap rocks of the Boulder Tops plateau. The three Row Lakes are part of a chain of several small lakes. The largest is 30 acres and all are less than 10 feet deep. They are stocked annually with catchable rainbow trout.

From the first Row Lake, the trail continues toward an open meadow and then swings north into the trees. The trail here climbs steeply to Purple Lake. There are

Tall conifers border the still waters of the Row Lakes

Mud can become deep and lumpy as the Purple and Blue Lakes Trail crosses this open meadow

some medium-size boulders, a loose surface, and ruts to be negotiated as you approach the lake. Once at the lake the trail swings along the south shore. This section can be very muddy, and some of the mud wallows are deep.

Purple Lake is probably the prettiest of the lakes on this trail, being set in a small tree-ringed depression. The lake is stocked with fingerling brook trout, and although many die when the lake freezes each winter, sufficient numbers survive each year to provide good fishing. There are limited backcountry campsites surrounding Purple Lake, but better sites are found around Blue and Row Lakes.

Half a mile farther is Blue Lake, which is set in a deep depression and is the smallest of the lakes along the trail. There are some good campsites on the east shore that are set among the trees. The lake is host to brook and cutthroat trout.

From Blue Lake, the trail descends back down to Row Lakes. This side is an easier slope than the climb to Purple Lake. The trail makes a loop past the second of the larger Row Lakes, back to where you began the climb to Purple Lake. From here, retrace your steps back to FR 162.

Current Road Information
Dixie National Forest
Fremont River Ranger District
PO Box 129; 138 South Main St.
Loa, UT 84747
(435) 425-3702

Dixie National Forest
Escalante Ranger District
PO Box 246
Escalante, UT 84726
(435) 826-5400

Map References
BLM   Loa
USFS   Dixie National Forest: Escalante
        and Teasdale Ranger Districts
USGS   1:24,000   Jacobs Reservoir
        1:100,000 Loa
Maptech CD-ROM: Escalante/Dixie
        National Forest
Trails Illustrated, #707
Utah Atlas & Gazetteer, p. 27

Route Directions

▼ 0.0   From FR 162, 5.8 miles east of
           Southwest #26: Posey Lake Road,
           turn northwest onto ungraded dirt trail,

SW Trail #30: Purple and Blue Lakes Trail

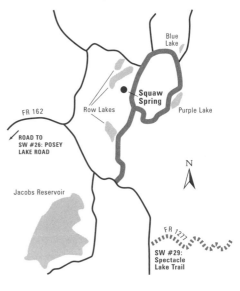

signed to Row Lakes. Zero trip meter.
GPS: N 38°03.50′ W 111°35.14′

▼ 0.6 SO Track on left to Row Lakes and campsite.
GPS: N 38°03.94′ W 111°35.05′

▼ 0.7 SO Track on left to lake and campsite.
▼ 0.8 SO Cattle guard and sign for Great
Western Trail. Trail leads across boulder-strewn meadow.
▼ 0.9 SO Muddy section of track.
▼ 1.2 TR Enter tall pines and spruce. Start of
loop section. Track ahead is end of
loop section. Turn right and zero trip
meter.
GPS: N 38°04.35′ W 111°34.85′

▼ 0.0 Continue along lumpy track.
▼ 0.7 BL Track on right. Purple Lake is directly in
front. Continue along western shore.
GPS: N 38°04.40′ W 111°34.32′

▼ 0.8 SO Muddy section along lakeshore.
▼ 1.0 SO Trail leaves Purple Lake.
▼ 1.5 BL Blue Lake directly ahead. Track on right
to good campsites. Continue around
southern shore.
GPS: N 38°04.93′ W 111°34.13′

▼ 1.6 SO Campsite on right. Trail leaves Blue
Lake.
▼ 2.2 TL Zero trip meter. Great Western Trail
goes to the right.
GPS: N 38°04.93′ W 111°34.69′

▼ 0.0 Continue along loop.
▼ 0.1 BL Track on right to Row Lakes (second
lake).
▼ 0.2 SO Cross through old fence line.
▼ 0.5 SO Muddy section with large boulders;
careful wheel placement needed.
▼ 0.6 SO Faint track on right.
GPS: N 38°04.46′ W 111°34.92′

▼ 0.7 Abandoned vehicle on left, then track
on left is start of loop to Purple and
Blue Lakes. Retrace your steps to join
FR 162.
GPS: N 38°04.35′ W 111°34.85′

Dark Valley Trail

STARTING POINT Southwest #26: Posey Lake
Road (FR 154)
FINISHING POINT Southwest #27: Boulder Tops
Road (FR 178)
TOTAL MILEAGE 12.2 miles
UNPAVED MILEAGE 12.2 miles
DRIVING TIME 1.5 hours
ELEVATION RANGE 9,000–9,700 feet
USUALLY OPEN May to November
DIFFICULTY RATING 4
SCENIC RATING 8
REMOTENESS RATING +0

Special Attractions
■ Interesting and varied scenery on the
Aquarius Plateau.
■ Aspen viewing in the fall.
■ ATV trail access and backcountry camping.

Description
This gentle, 12-mile route on the Aquarius
Plateau contains a wide variety of scenery.
The trail meanders along the wide valley of
Rock Draw, passing through stands of aspen,

Aspens climb away from the water's edge in the Potholes

A well-preserved log cabin at the foot of a tall pine in the Potholes

spruce, and pine, and over rolling meadows covered with sagebrush and grasslands. The road becomes tighter when it enters Dark Valley and passes between the rock cliffs of Rock Spring Ridge to the west and Dark Valley Shelf to the east. The Great Western Trail intersects the route.

After 8 miles, you reach the pretty Lava Spring, a natural spring near Birch Creek. There is private property at this point, but the trail passes around the boundaries. After Birch Creek, the trail traverses the area known as the Potholes, which are deep depressions in the lava cap of the Aquarius Plateau. The open bowl north of the Potholes before the intersection with FR 178 has some excellent backcountry campsites, which are accessible even with a trailer from FR 178. Many people use this area as a base for hiking or further exploration via ATV or 4WD.

The ungraded trail surface is generally moderate going, although a couple of spots require greater concentration. The crossing over Birch Creek can be tricky as the area is muddy more often than not, and deep ruts have formed in the crossing. After rain, the section along Rock Draw can be difficult. In the trees there are a couple of rocky sections that need care with wheel placement, but this is a good trail for less experienced drivers in high-clearance SUVs who want to move to harder trails. The trail is used by snowmobiles in winter.

Current Road Information

Dixie National Forest
Fremont River Ranger District
PO Box 129; 138 South Main St.
Loa, UT 84747
(435) 425-3702

Map References

BLM   Loa
USFS   Dixie National Forest: Teasdale
Ranger District
USGS   1:24,000   Big Lake, Jacobs
Reservoir, Government Point
1:100,000   Loa
Maptech CD-ROM: Escalante/Dixie
National Forest
Trails Illustrated, #707 (incomplete)
Utah Atlas & Gazetteer, p. 27
Utah Travel Council #4

Route Directions

▼ 0.0   From Southwest #26: Posey Lake
Road (FR 154), 21.8 miles from
Bicknell, turn northeast on FR 285 at
the sign for Rock Spring. Zero trip
meter.

9.0 ▲   Trail finishes at Southwest #26: Posey
Lake Road (FR 154). Turn left for
Escalante, right for Bicknell.
GPS: N 38°03.94' W 111°41.45'

▼ 1.3   SO Cross through wash.
7.7 ▲   SO Cross through wash.
GPS: N 38°04.60' W 111°40.17'

▼ 1.5   SO Rock Spring Pond on right.
7.5 ▲   SO Rock Spring Pond on left.
GPS: N 38°04.60' W 111°40.01'

▼ 1.6   SO Cross through Rock Spring Draw. Trail
enters trees, winding among stands of
trees and open meadows.
7.4 ▲   SO Cross through Rock Spring Draw. Trail
leaves trees and continues across the
open valley.

▼ 4.3   SO Exit trees and descend into Dark
Valley.
4.7 ▲   SO Leave Dark Valley and enter trees,

winding among stands of trees and open meadows.

▼ 5.4 SO Small dam on right.
3.6 ▲ SO Small dam on left.

▼ 5.6 SO Exclosure wildlife area on right.
3.4 ▲ SO Exclosure wildlife area on left.

▼ 6.2 SO Track on right is ATV trail to Blue Lake. Great Western Trail now follows along the route.
2.8 ▲ SO Track on left is ATV trail to Blue Lake. Great Western Trail leaves the route and goes left.
GPS: N 38°06.25' W 111°35.96'

▼ 6.4 SO Faint track on right.
2.6 ▲ BR Faint track on left.

▼ 7.1 BR Faint track on left. Rock Spring Ridge is to the left, Dark Valley Shelf to the right.
1.9 ▲ BL Faint track on right. Rock Spring Ridge is to the right, Dark Valley Shelf to the left.

▼ 7.3 SO Faint track on left.
1.7 ▲ BL Faint track on right.

▼ 7.6 SO Faint track on right.
1.4 ▲ SO Faint track on left.

▼ 8.4 SO Track on right, then cross through fence line.
0.6 ▲ SO Cross through fence line, then track on left.
GPS: N 38°07.69' W 111°35.52'

▼ 8.6 SO Lava Spring on right.
0.4 ▲ SO Lava Spring on left.

▼ 8.7 SO Cross over Birch Creek.
0.3 ▲ SO Cross over Birch Creek.
GPS: N 38°07.88' W 111°35.33'

▼ 9.0 SO Pass through gate. Entrance to private property on left. Zero trip meter.
0.0 ▲   Continue toward Dark Valley.
GPS: N 38°08.12' W 111°35.24'

▼ 0.0   Continue toward the Potholes.
3.2 ▲ SO Entrance to private property on right. Pass through gate and zero trip meter.

▼ 0.4 SO Cross through creek. Entering the Potholes area.
2.8 ▲ SO Cross through creek. Leaving the Potholes area.

▼ 0.7 SO Fork; tracks rejoin almost immediately.
2.5 ▲ SO Fork; tracks rejoin almost immediately.

▼ 1.0 SO Small dam on right.
2.2 ▲ SO Small dam on left.

SW Trail #31: Dark Valley Trail

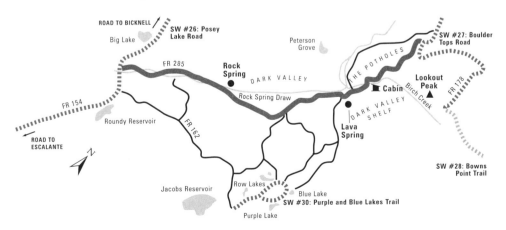

| ▼ 1.2 | BR | Small lake on right, then track on left. |
| 2.0 ▲ | SO | Track on right, then small lake on left. |

GPS: N 38°08.86′ W 111°34.94′

| ▼ 1.3 | SO | Old log cabin by clearing in aspens. |
| 1.9 ▲ | SO | Old log cabin by clearing in aspens. |

GPS: N 38°08.93′ W 111°34.85′

| ▼ 1.5 | SO | Track on right. |
| 1.7 ▲ | SO | Track on left. |

| ▼ 2.7 | SO | Track on left. |
| 0.5 ▲ | SO | Track on right. |

GPS: N 38°10.02′ W 111°34.74′

| ▼ 3.0 | SO | Track on left. |
| 0.2 ▲ | SO | Track on right. |

| ▼ 3.1 | SO | Track on left. |
| 0.1 ▲ | SO | Track on right. |

| ▼ 3.2 | | Trail ends at Southwest #27: Boulder Tops Road (FR 178). Turn right to continue to Boulder Tops, turn left for Southwest #26: Posey Lake Road and Bicknell. |
| 0.0 ▲ | | On Southwest #27: Boulder Tops Road (FR 178), turn south on FR 285 toward Dark Valley and zero trip meter. Trail enters the Potholes. |

GPS: N 38°10.39′ W 111°34.86′

SOUTHWEST REGION TRAIL #32

Chokecherry Point Trail

STARTING POINT Southwest #28: Bowns Point Trail (FR 178)
FINISHING POINT Utah 12
TOTAL MILEAGE 9.3 miles
UNPAVED MILEAGE 9.3 miles
DRIVING TIME 2.5 hours
ELEVATION RANGE 8,700–11,000 feet
USUALLY OPEN June 16 to October 31
DIFFICULTY RATING 7
SCENIC RATING 8
REMOTENESS RATING +0

Special Attractions

- Extremely challenging 4WD trail.
- One of the few through routes on the Boulder Tops.
- Spectacular views as you descend from Chokecherry Point.

Description

This difficult and technical 4WD trail should only be attempted by experienced drivers. It is passable with care by stock SUVs that have excellent clearance and good off-road tires. Additional lift is a definite advantage. The trail contains a long section of large boulders that twists tightly within the trees. However, the trail as far as Chokecherry Point is easier than the descent from that point to Utah 12. This steep descent has an extremely loose surface, making traction difficult. There are many rocky sections and some off-camber suspension-twisting ruts. It is easier to travel the trail from west to east, so that you descend from Chokecherry Point rather than climb up to it.

The trail leaves Southwest #28: Bowns Point Trail 2.8 miles past Elbow Lake. For

Looking back through the aspens at the lower end of the Chokecherry Point Trail

the first 2 miles, it is an ungraded, easy dirt road that crosses the appealingly named Stink Flats, followed by Beef Meadows and Willow Draw. After Willow Draw the track becomes fainter and hard to follow as it crosses the meadow. Follow the most well-used wheel ruts. After 3 miles, the trail enters the trees and gets progressively harder. This section is slow-going as it crawls over large boulders and rocks in the trees.

Just over 6 miles from the start, you reach Chokecherry Point. The actual point is north of the trail. The trail crosses through the logworm fence line and descends from Boulder Mountain. The first half mile is the steepest and loosest, and it is this section that will cause the most difficulties for vehicles traveling in the reverse direction. The trail continues to descend, crossing several hiking trails. The views are superb—on a clear day, you can see Mount Ellen and Mount Pennell in the Henry Mountains and even the La Sal Mountains. Closer by, you can see Lower Bowns Reservoir, the convolutions of the Waterpocket Fold in Capitol Reef National Park, and the stark, desolate Caineville Mesas. The lower you get, the easier the trail becomes. There are a couple of campsites tucked into the aspens on this section.

The trail receives no forest service maintenance. It is maintained as a 4WD trail by the Offroad Adventurers 4x4 Club from Richfield.

Motorized travel on the Boulder Tops is prohibited between November 1 and June 15, so the trail can only be traveled as a through route from June 16 to October 31.

Current Road Information
Dixie National Forest
Fremont River Ranger District
PO Box 129; 138 South Main St.
Loa, UT 84747
(435) 425-3702

Panoramic views of the Henry Mountains, Lower Bowns Reservoir, and Capitol Reef unfold to the east as the trail descends from Chokecherry Point

Map References
BLM   Loa
USFS Dixie National Forest: Teasdale
       Ranger District
USGS 1:24,000   Deer Creek Lake, Blind
       Lake, Grover
       1:100,000 Loa
Maptech CD-ROM: Escalante/Dixie
       National Forest
Trails Illustrated, #707 (incomplete)
Utah Atlas & Gazetteer, p. 28
Utah Travel Council #4 (incomplete)

Route Directions

▼ 0.0   On Southwest #28: Bowns Point Trail
       (FR 178), 2.8 miles past Elbow Lake,
       turn east on FR 177, following sign to
       Chokecherry Point. Trail crosses Stink
       Flats.
6.2 ▲   Trail finishes at Southwest #28:
       Bowns Point Trail (FR 178). Turn left to
       continue to Bowns Point, right to exit
       to Boulder Tops.
       GPS: N 38°07.41′ W 111°26.85′

▼ 1.2   SO Trail leaves trees and crosses the edge
       of Beef Meadows.
5.0 ▲   SO Beef Meadows on right.

▼ 1.6   SO Great Western Trail enters on left.
4.6 ▲   SO Great Western Trail leaves on right.
       GPS: N 38°07.80′ W 111°25.49′

SW Trail #32: Chokecherry Point Trail

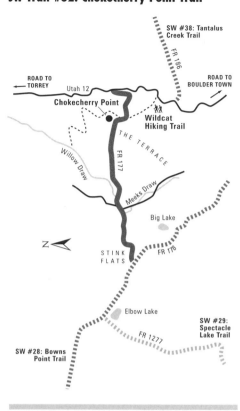

▼ 2.1   SO   Track on right to Meeks Draw.
4.1 ▲   SO   Track on left to Meeks Draw.
    GPS: N 38°07.77′ W 111°25.05′

▼ 2.3   SO   Two small dams on left.
3.9 ▲   SO   Two small dams on right.

▼ 2.5   BR   Fork at Willow Draw. Trail becomes fainter; follow most well used wheel ruts.
3.7 ▲   SO   Willow Draw. Trail is more defined.
    GPS: N 38°08.01′ W 111°24.63′

▼ 2.8   BR   Trail bears southeast.
3.4 ▲   SO   Trail bears northwest.
    GPS: N 38°08.09′ W 111°24.33′

▼ 3.1   SO   Reenter trees; FR 177 sign on tree on right, then track on right.
3.1 ▲   SO   Track on left, then leave trees and cross meadow.
    GPS: N 38°07.96′ W 111°24.09′

▼ 4.1   BL   Trail swings left.
2.1 ▲   BR   Trail swings right.
    GPS: N 38°08.21′ W 111°23.14′

▼ 4.4   SO   Leave trees and bear slightly right to southeast. Trail is faint across meadow.
1.8 ▲   SO   Leave the meadow and enter the trees.
    GPS: N 38°08.15′ W 111°22.88′

▼ 4.6   SO   Small dam on left.
1.6 ▲   SO   Small dam on right.

▼ 4.7   BL   Across meadow.
1.5 ▲   BR   Across meadow.
    GPS: N 38°08.26′ W 111°22.30′

▼ 5.1   SO   Faint track on left.
1.1 ▲   SO   Faint track on right.

▼ 6.2   SO   Chokecherry Point on left. Great Western Loop Trail on right. Trail crosses fence line and descends from Boulder Mountain. Zero trip meter.
0.0 ▲   Continue through the trees on lumpy trail.
    GPS: N 38°08.15′ W 111°21.12′

▼ 0.0   Descend from Boulder Mountain. Trail is steep and loose.
3.1 ▲   SO   End of climb. Chokecherry Point on right. Great Western Loop Trail on left. Trail crosses fence line. Zero trip meter.

▼ 0.4   SO   End of steepest part of descent.
2.7 ▲   SO   Trail gets a lot steeper and is loose.
    GPS: N 38°08.06′ W 111°20.89′

▼ 0.6   SO   Wildcat Hiking Trail (#140) joins main trail from the left.
2.5 ▲   SO   Wildcat Hiking Trail (#140) leaves main trail to the right.
    GPS: N 38°07.80′ W 111°20.85′

▼ 1.0   SO   Small saddle. Wildcat Hiking Trail (#140) leaves main trail to the right.
2.1 ▲   SO   Small saddle. Wildcat Hiking Trail (#140) joins main trail from the left.
    GPS: N 38°07.70′ W 111°20.81′

| ▼ 1.4 | SO | Cross through fence line. |
| 1.7 ▲ | SO | Cross through fence line. |

| ▼ 1.7 | SO | Cattletank on right in aspens. |
| 1.4 ▲ | SO | Cattletank on left in aspens. |

▼ 3.1		Trail finishes at Utah 12, 5.7 miles south of the Dixie National Forest boundary. Turn left for Torrey, turn right for Boulder Town.
0.0 ▲		On Utah 12, 5.7 miles south of the Dixie National Forest boundary, turn west at sign for Chokecherry 4x4 Road and zero trip meter.
		GPS: N 38°08.09′ W 111°19.66′

SOUTHWEST REGION TRAIL #33

Griffin Road

STARTING POINT Escalante Summit on Southwest #34: Escalante Summit Trail
FINISHING POINT Southwest #26: Posey Lake Road (FR 154)
TOTAL MILEAGE 21.1 miles
UNPAVED MILEAGE 21.1 miles
DRIVING TIME 1.5 hours
ELEVATION RANGE 9,200–10,600 feet
USUALLY OPEN May to October
DIFFICULTY RATING 1
SCENIC RATING 8
REMOTENESS RATING +0

Special Attractions

- Access to a network of 4WD tracks and backcountry campsites.
- Aspen viewing and fall colors.
- Wide-ranging scenic views and wildlife viewing.

Description

This beautiful drive crosses the high-altitude plateau of Griffin Top, with its long stretches of alpine meadows and wildlife viewing opportunities. The entire road surface is graded gravel and is suitable for a passenger car, but at the southern end some automobiles may find the grade steep.

The trail commences at Escalante Summit along Southwest #34: Escalante Summit Trail (FR 17), 13.8 miles from Utah 12. Turn north on FR 140 (Griffin Road), which immediately climbs steeply up a series of switchbacks around Horse Creek Top. As the road climbs, you get excellent views back down Main Canyon east of Escalante Summit.

The first couple miles are the steepest on the trail, which continues to climb until it reaches the plateau of Griffin Top, part of the Escalante Mountain Range. Johns Valley to the west is spread out below as the trail winds through stands of mature aspens. Horse Lake is 0.2 miles west of the trail near the top of the climb. You can park and walk down to the small lake.

After 4.7 miles you reach Griffin Top, a large alpine meadow running predominantly north to south. As it crosses the meadow,

A bend in Griffin Road reveals expansive views into Escalante Canyon

SW Trail #33: Griffin Road

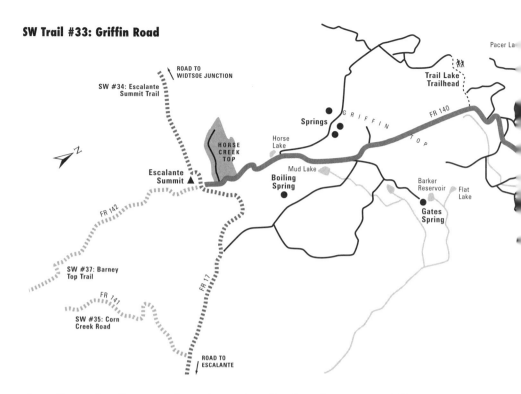

the trail occasionally passes through stands of pine and aspen. You can often see mule deer and elk grazing in these high plateaus in summer. Cattle also graze here in summer, so take care on blind corners. You may also see wild turkeys, which have been introduced into the forest. There are plenty of good secluded campsites tucked into the trees on both sides of the meadow. A variety of trails leads off from this road. There are plenty of small trails, mainly dead ends, that are suitable for SUVs, and a network of 4WD trails leads northwest into the Poison Creek area of the Dixie National Forest. Many trails are suitable for ATV use or snowmobiles in the winter.

The trail continues to undulate across open meadows, finishing at Southwest #26: Posey Lake Road (FR 154).

Current Road Information

Dixie National Forest
Escalante Ranger District
PO Box 246
Escalante, UT 84726
(435) 826-5400

Escalante Interagency Office
755 West Main
Escalante, UT 84726
(435) 826-5499

Map References

BLM   Escalante, Loa
USFS   Dixie National Forest: Escalante
    Ranger District
USGS   1:24,000   Sweetwater Creek,
    Griffin Point, Barker Reservoir
    1:100,000 Escalante, Loa
Maptech CD-ROM: Escalante/Dixie
    National Forest
Utah Atlas & Gazetteer, p. 27
Utah Travel Council #4
Other: BLM Map of the Grand Staircase–
    Escalante National Monument

Route Directions

▼ 0.0   At Escalante Summit on Southwest #34:
    Escalante Summit Trail (FR 17), turn north
    on Griffin Road (FR 140), following sign
    for Griffin Top. Zero trip meter.

4.7 ▲   Trail finishes at Escalante Summit on

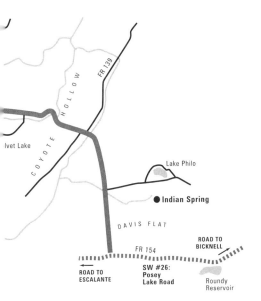

Southwest #34: Escalante Summit Trail (FR 17). Turn left for Escalante, right for Widtsoe Junction. Straight ahead is Southwest #37: Barney Top Trail (FR 142).
GPS: N 37°49.53′ W 111°52.89′

▼ 0.8   SO Track on left, then wide shelf road with excellent views down Main Canyon.
3.9 ▲   SO Track on right. End of shelf road.

▼ 1.1   SO Track on left. End of shelf road.
3.6 ▲   SO Track on right, then wide shelf road with excellent views down Main Canyon.

▼ 1.6   SO Great Western Trail on left to Sweetwater Road.
3.1 ▲   SO Great Western Trail on right to Sweetwater Road.
GPS: N 37°50.64′ W 111°52.69′

▼ 1.7   SO Track on right.
3.0 ▲   SO Track on left.

▼ 2.1   SO Pull-in on left gives views west over Johns Valley.

▼ 2.6   SO Pull-in on right gives views west over Johns Valley.

▼ 2.5   SO Small track on left.
2.2 ▲   SO Small track on right.

▼ 3.5   SO Hiking trail on left leads to Horse Lake (0.2 miles).
1.2 ▲   SO Hiking trail on right leads to Horse Lake (0.2 miles).
GPS: N 37°51.65′ W 111°52.77′

▼ 4.5   SO Cattle guard.
0.2 ▲   SO Cattle guard.

▼ 4.6   SO Small track on left.
0.1 ▲   SO Small track on right; trail descends to Escalante Summit.

▼ 4.7   BL Entering Griffin Top—large, open meadow. Two tracks on right, campsite on left. Zero trip meter.
0.0 ▲   Leave Griffin Top and enter trees.
GPS: N 37°52.52′ W 111°52.30′

▼ 0.0   Continue along open meadow.
5.3 ▲   BR Two tracks on left, campsite on right. Leave open meadow and zero trip meter.

▼ 0.9   SO Track on right.
4.4 ▲   SO Track on left.

▼ 1.0   SO Track on right, then track on left.
4.3 ▲   SO Track on right, then track on left.

▼ 1.3   SO North Creek Lakes Trail on right.
4.0 ▲   SO North Creek Lakes Trail on left.

▼ 2.1   SO Track on left to Griffin Spring.
3.2 ▲   SO Track on right to Griffin Spring.
GPS: N 37°54.35′ W 111°52.08′

▼ 2.6   SO Track on left goes past shallow lake.
2.7 ▲   SO Track on right goes past shallow lake.
GPS: N 37°54.84 W 111°51.87′

▼ 3.2   SO Track on left.
2.1 ▲   SO Track on right.

▼ 3.9   SO Track on left.
1.4 ▲   SO Track on right.

▼ 4.4   SO Track on right.
0.9 ▲   SO Track on left.

▼ 5.3   SO Cattle guard, then track on left is Trail
            Lake trailhead. Zero trip meter.
0.0 ▲   Continue along main trail.
            GPS: N 37°57.26′ W 111°51.86′

▼ 0.0   Continue along main trail.
7.3 ▲   SO Track on right is Trail Lake trailhead.
            Zero trip meter at cattle guard.

▼ 1.2   SO Track on left.
6.1 ▲   SO Track on right.

▼ 2.0   SO Track on right to the Sinkholes. Crossing
            the Salt Lake Meridian (longitude line).
5.3 ▲   SO Track on left to the Sinkholes. Crossing
            the Salt Lake Meridian (longitude line).
            GPS: N 37°57.73′ W 111°50.53′

▼ 2.2   SO Track on left.
5.1 ▲   SO Track on right.

▼ 2.6   SO Track on left gives access to Poison
            Creek. Also goes to snowmobile rest
            station.
4.7 ▲   SO Track on right gives access to Poison
            Creek. Also goes to snowmobile rest
            station.
            GPS: N 37°58.03′ W 111°49.97′

▼ 3.0   SO The Gap trailhead on right, Great
            Western Trail access point.
4.3 ▲   SO The Gap trailhead on left, Great
            Western Trail access point.
            GPS: N 37°58.18′ W 111°49.59′

▼ 3.2   SO Track on left.
4.1 ▲   SO Track on right.

▼ 3.7   SO Track on right to Velvet Lake.
3.6 ▲   SO Track on left to Velvet Lake.
            GPS: N 37°58.41′ W 111°48.91′

▼ 3.9   SO Intersection.
3.4 ▲   SO Intersection.

▼ 4.5   SO Track on left.
2.8 ▲   SO Track on right.

▼ 6.1   SO Cattle guard.
1.2 ▲   SO Cattle guard.

▼ 7.1   SO FR 465 on left to Coyote Hollow.
0.2 ▲   SO FR 465 on right to Coyote Hollow.

▼ 7.3   SO FR 139 on left to Pollywog Lake. Zero
            trip meter.
0.0 ▲   Continue along main trail.
            GPS: N 38°00.82′ W 111°46.52′

▼ 0.0   Continue on main trail.
3.8 ▲   SO FR 139 on right to Pollywog Lake. Zero
            trip meter.

▼ 1.3   SO Track on right.
2.5 ▲   SO Track on left.

▼ 1.9   SO Track on left to Lake Philo. Small dam
            on right is Indian Spring Reservoir.
1.9 ▲   SO Track on right to Lake Philo. Small dam
            on left is Indian Spring Reservoir.
            GPS: N 38°00.71′ W 111°44.44′

▼ 2.8   SO Track on right.
1.0 ▲   SO Track on left.

▼ 3.0   SO Cattle guard; trail crosses Davis Flat.
0.8 ▲   SO Cattle guard; trail crosses Davis Flat.

▼ 3.3   SO Track on left.
0.5 ▲   SO Track on right.

▼ 3.5   SO Corral on left.
0.3 ▲   SO Corral on right.

▼ 3.8   Trail ends at Southwest #26: Posey
            Lake Road (FR 154). Turn right for
            Escalante, left for Bicknell.
0.0 ▲   On Southwest #26: Posey Lake Road
            (FR 154), 26.5 miles south of Bicknell,
            zero trip meter and turn northwest on
            FR 140, following sign for Escalante
            Summit.
            GPS: N 38°00.20′ W 111°42.42′

Escalante Summit Trail

STARTING POINT Utah 12, 4 miles west of Escalante
FINISHING POINT Widtsoe Junction on Utah 22
TOTAL MILEAGE 21.1 miles
UNPAVED MILEAGE 21.1 miles
DRIVING TIME 1.5 hours
ELEVATION RANGE 6,100–9,500 feet
USUALLY OPEN May to October
DIFFICULTY RATING 1
SCENIC RATING 8
REMOTENESS RATING +0

Special Attractions
- Access to a network of trails in the Dixie National Forest.
- Interesting drive down two different canyons.
- Backcountry camping opportunities.

Description
This trail runs through the Dixie National Forest and provides a more northern, backcountry alternative to the highway between Escalante and Bryce Canyon National Park. It leaves Utah 12, 4 miles west of Escalante, at the sign for Main Canyon Road. The entire trail is a graded gravel road that is suitable for passenger vehicles. For the first few miles, the trail runs through Main Canyon following along Birch Creek. It gradually climbs until it reaches Escalante Summit, the high point of the trail at 9,302 feet. From here, Southwest #33: Griffin Road leads north and Southwest #37: Barney Top Trail leads south.

The trail continues down into Escalante Canyon. The first mile is a fairly steep descent along switchbacks; then the trail eases off to follow Sweetwater Creek through the canyon. A variety of backcountry campsites are scattered along here, and they offer better camping opportunities than the east end of the trail.

After the summit, you reach Widtsoe Junction and Utah 22 in 7.3 miles. There is

The remains of an old log cabin stand to the northeast of the Escalante Summit Trail

little left of Widtsoe these days—just a few cabins and some more recent but still abandoned housing.

Current Road Information
Dixie National Forest
Escalante Ranger District
PO Box 246
Escalante, UT 84726
(435) 826-5400

Escalante Interagency Office
755 West Main
Escalante, UT 84726
(435) 826-5499

Map References
BLM Escalante, Panguitch
USFS Dixie National Forest: Escalante Ranger District
USGS 1:24,000 Flake Mt. East, Sweetwater Creek, Griffin Point, Wide Hollow Reservoir
1:100,000 Panguitch, Escalante
Maptech CD-ROM: Escalante/Dixie National Forest
Utah Atlas & Gazetteer, pp. 19, 27
Utah Travel Council #4
Other: BLM Map of the Grand Staircase–Escalante National Monument

Two small waterfalls punctuate the course of the Escalante River

Route Directions

▼ 0.0   From Utah 12, 4 miles west of Escalante, turn west onto the graded gravel road at sign for Main Canyon Road and zero trip meter.

5.0 ▲   Trail ends at Utah 12. Turn left for Escalante, right for Bryce Canyon National Park.

GPS: N 37°45.91 W 111°40.93'

▼ 0.1   SO Gravel road on right to Barker Reservoir.

4.9 ▲   SO Gravel road on left to Barker Reservoir.

▼ 5.0   SO Cattle guard, then enter Dixie National Forest and zero trip meter. The trail is now FR 17.

0.0 ▲   Continue along FR 17.

GPS: N 37°46.86' W 111°46.03'

▼ 0.0   Continue along FR 17.

1.6 ▲   SO Leave Dixie National Forest, zero trip meter, and cross cattle guard.

▼ 1.2   SO Faint track on left.

0.4 ▲   SO Faint track on right.

▼ 1.6   SO Gravel road on left is Southwest #35: Corn Creek Road (FR 141). Zero trip meter.

0.0 ▲   Continue along FR 17.

GPS: N 37°47.56' W 111°47.65'

▼ 0.0   Continue along FR 17.

7.2 ▲   SO Gravel road on right is Southwest #35: Corn Creek Road (FR 141). Zero trip meter.

▼ 0.8   SO Mill site on right.

6.4 ▲   SO Mill site on left.

▼ 0.9   SO Small track on right.

6.3 ▲   SO Small track on left.

▼ 1.2   SO Two old cabins on right of trail and one on left of trail.

6.0 ▲   SO Two old cabins on left of trail and one on right of trail.

GPS: N 37°48.27' W 111°48.66'

▼ 1.8   BL Track on right.

5.4 ▲   SO Track on left.

▼ 2.5   SO Track on right.

4.7 ▲   SO Track on left.

▼ 2.7   SO Track on right.

4.5 ▲   SO Track on left.

▼ 3.4   SO Griffin Point Hiking Trail on right to Barker Reservoir; also track on left.

3.8 ▲   SO Griffin Point Hiking Trail on left to Barker Reservoir; also track on right.

GPS: N 37°49.47' W 111°50.65'

▼ 4.2   SO Track on left.

3.0 ▲   SO Track on right.

▼ 4.4   SO Track on left.

2.8 ▲   SO Track on right.

▼ 5.3   SO Track on right.

1.9 ▲   SO Track on left.

▼ 7.1	SO	Cattle guard.
0.1 ▲	SO	Cattle guard.

▼ 7.2	SO	Escalante Summit. Track on right is Southwest #33: Griffin Road (FR 140), main track on left is Southwest #37: Barney Top Trail (FR 142). Zero trip meter.
0.0 ▲		Continue toward Escalante.
		GPS: N 37°49.51' W 111°52.90'

▼ 0.0		Continue toward Widtsoe Junction.
7.3 ▲	SO	Escalante Summit. Track on left is Southwest #33: Griffin Road (FR 140), main track on right is Southwest #37: Barney Top Trail (FR 142). Zero trip meter.

▼ 0.3	SO	Track on left.
7.0 ▲	SO	Track on right.

▼ 0.4	SO	Track on left.
6.9 ▲	SO	Track on right.

▼ 0.7	SO	Track on right.
6.6 ▲	SO	Track on left.

▼ 1.1	SO	Track on left to campsite.
6.2 ▲	SO	Track on right to campsite.

▼ 1.6	SO	Track on left to campsite.

5.7 ▲	SO	Track on right to campsite.

▼ 2.1	SO	Campsite on left.
5.2 ▲	SO	Campsite on right.

▼ 2.2	SO	Track on left to campsite.
5.1 ▲	SO	Track on right to campsite. Trail climbs toward Escalante Summit.

▼ 2.7	SO	Track on right to corral.
4.6 ▲	SO	Track on left to corral.

▼ 3.0	SO	Track on left.
4.3 ▲	SO	Track on right.

▼ 3.6	SO	Track on right.
3.7 ▲	SO	Track on left.

▼ 3.8	SO	Track on right.
3.5 ▲	SO	Track on left.

▼ 4.2	SO	Great Western Trail crosses. Vehicle track on right goes to Southwest #33: Griffin Road; then track on left.
3.1 ▲	SO	Track on right. Road on left is a vehicle track that goes to Southwest #33: Griffin Road. Great Western Trail crosses.
		GPS: N 37°49.61' W 111°56.74'

▼ 4.7	SO	Track on right.
2.6 ▲	SO	Track on left.

SW Trail #34: Escalante Summit Trail

▼ 4.9	SO	Track on right.
2.4 ▲	SO	Track on left.

▼ 5.3	SO	Track on left.
2.0 ▲	SO	Track on right.

▼ 5.7	SO	Leaving Dixie National Forest over cattle guard.
1.6 ▲	SO	Entering Dixie National Forest over cattle guard. Road is now FR 17.

▼ 6.6	SO	Track on left.
0.7 ▲	SO	Track on right.

▼ 6.8	SO	Track on left, then old cabins on left.
0.5 ▲	SO	Old cabins on right, then track on right.

▼ 6.9	SO	Track on left to the remains of Widtsoe.
0.4 ▲	SO	Track on right to the remains of Widtsoe.

▼ 7.1	SO	Track on left.
0.2 ▲	SO	Track on right.

▼ 7.3		Trail finishes at Widtsoe Junction on Utah 22. Turn left for Bryce Canyon National Park.
0.0 ▲		At Widtsoe Junction on Utah 22, turn east up FR 17 signed toward Escalante and zero trip meter.
		GPS: N 37°50.03' W 112°00.11'

Table Cliff Plateau towers above this stretch of Corn Creek Road

SOUTHWEST REGION TRAIL #35

Corn Creek Road

STARTING POINT Southwest #34: Escalante Summit Trail, 6.6 miles west of Utah 12

FINISHING POINT Utah 12, 12.3 miles west of Escalante

TOTAL MILEAGE 14.4 miles

UNPAVED MILEAGE 14.4 miles

DRIVING TIME 1.5 hours

ELEVATION RANGE 7,100–8,700 feet

USUALLY OPEN May to November

DIFFICULTY RATING 1

SCENIC RATING 8

REMOTENESS RATING +0

Special Attractions

■ Easy, scenic route with spectacular views over Table Cliffs.

■ Backcountry alternative route to Utah 12.

Description

This graded road leaves Southwest #34: Escalante Summit Trail (or FR 17, Main Canyon Road) 6.6 miles west of Utah 12. It winds south and rejoins Utah 12 about 12 miles west of Escalante. The trail runs along Corn Creek for 2 miles before climbing up along the eastern flank of the Escalante Mountains. There are striking views to the west of the red-and-white striated Table Cliffs, part of the promontory leading down to Powell Point.

The trail then descends from the pine forest to enter the juniper and sagebrush sloping benches. A multitude of small tracks lead off from this section, and the graded road surface becomes rougher and slightly washed out. In wet weather, there can be muddy sections, but in dry weather the trail is suitable for passenger vehicles.

Current Road Information

Dixie National Forest
Escalante Ranger District
PO Box 246
Escalante, UT 84726
(435) 826-5400

Map References

BLM   Escalante
USFS Dixie National Forest: Escalante
      Ranger District
USGS 1:24,000   Griffin Point, Upper
      Valley
      1:100,000 Escalante
Maptech CD-ROM: Escalante/Dixie
      National Forest
Utah Atlas & Gazetteer, p. 19
Utah Travel Council #4 (incomplete)

Route Directions

▼ 0.0   From Southwest #34: Escalante
         Summit Trail (FR 17, Main Canyon
         Road), turn southwest onto graded
         gravel Corn Creek Road (FR 141)
         following the sign to Upper Valley
         Guard Station, and zero trip meter.
7.5 ▲   Trail finishes at Southwest #34:
         Escalante Summit Trail (FR 17, Main
         Canyon Road). Turn right for Utah 12,
         left for Escalante Summit.
         GPS: N 37°47.56' W 111°47.65'

▼ 0.1   SO Old cabin on left.
7.4 ▲   SO Old cabin on right.

▼ 2.2   BL Fork, unsigned. Road is now graded
           dirt.
5.3 ▲   SO Junction is unsigned. Road is now
           graded gravel.
           GPS: N 37°47.02' W 111°49.95'

▼ 3.7   SO Track on left.
3.8 ▲   SO Track on right.

▼ 5.2   SO Track on left.
2.3 ▲   SO Track on right.

▼ 5.4   SO Track on right.
2.1 ▲   SO Track on left.

▼ 5.7   SO Track on left. Continue around right-
           hand bend for striking view of Table
           Cliffs.
1.8 ▲   SO Striking view of Table Cliffs from left-
           hand bend, then track on right.
           GPS: N 37°45.00' W 111°50.55'

▼ 5.9   SO Cattle guard.
1.6 ▲   SO Cattle guard.

▼ 7.5   TR T-intersection. Turn right on FR 144 to
           Stump Spring; left is FR 147 to Utah
           12. Zero trip meter.
0.0 ▲   Continue on Corn Creek Road (FR 141).
           GPS: N 37°43.83' W 111°50.87'

▼ 0.0   Continue toward Stump Spring
         (FR 144).
3.0 ▲   TL Ahead is FR 147 to Utah 12. Turn left
           onto FR 141, signed as Corn Creek Road.

SW Trail #35: Corn Creek Road

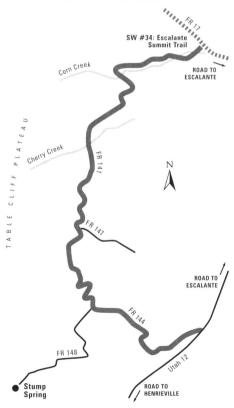

| ▼ 0.9 | SO | Track on left. |
| 2.1 ▲ | SO | Track on right. |

| ▼ 1.0 | SO | Track on left. |
| 2.0 ▲ | SO | Track on right. |

| ▼ 1.2 | SO | Track on left, then track on right. |
| 1.8 ▲ | SO | Track on left, then track on right. |

| ▼ 1.4 | SO | Track on right. |
| 1.6 ▲ | SO | Track on left. |

| ▼ 2.1 | SO | Track on left. |
| 0.9 ▲ | SO | Track on right. |

▼ 3.0	TR	T-intersection, turn right. Zero trip meter.
0.0 ▲		Continue northwest.
		GPS: N 37°42.40′ W 111°50.62′

| ▼ 0.0 | | Continue southeast. |
| 3.9 ▲ | TL | Turn left at intersection. Zero trip meter. |

▼ 0.2	SO	Track on right is FR 148 to Stump Spring.
3.7 ▲	SO	Track on left is FR 148 to Stump Spring.
		GPS: N 37°42.23′ W 111°50.55′

| ▼ 0.7 | SO | Track on left. |
| 3.2 ▲ | SO | Track on right. |

| ▼ 1.2 | SO | Track on left. |
| 2.7 ▲ | SO | Track on right. |

| ▼ 1.6 | SO | Track on left. |
| 2.3 ▲ | SO | Track on right. |

| ▼ 2.5 | SO | Entering private property; remain on main track. |
| 1.4 ▲ | SO | Leaving private property into national forest. |

| ▼ 3.2 | SO | Old cabin on right is private property. |
| 0.7 ▲ | SO | Old cabin on left is private property. |

| ▼ 3.8 | BR | Track on left. |

| 0.1 ▲ | BL | Track on right. |

▼ 3.9		Cross cattle guard, then trail ends at Utah 12. Turn left for Escalante, right for Henrieville.
0.0 ▲		From Utah 12, 12.3 miles west of Escalante, turn onto FR 144 signed toward Upper Valley Guard Station and Stump Spring. The first 1.4 miles cross private property; remain on main track.
		GPS: N 37°41.72′ W 111°47.67′

Powell Point Trail

STARTING POINT Utah 22 (Johns Valley Road) and FR 132
FINISHING POINT Powell Point
TOTAL MILEAGE 14.4 miles
UNPAVED MILEAGE 14.4 miles
DRIVING TIME 1.5 hours
ELEVATION RANGE 7,500–10,100 feet
USUALLY OPEN June to October
DIFFICULTY RATING 3
SCENIC RATING 9
REMOTENESS RATING +0

Special Attractions
- Powell Point lookout.
- Pine Lake camping and fishing.
- Access to ATV and hiking trails.

History
Powell Point, named after American explorer John Wesley Powell, is a prominent bluff on the landscape. Its pink-tinged cliffs are visible for many miles. The point itself is the narrow end to the broad 10,000-foot summit of Table Cliffs.

The highly visible cliffs were used as a navigation reference point by Powell, who led the first exploratory trips down the Colorado River in 1869 and 1871. The expedition geologist, Clarence Dutton, described Powell Point as "the aspect of a vast acropolis crowned with a parthenon."

Description

This route commences in Johns Valley on FR 132, a graded gravel road that climbs gradually into Dixie National Forest. After 5 miles it passes by the popular camping and fishing spot of Pine Lake. The developed national forest campground here (fee required) has secluded sites set among tall pines; it's a short walk to the lake. After the campground, the trail standard becomes a rougher dirt road, which climbs up Pine Canyon and follows along Clay Creek. Many of the tributaries of Clay Creek can wash out quite severely, and the crossings through the wash can be very rough, since large boulders and quantities of rock often wash down. However, this part of the trail is normally suitable for a high-clearance vehicle. There are some sections of shelf road, but although rough, they are wide enough for a full-size vehicle and have ample passing places.

After 11 miles, you reach the turn for Powell Point; Southwest #37: Barney Top Trail also connects here from the north. The sign for Powell Point is very small and easily missed, and the start of the trail looks too narrow to be a proper vehicle trail. This first section is the narrowest, winding through dense pines and aspens. It is bumpy—not from rocks, but from tree roots growing across the track. This first section can also be muddy after rain, with several deep depressions, and you may want to avoid it then. The lack of traction from mud, combined with the tight clearance between the trees, might result in vehicle damage.

After a mile, the trail becomes less twisty, the trees sparser, and the trail surface rockier as it follows the eastern edge of Table Cliff Plateau, affording great views east. There are several campsites tucked into the trees along the edge of the escarpment. The trail ends at a turnaround. From here, you can hike just over half a mile to Powell Point proper at the end of the plateau.

The Powell Point Trail winds through thick stands of aspen and pine

Current Road Information

Dixie National Forest
Escalante Ranger District
PO Box 246
Escalante, UT 84726
(435) 826-5400

Escalante Interagency Office
755 West Main
Escalante, UT 84726
(435) 826-5499

Map References

BLM Panguitch, Escalante
USFS Dixie National Forest: Escalante
      Ranger District
USGS: 1:24,000 Flake Mt. East,
      Sweetwater Creek, Pine Lake,
      Upper Valley
      1:100,000 Panguitch, Escalante
Maptech CD-ROM: Escalante/Dixie
      National Forest
Utah Atlas & Gazetteer, pp. 27, 19
Utah Travel Council # 4 (incomplete)
Other: BLM Map of the Grand Staircase–
      Escalante National Monument
      (incomplete)

Pine Lake at Sunset

Route Directions

▼ 0.0   On Utah 22 (Johns Valley Road), 2.5 miles south of Widtsoe Junction, turn east onto FR 132 (signed toward Pine Lake) and zero trip meter.

5.1 ▲   Trail finishes at Utah 22. Turn right for Widtsoe Junction, left for Tropic.

         GPS: N 37°47.84' W 112°01.20'

▼ 0.4   SO   Enter Dixie National Forest over cattle guard.

4.7 ▲   SO   Leaving Dixie National Forest over cattle guard.

▼ 0.6   SO   Track on right.
4.5 ▲   SO   Track on left.

▼ 1.0   SO   Track on left, then track on right.
4.1 ▲   SO   Track on left, then track on right.

▼ 1.5   SO   Track on left, then faint track on right.
3.6 ▲   SO   Faint track on left, then track on right.

▼ 2.3   SO   Track on left to campsite.
2.8 ▲   SO   Track on right to campsite.

▼ 3.0   SO   Cattle guard.
2.1 ▲   SO   Cattle guard.

▼ 4.6   SO   Cross over Clay Creek on culvert.
0.5 ▲   SO   Cross over Clay Creek on culvert.

▼ 4.7   SO   Track on left.
0.4 ▲   SO   Track on right.

▼ 5.0   SO   Track on right to Pine Lake (0.2 miles).
0.1 ▲   SO   Track on left to Pine Lake (0.2 miles).

▼ 5.1   BL   Road on right to Pine Lake Campground. Zero trip meter.
0.0 ▲   Continue along graded gravel road.

         GPS: N 37°44.78' W 111°57.13'

▼ 0.0   Continue along rougher trail away from Pine Lake.
5.8 ▲   TR   Road on left to Pine Lake Campground. Zero trip meter.

SW Trail #36: Powell Point Trail

▼ 0.1   SO   Track on left is part of the Great Western Trail and goes to Sweetwater.

5.7 ▲   SO   Track on right is part of the Great Western Trail and goes to Sweetwater.

▼ 0.4   SO   ATV staging area and trailhead on right.

5.4 ▲   SO   ATV staging area and trailhead on left.

▼ 0.6   SO   Track on left, then track on right.

5.2 ▲   SO   Track on left, then track on right.

GPS: N 37°44.68′ W 111°56.51′

▼ 0.7   SO   Cross through rough stony wash.

5.1 ▲   SO   Cross through rough stony wash.

▼ 0.8   SO   Track on right.

5.0 ▲   SO   Track on left.

▼ 1.0   SO   Track on right.

4.8 ▲   SO   Track on left.

▼ 1.3   SO   Cross through rough stony wash.

4.5 ▲   SO   Cross through rough stony wash.

▼ 1.6   SO   Cross through rough stony wash.

4.2 ▲   SO   Cross through rough stony wash.

▼ 1.8   SO   Cross through rough stony wash.

4.0 ▲   SO   Cross through rough stony wash.

▼ 2.2   SO   Cattle guard.

3.6 ▲   SO   Cattle guard.

▼ 3.1   SO   Track right to camping area.

2.7 ▲   SO   Track left to camping area.

▼ 5.8   TR   Turn right onto small trail signed for Powell Point. Straight ahead is Southwest #37: Barney Top Trail (FR 142). Zero trip meter.

0.0 ▲   TL   Return from Powell Point. Turn left for Pine Lake and Utah 22, turn right on FR 142 for Southwest #37: Barney Top Trail. Zero trip meter.

GPS: N 37°44.06′ W 111°52.24′

▼ 0.0   Continue on small trail as it winds through the trees.

▼ 0.3   SO   Muddy section.

▼ 1.4   SO   Water Canyon hiking trail on left.

GPS: N 37°43.31′ W 111°53.31′

▼ 1.8   SO   Trail runs on eastern edge of Table Cliff Plateau.

▼ 3.1   SO   Campsite with views on left. Many small campsites are on the edge tucked into the trees.

▼ 3.5   UT   End of vehicle trail. Scenic overlook is 3,000 feet along a hiking trail. Return to the junction of FR 132 and FR 142.

GPS: N 37°41.61′ W 111°53.79′

<hr>

SOUTHWEST REGION TRAIL #37

Barney Top Trail

STARTING POINT Intersection of Southwest #33: Griffin Road and Southwest #34: Escalante Summit Trail

FINISHING POINT Southwest #36: Powell Point Trail (FR 132)

TOTAL MILEAGE 8.3 miles

UNPAVED MILEAGE 8.3 miles

DRIVING TIME 2 hours

ELEVATION RANGE 9,000–10,700 feet

USUALLY OPEN June to October

DIFFICULTY RATING 5

SCENIC RATING 9

REMOTENESS RATING +0

Special Attractions

■ Moderately challenging trail with a variety of driving conditions.

■ A wide range of backcountry campsites on Barney Top.

■ Panoramic views east over the Upper Valley.

Description

This exciting trail connects Southwest #34: Escalante Summit Trail and Southwest #33: Griffin Road with Southwest #36: Powell Point Trail. The trail is a moderately difficult drive over a variety of surfaces and conditions, but in dry conditions it is suitable for most high-clearance 4WDs.

A white cliff face falls away to the side of the Barney Top Trail

The trail starts from Southwest #34: Escalante Summit Trail (FR 17) at Escalante Summit, 7.3 miles east of Widtsoe Junction. The trail is marked as FR 142 on the ground; yet Dixie National Forest maps show it as FR 143. There are three alternatives at the junction; follow the sign for Barney Top, taking the middle trail south.

The narrow trail is only wide enough for a single vehicle, and it climbs almost immediately, winding around the eastern edge of the ridge top. It can be very muddy if there has been recent rain and may be impassable. On a clear day, you can see east to the Henry Mountains. After 2.7 miles, the trail be-

comes harder, has larger rocks, and then there's a section of narrow shelf road that crosses a rocky scree slope. The shelf road climbs steeply and the surface can be loose—this is the most difficult part of the trail. Passing places are limited, and you may need to reverse to let on-coming vehicles pass. Passengers will enjoy the views east even if the driver doesn't! After 3 miles you reach Barney Top, and the trail becomes easier as it traverses open meadows and pine and aspen forest. There are ample backcountry campsites along this section.

After passing by the communications tower, the trail descends to join Southwest #36: Powell Point Trail. The descent is easier than the ascent, as the shelf road is wider and the surface offers better traction. The trail finishes where the Powell Point Trail turns toward the Powell Point spur.

Current Road Information

Dixie National Forest
Escalante Ranger District
PO Box 246
Escalante, UT 84726
(435) 826-5400

Map References

BLM   Escalante
USFS   Dixie National Forest: Escalante
       Ranger District
USGS   1:24,000   Sweetwater Creek,
       Griffin Point, Upper Valley
       1:100,000 Escalante
Maptech CD-ROM: Escalante/Dixie
       National Forest
Utah Atlas & Gazetteer, pp. 19, 27

Route Directions

▼ 0.0   On Southwest #34: Escalante Summit
         Trail (FR 17), 7.3 miles east of Widtsoe
         Junction, zero trip meter and turn
         south on FR 142, following sign to
         Barney Top.

View to the east through the rocky crags and small aspens of Barney Top

5.7 ▲		Trail finishes at Escalante Summit and Southwest #34: Escalante Summit Trail (FR 17). Turn left for Widtsoe Junction, right for Escalante. Straight ahead is Southwest #33: Griffin Road.

GPS: N 37°49.51' W 111°52.90'

▼ 0.1 SO Campsite on left with good views. Trail starts to climb.
5.6 ▲ SO Campsite on right with good views.

▼ 1.0 SO Track on left.
4.7 ▲ SO Track on right.
GPS: N 37°48.75' W 111°53.01'

▼ 1.2 SO Track on right.
4.5 ▲ SO Track on left.

▼ 1.6 SO Viewpoint on left. Views east to the Henry Mountains.
4.1 ▲ SO Viewpoint on right. Views east to the Henry Mountains.
GPS: N 37°48.47' W 111°53.27'

▼ 2.0 SO Track on right at clearing.
3.7 ▲ SO Track on left at clearing.

▼ 2.3 SO Cross over small scree face.
3.4 ▲ SO Cross over small scree face.

▼ 2.7 SO Cross scree slope on narrow shelf road.
3.0 ▲ SO End of shelf road.

▼ 3.0 SO End of shelf road, trail levels out. Track on right.
2.7 ▲ SO Track on left. Cross scree slope on narrow shelf road; descend to Escalante Summit.
GPS: N 37°47.45' W 111°53.21'

▼ 3.5 SO Track on right crosses Barney Top (open meadow).
2.2 ▲ SO Track on left crosses Barney Top.

▼ 3.7 SO Track on right across meadow. Many backcountry campsites.
2.0 ▲ SO Track on left across meadow. Many backcountry campsites.

▼ 4.5 BL Track on right into grassy area.
1.2 ▲ BR Track on left into grassy area.

▼ 4.9 SO Track on right.
0.8 ▲ BR Track on left.

▼ 5.7 SO Track on right, then communications tower immediately on left of trail. Zero trip meter at tower.
0.0 ▲ Continue north.
GPS: N 37°45.52' W 111°52.35'

▼ 0.0 Continue south.
2.6 ▲ SO Pass second communications tower immediately on right of trail and zero trip meter. Track on left after tower.

SW Trail #37: Barney Top Trail

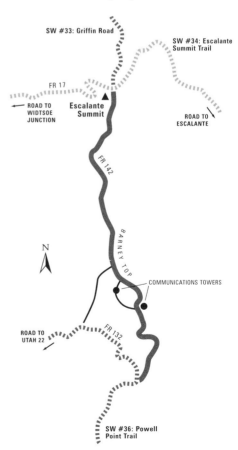

| ▼ 0.1 | SO | Track on right to second communications tower. |
| 2.5 ▲ | SO | Track on left to communications tower. |

| ▼ 0.5 | SO | Trail descends wide shelf road. |
| 2.1 ▲ | SO | End of ascent. |

| ▼ 0.9 | SO | Views right to Pine Lake. Trail standard is now easier. |
| 1.7 ▲ | SO | Views left to Pine Lake. Trail ascends wide shelf road; standard becomes harder. |

| ▼ 1.3 | SO | Track on right. |
| 1.3 ▲ | SO | Track on left. |

| ▼ 1.8 | SO | Track on left. |
| 0.8 ▲ | SO | Track on right. |

| ▼ 2.5 | SO | Campsite and views on left. |
| 0.1 ▲ | SO | Campsite and views on right. |

| ▼ 2.6 | | Trail finishes at Southwest #36: Powell Point Trail (FR 132). Turn left to visit Powell Point, right for Pine Lake and Utah 22. |
| 0.0 ▲ | | 10.9 miles from the western end of Southwest #36: Powell Point Trail (FR 132) at the spur to Powell Point, zero trip meter and continue north on FR 142. |

GPS: N 37°44.06′ W 111°52.24′

Tantalus Creek Trail

STARTING POINT Utah 12, 16.2 miles south of Utah 24

FINISHING POINT Capitol Reef National Park

TOTAL MILEAGE 17.8 miles

UNPAVED MILEAGE 17.8 miles

DRIVING TIME 2 hours

ELEVATION RANGE 5,800–8,600 feet

USUALLY OPEN May to November

DIFFICULTY RATING 4

SCENIC RATING 10

REMOTENESS RATING +1

Special Attractions

- Exciting trail partly within Capitol Reef National Park.
- Range of scenery from pine forest to red rock desert.
- Fishing and camping opportunities at Lower Bowns Reservoir.

Description

This trail sees surprisingly little use considering that it is partly within a popular national park. Moderately difficult, the trail encompasses a wide variety of scenery and trail surfaces. It starts from Utah 12, 16.2 miles south of its junction with Utah 24 near Torrey. Turn east on FR 186 (on *Delorme* it says 181 but on

Smooth section of the Tantalus Creek Trail overlooking Capitol Reef

the Dixie NF it is 186), which begins as a graded gravel road and gradually descends through the shady pine forest toward Lower Bowns Reservoir. ATVs have their own trail, the Rosebud ATV trail, which takes a slightly more meandering route to the reservoir. Dispersed camping is permitted along the trail, and there are several pretty sites in pine clearings on the banks of a small creek. The trail passes the Wildcat Revegetation Program, an area cleared and then reseeded with grass and shrubbage to provide improved forage for deer and grazing livestock.

Driving below the protruding rock formations along South Draw Wash

After 3 miles the trail forks, with the right-hand track going to Lower Bowns Reservoir. The reservoir has more lovely camping areas (no facilities), some under the shade of large pines, but most in the open around its shores. The area is very popular in the summer for both camping and fishing. From the fork to the reservoir, the trail is smaller, with long stretches of a very fine, powdery surface. The grader stops at a large corral at the start of Jorgensen Flat. From there the trail is formed and narrower. There are some rocky sections as it drops further to cross Tantalus Creek, 2,000 feet lower than Utah 12.

Jorgensen Flat is very pretty; the sagebrush benches are surrounded by red rocks and sandstone. Pleasant Creek cuts a deep canyon on the left-hand side of the trail. The approach to Tantalus Creek zigzags down a sandy gully, which can be washed out; it is also hard to climb back out—both in very dry and very wet weather!

From the creek, the trail gently climbs as it runs along Tantalus Flats. This section can be very muddy when wet. The trail then swings east and enters Capitol Reef National Park, 10 miles from the start of the trail. Dispersed camping is not permitted in the park, but there are some lovely sites at the end of the valley before the trail enters the park. The first part of the trail within the national park is the roughest section, as it climbs through a rocky gap toward the Waterpocket Fold and then drops to enter

South Draw. Once in the draw, the trail follows the creekbed for the next 3.5 miles before crossing Pleasant Creek. After Pleasant Creek, the road returns to graded dirt until it finishes at the end of the paved scenic drive from Fruita and the park's information center. The portion of the trail within Capitol Reef National Park is subject to park fees.

Current Road Information

Capitol Reef National Park
HC-70 Box 15
Torrey, UT 84775
(435) 425-3791

Dixie National Forest
Fremont River Ranger District
PO Box 129; 138 South Main St.
Loa, UT 84747
(435) 425-3702

Map References

BLM   Loa
USFS   Dixie National Forest: Teasdale
      Ranger District
USGS   1:24,000   Lower Bowns Reservoir,
      Grover, Golden Throne, Bear Canyon
      1:100,000 Loa
Maptech CD-ROM: Escalante/Dixie
      National Forest
Trails Illustrated, #707
Utah Atlas & Gazetteer, p. 28
Utah Travel Council #5
Other: Capitol Reef National Park map

Route Directions

▼ 0.0   From Utah 12, 16.2 miles south of Utah 24, turn southeast along the graded gravel FR 186, following sign to Lower Bowns Reservoir. Zero trip meter.

3.0 ▲   Trail ends at Utah 12. Turn right for Torrey, left for Boulder Town.

GPS: N 38°06.01' W 111°20.22'

▼ 0.2 SO Rosebud ATV trail on left. ATV unloading and parking at the trailhead. No ATVs on the graded road past this point.

2.8 ▲ SO Rosebud ATV trail on right. ATV unloading and parking at the trailhead.

GPS: N 38°05.86' W 111°20.10'

▼ 0.3 SO Track on right to Park Ridge.

2.7 ▲ SO Track on left to Park Ridge.

GPS: N 38°05.82' W 111°20.04'

▼ 0.6 SO Track on left.

2.4 ▲ SO Track on right.

▼ 0.9 SO Track on right to campsite.

2.1 ▲ SO Track on left to campsite.

▼ 1.2 SO Start of dispersed camping area alongside trail.

1.8 ▲ SO End of dispersed camping area.

▼ 2.2 SO Cattle guard.

0.8 ▲ SO Cattle guard.

▼ 2.3 SO Slickrock Trail (hiking, pack, and ATV only) enters on left and leaves on right.

0.7 ▲ SO Slickrock Trail (hiking, pack, and ATV only) enters on left and leaves on right.

GPS: N 38°06.28' W 111°17.85'

▼ 2.5 SO Wildcat Revegetation Project on left.

0.5 ▲ SO Wildcat Revegetation Project on right.

▼ 3.0 BL Track on right to Lower Bowns Reservoir. Proceed along FR 168 on left marked as Tantalus 4x4 Road. Zero trip meter.

0.0 ▲   Continue toward Utah 12.

▼ 0.0   Continue toward Jorgensen Flat.

4.2 ▲ SO Track on left to Lower Bowns Reservoir.

▼ 0.2 SO Track on right is Rosebud ATV trail. ATVs are permitted on the main trail from this point.

4.0 ▲ SO Track on left is Rosebud ATV trail. ATVs are not permitted on the main trail from this point.

▼ 0.5 SO Slaughter Flat. Track on left is Rosebud ATV trail.

3.7 ▲ SO Slaughter Flat. Track on right is Rosebud ATV trail.

GPS: N 38°06.84' W 111°16.81'

▼ 1.1 SO Track on right to the north end of Lower Bowns Reservoir.

3.1 ▲ SO Track on left to the north end of Lower Bowns Reservoir.

GPS: N 38°07.12' W 111°16.34'

▼ 2.2 SO Cattle guard, then corral on right. Trail is now ungraded.

2.0 ▲ SO Corral on left, then cattle guard. Trail is now graded.

▼ 2.4 SO Track on left. Pleasant Creek is on left in a deep gorge.

1.8 ▲ SO Track on right.

▼ 3.7 SO Faint track on left to campsites along the ridge overlooking Pleasant Creek.

0.5 ▲ SO Faint track on right to campsites along the ridge overlooking Pleasant Creek.

▼ 4.2 SO Track on left is recommended only for vehicles fewer than 50 inches wide. Zero trip meter.

0.0 ▲   Continue along Jorgensen Flat. Pleasant Creek is on right in a deep gorge.

GPS: N 38°08.65' W 111°13.49'

▼ 0.0   Continue toward Capitol Reef National Park.

3.0 ▲ SO Track on right is recommended only for

vehicles fewer than 50 inches wide. Zero trip meter.

▼ 0.1   SO   Cross through wash.
2.9 ▲   SO   Cross through wash.

▼ 0.4   SO   Trail winds down to Tantalus Creek.
2.6 ▲   SO   End of climb from Tantalus Creek.

▼ 0.5   SO   Track on right.
2.5 ▲   SO   Track on left.

▼ 0.7   BL   Down at the creek, bear north alongside creek.
2.3 ▲   BR   Sandy climb out of Tantalus Creek gully.
    GPS: N 38°08.42′ W 111°13.17′

▼ 0.8   SO   Cross through Tantalus Creek. Small spring on right at exit flows out of a crack in the rock. Trail climbs out of creek gully.
2.2 ▲   SO   Cross through Tantalus Creek. Small spring on left at entrance flows out of a crack in the rock. Trail follows south alongside creek.
    GPS: N 38°08.39′ W 111°13.12′

▼ 0.9   SO   Cattle guard.
2.1 ▲   SO   Cattle guard.

▼ 2.3   BL   Track on right.
0.7 ▲   SO   Track on left.

▼ 2.6   BL   Track on right. Small arch on top of cliff on right.
0.4 ▲   SO   Second entrance to track on left. Small arch on top of cliff on left.
    GPS: N 38°07.42′ W 111°11.63′

▼ 2.7   SO   Second entrance to track on right, then cattle guard.
0.3 ▲   BR   Cattle guard, then track on left.

▼ 3.0   SO   Entering Capitol Reef National Park. Zero trip meter.
0.0 ▲   Continue toward Tantalus Creek.
    GPS: N 38°07.54′ W 111°11.29′

▼ 0.0   Continue into Capitol Reef National Park.
4.9 ▲   SO   Leaving Capitol Reef National Park. Zero trip meter.

▼ 1.4   SO   Cross through wash. Trail crosses wash numerous times and runs alongside or in the wash for the next 2.5 miles.
3.5 ▲   SO   Trail leaves South Draw.

▼ 3.9   SO   Trail leaves South Draw.
1.0 ▲   SO   Trail enters South Draw. Trail runs in or alongside the wash and crosses it numerous times for the next 2.5 miles.
    GPS: N 38°10.04′ W 111°10.58′

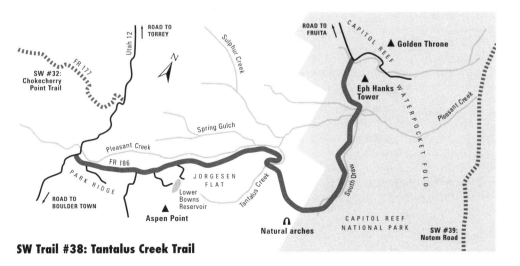

SW Trail #38: Tantalus Creek Trail

▼ 4.2   SO Cross through small, tight wash.
0.7 ▲   SO Cross through small, tight wash.

▼ 4.5   SO Cross through South Draw.
0.4 ▲   SO Cross through South Draw.

▼ 4.6   SO Enter wash.
0.3 ▲   SO Exit wash.

▼ 4.8   SO Exit wash.
0.1 ▲   SO Enter wash.

▼ 4.9   SO Cross through Pleasant Creek. Parking area and pit toilets on left. Zero trip meter.
0.0 ▲   Continue on South Draw 4x4 Road.
      GPS: N 38°10.81′ W 111°10.81′

▼ 0.0   Continue on graded dirt road.
2.7 ▲   SO Parking area and pit toilets on right. Zero trip meter and cross through Pleasant Creek.

▼ 0.1   SO Track on left.
2.6 ▲   SO Track on right.

▼ 0.2   SO Pass through stockyards and ranch buildings.
2.5 ▲   SO Pass through stockyards and ranch buildings.

▼ 0.4   SO Track on right is for authorized vehicles only. Trail is now graded dirt.
2.3 ▲   SO Track on left is for authorized vehicles only. Trail is now ungraded dirt.

▼ 0.5   SO Cross through wash.
2.2 ▲   SO Cross through wash.

▼ 0.6   SO Cross through fence line. Track on right is for authorized vehicles only.
2.1 ▲   SO Track on left is for authorized vehicles only; then cross through fence line.

▼ 1.8   SO Golden Throne viewpoint.
0.9 ▲   SO Golden Throne viewpoint.

▼ 1.9   SO Cross through wash.
0.8 ▲   SO Cross through wash.

▼ 2.2   SO Cross through wash.

▼ 0.5 ▲   SO Cross through wash.

▼ 2.6   SO Cross through wash.
0.1 ▲   SO Cross through wash.

▼ 2.7   Trail ends at the paved scenic national park drive from Fruita. Turn left for Fruita and for park information center.
0.0 ▲   At end of the paved scenic national park drive from Fruita and the Capitol Reef National Park information center, zero trip meter and turn south, following the sign for Pleasant Creek Road.
      GPS: N 38°12.50′ W 111°11.66′

Notom Road

STARTING POINT Notom Road at Utah 24, eastern edge of Capitol Reef National Park
FINISHING POINT Southwest #40: Burr Trail
TOTAL MILEAGE 31 miles
UNPAVED MILEAGE 26.3 miles
DRIVING TIME 2 hours
ELEVATION RANGE 5,000–5,700 feet
USUALLY OPEN Year-round
DIFFICULTY RATING 2
SCENIC RATING 9
REMOTENESS RATING +0

Special Attractions
- Old town site of Notom.
- Views of the Waterpocket Fold and Oyster Shell Reef within Capitol Reef National Park.

History
Notom evolved from the settlement of Pleasant Creek, which was first settled in 1886 by Jorgen Christian Smith. When a post office was built, the state would not allow the name Pleasant Creek to be used, as there were already other settlements by that name. Smith suggested the name Notom for reasons unknown, and that is what the settlement came to be called.

The well-maintained trail drops down onto Notom Bench

Notom in the early days didn't amount to much, and many of the original families moved away. In 1904, an ex-cattleman, William Bowns, purchased land at Notom and farther to the south and built a large sheep property he named Sandy Ranch. The flocks, numbering an estimated 21,000 total animals, grazed on Boulder Mountain to the west and the Henry Mountains to the east and in the desert in between. The wool was taken to Salina for sale, while sheep for market were taken to the railroad in Green River or driven to Marysvale or Salina. Coyotes were a constant threat, but the state paid a bounty of six dollars per coyote skin, which helped to keep the problem in check. Following the Great Depression, sheep were deemed unprofitable, and the ranch slowly returned to cattle.

Another major ranching family around Notom was the Durfey family, which settled in the area in 1919. They, too, concentrated on sheep, but moved to cattle when the grazing rights for sheep were cut back by the forest service.

Sandy Ranch and Notom shared the water rights for Oak and Pleasant Creeks in an unusual arrangement. Notom had rights to the water from April 1 to October 30; the remainder of the year the water was diverted into Bowns Reservoir and used by Sandy Ranch.

In the 1950s the demand for uranium was so strong that a special use permit allowed mining within what was then the Capitol Reef National Monument. Notom Road saw a lot of traffic as Jeeps drove in and out of the park all day, and ore trucks passed by on their way to the processing plants at Moab and Marysvale.

Today, there is little to see in Notom; the town is mainly ranch property owned by the Durfey family.

Description

This easygoing route passes through the old town site of Notom and across the Sandy Creek Benches to travel along inside the Waterpocket Fold in Capitol Reef National Park. It is often suitable for passenger cars in dry weather, but loose sand, bulldust, and a couple of rough wash crossings make it preferable to have a high-clearance vehicle.

Notom Road leaves Utah 24 on the eastern edge of Capitol Reef National Park. The first part of the trail is paved road as it crosses over

An old uranium mining truck in Notom

Pleasant Creek and enters the settlement of Notom, now just a few private houses and ranch buildings. The trail crosses Notom Bench with spectacular and wide-ranging views east over Thompson Mesa to the Henry Mountains and west to the Waterpocket Fold in Capitol Reef National Park.

At Sandy Junction, a major trail leads east into the Henry Mountains and joins up with Southwest #47: Bull Creek Pass Trail. Notom Road continues south and enters Capitol Reef National Park. It goes through the Narrows and runs inside the Waterpocket Fold, with the Oyster Shell Reef to the west. The reef, named for the fossilized oyster shells found along its length, is a jagged yet delicate spine of rock that parallels the main Waterpocket Fold. The trail finishes at Southwest #40: Burr Trail, a few miles from the base of the Burr Trail switchbacks.

If you are planning to camp along this route, be aware that there is a lot of private property interspersed with the federal lands. There are some pleasant sites to be found on some of the side trails. Within the park, camping is restricted to the free Cedar Mesa Campground, which you pass 2 miles after entering the park.

Current Road Information

Capitol Reef National Park
HC-70 Box 15
Torrey, UT 84775
(435) 425-3791

Escalante Interagency Office
755 West Main
Escalante, UT 84726
(435) 826-5499

Map References

BLM   Loa, Escalante
USGS 1:24,000   Fruita, Caineville, Notom,
      Sandy Creek Benches, Bitter Creek
      Divide, Wagon Box Mesa
      1:100,000 Loa, Escalante
Maptech CD-ROM: Escalante/Dixie
      National Forest
Trails Illustrated, #213
Utah Atlas & Gazetteer, p. 28

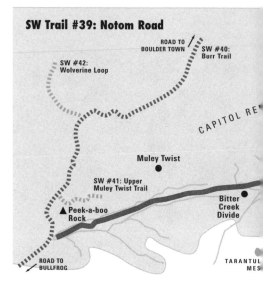

SW Trail #39: Notom Road

Utah Travel Council #5
Other: Capitol Reef National Park map
        Recreation Map of the Henry
        Mountains Area
        BLM Map of the Grand Staircase–
        Escalante National Monument
        (incomplete)

Route Directions

▼ 0.0   From Utah 24, turn south on paved
          Notom Road at the eastern edge of
          Capitol Reef National Park, following
          sign for Bullfrog. Zero trip meter.
4.7 ▲   Trail ends at Utah 24. Turn left for
          Capitol Reef National Park, turn right
          for Hanksville.
          GPS: N 38°17.01′ W 111°07.66′

▼ 1.4 SO Track on right.
3.3 ▲ SO Track on left.

▼ 2.0 SO Track on left, then cross over Pleasant
          Creek on bridge. Track on right after
          bridge.
2.7 ▲ SO Track on left, then cross over Pleasant
          Creek on bridge. Track on right after
          bridge.
          GPS: N 38°15.49′ W 111°07.13′

▼ 2.1 SO Track on left.

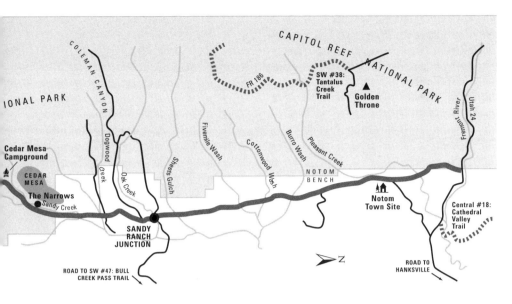

2.6 ▲   SO Track on right.

▼ 3.0   SO Track on left.
1.7 ▲   SO Track on right.

▼ 3.4   SO Notom. Track on left, then track on
              right.
1.3 ▲   SO Notom. Track on left, then track on
              right.

▼ 3.7   SO Track on right, then track on left.
1.0 ▲   SO Track on right, then track on left.

▼ 4.6   SO Track on right, then track on left.
0.1 ▲   SO Track on right, then track on left.

▼ 4.7   SO Road turns to graded gravel. Zero trip
              meter.
0.0 ▲   Continue north.
              GPS: N 38°13.13′ W 111°06.67′

▼ 0.0   Continue south.
8.1 ▲   SO Road turns to pavement. Zero trip meter.

▼ 1.0   SO Track on left.
7.1 ▲   SO Track on right.

▼ 1.1   SO Tracks on right and left.
7.0 ▲   SO Tracks on right and left.

▼ 1.5   SO Tracks on right and left.

6.6 ▲   SO Tracks on right and left.

▼ 2.3   SO Track on left.
5.8 ▲   SO Track on right.

▼ 2.7   SO Cross through Burro Wash.
5.4 ▲   SO Cross through Burro Wash.
              GPS: N 38°10.86′ W 111°05.60′

▼ 3.8   SO Cross through Cottonwood Wash, then
              track on right.
4.3 ▲   SO Track on left, then cross through
              Cottonwood Wash.

▼ 4.7   SO Cattle guard.
3.4 ▲   SO Cattle guard.

▼ 4.8   SO Cross through Fivemile Wash and
              enter Garfield County.
3.3 ▲   SO Enter Wayne County and cross through
              Fivemile Wash.

▼ 5.6   SO Cross through wash.
2.5 ▲   SO Cross through wash.

▼ 5.9   SO Cross through wash.
2.2 ▲   SO Cross through wash.

▼ 7.4   SO Cross through Sheets Gulch.
0.7 ▲   SO Cross through Sheets Gulch.
              GPS: N 38°06.85′ W 111°04.20′

▼ 8.1   BR   Sandy Ranch Junction. Track on left to McMillan Springs Campground and Southwest #47: Bull Creek Pass Trail in the Henry Mountains. Zero trip meter.

0.0 ▲   Continue north.

        GPS: N 38°06.23′ W 111°04.12′

▼ 0.0   Continue south.

5.4 ▲   SO   Sandy Ranch Junction. Track on right to McMillan Springs Campground and Southwest #47: Bull Creek Pass Trail in the Henry Mountains. Zero trip meter.

▼ 0.1   SO   Track on right to Oak Creek Canyon, then cross over Oak Creek on bridge.

5.3 ▲   SO   Cross over Oak Creek on bridge, then track on left to Oak Creek Canyon.

▼ 0.3   SO   Track on left is private.

5.1 ▲   SO   Track on right is private.

▼ 0.5   SO   Cattle guard.

4.9 ▲   SO   Cattle guard.

▼ 0.8   SO   Track on right is private.

4.6 ▲   SO   Track on left is private.

▼ 1.0   SO   Track on left is private.

4.4 ▲   SO   Track on right is private.

▼ 1.7   SO   Tracks on right and left are private.

3.7 ▲   SO   Tracks on right and left are private.

▼ 2.2   SO   Track on right is private.

3.2 ▲   SO   Track on left is private.

▼ 2.8   SO   Track on left, then cross cattle guard, then track on right.

2.6 ▲   SO   Track on left, then cross cattle guard, then track on right.

        GPS: N 38°04.15′ W 111°03.86′

▼ 2.9   SO   Cross through Dogwood Creek.

2.5 ▲   SO   Cross through Dogwood Creek.

▼ 3.9   SO   Cross through Sandy Creek.

1.5 ▲   SO   Cross through Sandy Creek.

▼ 4.5   SO   Track on left.

0.9 ▲   SO   Track on right.

▼ 5.4   SO   Entering Capitol Reef National Park over cattle guard. Zero trip meter.

0.0 ▲   Continue toward Notom.

        GPS: N 38°01.83′ W 111°03.88′

▼ 0.0   Continue into Capitol Reef National Park.

12.8 ▲   SO   Leaving Capitol Reef National Park over cattle guard. Zero trip meter.

▼ 0.1   SO   Cross twice through Sandy Creek wash. Entering The Narrows.

12.7 ▲   SO   Cross twice through Sandy Creek wash. Exit Narrows.

▼ 0.5   SO   Track on left. Exit Narrows.

12.3 ▲   SO   Track on right. Entering The Narrows.

▼ 0.6   SO   Cross through wash.

12.2 ▲   SO   Cross through wash.

▼ 1.3   SO   Cross through wash.

11.5 ▲   SO   Cross through wash.

▼ 1.4   SO   Cross through wash.

11.4 ▲   SO   Cross through wash.

▼ 2.0   SO   Cedar Mesa Campground (free) on right.

10.8 ▲   SO   Cedar Mesa Campground (free) on left.

        GPS: N 38°00.42′ W 111°04.91′

▼ 3.0   SO   Cross through Sandy Creek.

9.8 ▲   SO   Cross through Sandy Creek.

▼ 3.2   SO   Dam on left.

9.6 ▲   SO   Dam on right.

▼ 4.9   SO   Dam on left.

7.9 ▲   SO   Dam on right.

▼ 5.4   SO   Bitter Creek Divide.

7.4 ▲   SO   Bitter Creek Divide.

        GPS: N 37°57.51′ W 111°03.89′

▼ 12.7   SO Cross through wash.

0.1 ▲   SO Cross through wash.

▼ 12.8   Trail ends at Southwest #40: Burr Trail. Turn left for Bullfrog, right to ascend the switchbacks and continue to Boulder Town.

0.0 ▲   From Southwest #40: Burr Trail at the sign for Hanksville, 0.7 miles east of the Burr Trail switchbacks, zero trip meter and turn north on graded road.
    GPS: N 37°51.32' W 111°00.68'

Driving past Circle Cliffs at the eastern end of Long Canyon

SOUTHWEST REGION TRAIL #40

Burr Trail

STARTING POINT Utah 276, 5 miles north of Bullfrog Marina
FINISHING POINT Boulder Town on Utah 12
TOTAL MILEAGE 62.6 miles
UNPAVED MILEAGE 16.8 miles
DRIVING TIME 2 hours
ELEVATION RANGE 3,900–6,600 feet
USUALLY OPEN Year-round
DIFFICULTY RATING 1
SCENIC RATING 10
REMOTENESS RATING +0

Special Attractions
- Long and historic pioneer route.
- Capitol Reef National Park.
- Wide variety of canyon and desert scenery.

History
The Burr Trail was created in the late 1800s as a cow path to move cattle to market and between summer and winter pastures. The trail is named after John Atlantic Burr, a rancher of Burrville, Utah, who was born on board the SS *Brooklyn* in the Atlantic Ocean.

The most striking feature along the route is the Waterpocket Fold, and the most prominent aspect of the trail itself are the Burr Trail switchbacks, which ascend some 1,500 feet in one mile up a cleft in the Waterpocket Fold. This section alone was the

original Burr Trail, though today the entire road from Boulder Town to Bullfrog is known as the Burr Trail. The Waterpocket Fold, a hundred-mile long section of uplift in the earth's crust, was named by explorer John Wesley Powell. Powell observed many "pockets," or hollows, in the rock that retained water. The Waterpocket Fold is several miles wide and consists of weathered, exposed layers of sedimentary rock forming a jagged fin running from Thousand Lake Mountain in the north to Lake Powell in the south.

Just south of the switchbacks on the eastern side of Waterpocket Fold is the site of an old cabin and roundup corral known as "the Post." Nowadays nothing remains except the point of reference on maps.

For more than a hundred years, the Burr Trail was a dirt path. In the early 1990s the trail entered a new era, thanks to judicial courtrooms. Garfield County, in which the entire trail is contained, claimed that the trail was a highway under the Mining Act of 1866, and so it was entitled to improve the road for safety reasons. Despite strong opposition, all but 18 miles of the Burr Trail was paved. The only remaining dirt road section is within Capitol Reef National Park, plus a short section to the east.

Just past the southern end of the trail is Bullfrog and the western shore of Lake Powell across from Hall's Crossing. Charles Hall was an early pioneer in southern Utah. His first venture was to build the ferry that carried the Mormon pioneers across the river at the Hole-in-the-Rock in 1870. He operated his second Colorado River ferry from here in 1881. Hall's ferry ceased operation in 1884 when the Denver & Rio Grande Railroad crossed central Utah and reduced the need for the lower, more difficult route through the south. Hall's ranch in nearby Halls Creek was acquired by Eugene Baker at the turn of the century, but it was swallowed by the rising waters following the damming of Lake Powell.

Description

This long and easy route offers a great variety of scenery. Although it is now predominantly paved road, there are rough sections through Capitol Reef National Park on

A series of switchbacks along the remote Burr Trail

which low-slung vehicles will need to exercise care.

The trail commences 5 miles north of Bullfrog Marina and leads west, traveling within the Glen Canyon National Recreation Area. After crossing Bullfrog Creek, the road gradually climbs to travel along a ridge top. You can see Lake Powell to the south, and there are views to the north over the deep Bullfrog Canyon to the Henry Mountains.

After 7 miles the trail leaves the Glen Canyon National Recreation Area. There are some small 4WD side trails that lead to impressive viewpoints over the deep Bullfrog Canyon. After 18.4 miles of paved road, the trail intersects with Southwest #43: Clay Point Road and becomes a good, graded gravel road that runs north, parallel to Waterpocket Fold.

The trail enters Capitol Reef National Park and passes by a point on maps named "the Post." After the junction with Southwest #39: Notom Road, the trail climbs up the infamous Burr Trail switchbacks. This is the only part of the trail likely to challenge a passenger car in dry weather. The switchbacks climb steeply up a notch in the Waterpocket Fold. The upper end is rough, and rocks in the track bear the marks of undercarriage scrapes from low-slung vehicles. Ideally, travelers should have high-clearance vehicles, but many passenger cars successfully traverse this section.

At the top of the switchbacks, there are a couple of very pleasant picnic areas. The Burr Trail passes by hiking trailheads and a short 4WD spur, Southwest #41: Upper Muley Twist Trail; then it exits Capitol Reef National Park and immediately enters the newly formed Grand Staircase–Escalante National Monument, which is managed by the BLM. The road becomes paved from here all the way to Boulder Town, and it first traverses the plateau, passing by the jagged range of the Studhorse Peaks and Southwest #42: Wolverine Loop, which leads to Wolverine Petrified Wood Area. Several tracks to the right and left access remote areas of the monument.

The Burr Trail passes by the northern end

of Circle Cliffs, also named by John Wesley Powell, and then descends the narrow Long Canyon, enclosed on both sides by sheer cliffs of Wingate sandstone. The trail ends at the southern edge of Boulder Town at Utah 12.

Current Road Information
Capitol Reef National Park
HC-70 Box 15
Torrey, UT 84775
(435) 425-3791

Escalante Interagency Office
755 West Main
Escalante, UT 84726
(435) 826-5499

Map References
BLM   Hite Crossing, Escalante
USFS   Dixie National Forest: Escalante
       Ranger District (incomplete)
USGS   1:24,000   Bull Frog, Hall Mesa,
       Clay Point, Deer Point
       1:100,000 Hite Crossing, Escalante
Maptech CD-ROM: Moab/Canyonlands;
       Escalante/Dixie National Forest
Trails Illustrated, #213
Utah Atlas & Gazetteer, pp. 28, 20, 21
Utah Travel Council #5
Other: Recreation Map of the Henry
       Mountains Area (incomplete)
       BLM Map of the Grand Staircase–
       Escalante National Monument
       (incomplete)

Route Directions

▼ 0.0   Trail commences from Utah 276, 5
         miles north of Bullfrog Marina. Zero
         trip meter and turn west on paved
         road.
18.4 ▲   Trail ends at Utah 276. Turn right for
         Bullfrog Marina, turn left for Hanksville.
         GPS: N 37°34.54' W 110°42.88'

▼ 0.2   SO Track on left and right.
18.2 ▲   SO Track on right and left.

▼ 0.3   SO Track on left.
18.1 ▲   SO Track on right.

▼ 2.0   SO Track on left to Bullfrog Bay South,
         primitive camping area (fee required).
16.4 ▲   SO Track on right to Bullfrog Bay South,
         primitive camping area (fee required).
         GPS: N 37°34.66' W 110°44.75'

▼ 2.1   SO Cross over Bullfrog Canyon.
16.3 ▲   SO Cross over Bullfrog Canyon.

▼ 3.4   SO Track on left to Bullfrog Bay North,
         primitive camping area (fee required).
15.0 ▲   SO Track on right to Bullfrog Bay North,
         primitive camping area (fee required).
         GPS: N 37°35.02' W 110°46.25'

▼ 4.5   SO Pedestal Alley hiking trail on right.
13.9 ▲   SO Pedestal Alley hiking trail on left.
         GPS: N 37°35.89' W 110°46.67'

▼ 4.8   SO Enter Bullfrog Wash; wash is dirt and
         can be rough.
13.6 ▲   SO Leave wash; road is paved again.

▼ 4.9   SO Leave wash; road is paved again.
13.5 ▲   SO Enter Bullfrog Wash; wash is dirt and
         can be rough.

▼ 7.1   SO Cattle guard.
11.3 ▲   SO Cattle guard.

▼ 7.3   SO Leaving Glen Canyon National
         Recreation Area.
11.1 ▲   SO Entering Glen Canyon National
         Recreation Area.
         GPS: N 37°37.73' W 110°48.02'

▼ 9.3   SO Track on left.
9.1 ▲   SO Track on right.

▼ 9.9   SO Track on right to campsite with view.
8.5 ▲   SO Track on left to campsite with view.

▼ 11.4   SO Track on right to campsite and Bullfrog
         Canyon Overlook.
7.0 ▲   SO Track on left to campsite and Bullfrog
         Canyon Overlook.
         GPS: N 37°40.40' W 110°50.93'

▼ 11.7   SO Track on left.

SW Trail #40: Burr Trail

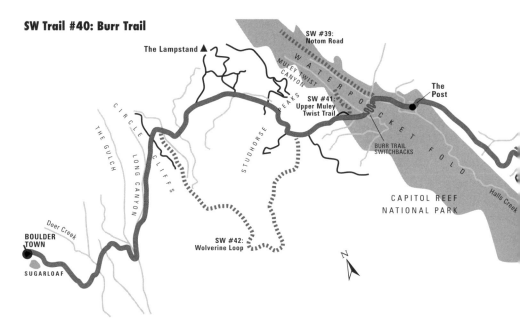

The Lampstand ▲

SW #39:
Notom Road

WATERPOCKET

MULEY TWIST CANYON

The Post

SW #41:
Upper Muley
Twist Trail

PEAKS

CIRCLE CLIFFS

THE GULCH

LONG CANYON

STUDHORSE

BURR TRAIL
SWITCHBACKS

FOLD

Halls Creek

CAPITOL REEF
NATIONAL PARK

Deer Creek

BOULDER
TOWN

SUGARLOAF

SW #42:
Wolverine Loop

N

6.7 ▲	SO	Track on right.

▼ 11.8	SO	Track on left.
6.6 ▲	SO	Track on right.

▼ 17.6	SO	Track on left to Halls Creek Overlook and trailhead.
0.8 ▲	SO	Track on right to Halls Creek Overlook and trailhead.
		GPS: N 37°44.78' W 110°54.52'

▼ 18.4	TL	Track on right is Southwest #43: Clay Point Road. Zero trip meter.
0.0 ▲		Continue up paved road toward Bullfrog Basin.
		GPS: N 37°45.56' W 110°54.44'

▼ 0.0		Continue along graded gravel road toward Capitol Reef National Park.
7.3 ▲	TR	Track ahead is Southwest #43: Clay Point Road. Zero trip meter.

▼ 1.5	SO	Track on left to flat area for primitive camping.
5.8 ▲	SO	Track on right to flat area for primitive camping.

▼ 3.2	SO	Track on left.
4.1 ▲	SO	Track on right.

▼ 5.1	SO	Track on right.
2.2 ▲	SO	Track on left.

▼ 7.3	SO	Entering Capitol Reef National Park. Zero trip meter.
0.0 ▲		Continue out of park.
		GPS: N 37°49.95' W 110°58.01'

▼ 0.0		Continue into park. The Waterpocket Fold is on left.
3.0 ▲	SO	Leaving Capitol Reef National Park. Zero trip meter.

▼ 0.1	SO	Cross through wash.
2.9 ▲	SO	Cross through wash.

▼ 0.2	SO	Cross through wash.
2.8 ▲	SO	Cross through wash.

▼ 0.5	SO	Cross through wash, then cattle guard.
2.5 ▲	SO	Cattle guard, then cross through wash.

▼ 0.9	SO	Track on left to Lower Muley Twist hiking trail. Cross cattle guard.
2.1 ▲	SO	Cattle guard, then track on right to Lower Muley Twist hiking trail.
		GPS: N 37°50.00' W 110°58.85'

SW #43: Clay Point Road

ROAD TO HANKSVILLE

Bullfrog Wash

CANYON

Utah 276

GULCH

Bullfrog Marina

Bullfrog Bay

Lake Powell

GLEN CANYON NATIONAL RECREATION AREA

▼ 1.4   SO   Surprise Canyon hikers area on left.
1.6 ▲   SO   Surprise Canyon hikers area on right.

▼ 3.0   BL   Right fork is Southwest #39: Notom Road to Utah 24. Zero trip meter.
0.0 ▲   Continue south.
       GPS: N 37°51.29' W 111°00.65'

▼ 0.0   Continue west toward Burr Trail switchbacks.
2.9 ▲   BR   Left fork is Southwest #39: Notom Road to Utah 24. Zero trip meter.

▼ 0.1   SO   Cross through creek, then service road on right.
2.8 ▲   SO   Service road on left, then cross through creek.

▼ 0.2   SO   Enter gap in Waterpocket Fold; Burr Canyon Creek on right.
2.7 ▲   SO   Leave gap in Waterpocket Fold.

▼ 0.7   SO   Climb Burr Trail switchbacks. Trail is rougher; care needed for low-clearance vehicles.
2.2 ▲   SO   End of switchbacks.

▼ 1.9   SO   End of switchbacks. Track on left to picnic area.

▼ 1.0 ▲   SO   Track on right to picnic area. Descend Burr Trail switchbacks. Trail is rougher; care needed for low-clearance vehicles.
       GPS: N 37°50.82' W 111°01.50'

▼ 2.0   SO   Lower Muley Twist Canyon hikers parking area on left.
0.9 ▲   SO   Lower Muley Twist Canyon hikers parking area on right.

▼ 2.1   SO   Cross through Muley Twist Wash.
0.8 ▲   SO   Cross through Muley Twist Wash.

▼ 2.4   SO   Track on left.
0.5 ▲   SO   Second entry to track on right.

▼ 2.6   SO   Second entry to track on left.
0.3 ▲   SO   Track on right.

▼ 2.9   SO   Track on right is Southwest #41: Upper Muley Twist Trail. Zero trip meter.
0.0 ▲   Continue east.
       GPS: N 37°51.21' W 111°02.50'

▼ 0.0   Continue west.
2.0 ▲   SO   Track on left is Southwest #41: Upper Muley Twist Trail. Zero trip meter.

▼ 1.6   SO   Picnic area on right.
0.4 ▲   SO   Picnic area on left.

▼ 2.0   SO   Leaving Capitol Reef National Park. Road is now paved. Zero trip meter.
0.0 ▲   Continue on gravel road into Capitol Reef National Park.
       GPS: N 37°51.79' W 111°04.60'

▼ 0.0   Continue on paved road.
1.6 ▲   SO   Entering Capitol Reef National Park. Road is now graded dirt. Zero trip meter.

▼ 0.1   SO   Entering Grand Staircase–Escalante National Monument.
1.5 ▲   SO   Leaving Grand Staircase–Escalante National Monument.

▼ 0.2   SO   Track on right to nice campsite with good views.

1.4 ▲	SO	Track on left to nice campsite with good views.

▼ 0.8	SO	Tracks on right and left.
0.8 ▲	SO	Tracks on left and right.

▼ 1.3	SO	Track on left.
0.3 ▲	SO	Track on right.

▼ 1.6	SO	Track on left is Southwest #42: Wolverine Loop. Zero trip meter.
0.0 ▲		Continue toward Capitol Reef National Park.
		GPS: N 37°51.93′ W 111°06.19′

▼ 0.0		Continue northwest.
9.9 ▲	SO	Track on right is Southwest #42: Wolverine Loop. Zero trip meter.

▼ 0.4	SO	Track left on right-hand bend goes to old dugouts and some pleasant campsites.
9.5 ▲	SO	Track right on left-hand bend goes to old dugouts and some pleasant campsites.

▼ 0.8	SO	Dam on right. Road winds through the Studhorse Peaks.
9.1 ▲	SO	Dam on left. Road winds through the Studhorse Peaks.

▼ 1.0	SO	Cattle guard.
8.9 ▲	SO	Cattle guard.

▼ 2.0	SO	Track on right.
7.9 ▲	SO	Track on left.

▼ 2.7	SO	Tracks on right and left.
7.2 ▲	SO	Tracks on left and right.

▼ 3.4	SO	Track on left.
6.5 ▲	SO	Track on right.

▼ 4.2	SO	Track on right.
5.7 ▲	SO	Track on left.

▼ 4.4	SO	Track on right to the Lampstand.
5.5 ▲	SO	Track on left to the Lampstand.
		GPS: N 37°55.04′ W 111°07.90′

▼ 4.7	SO	Dam, then track on left.

5.2 ▲	SO	Track on right, then dam.

▼ 5.9	SO	Cattle guard.
4.0 ▲	SO	Cattle guard.

▼ 6.7	SO	Track on left to the Lampstand.
3.2 ▲	SO	Track on right to the Lampstand.
		GPS: N 37°55.77′ W 111°10.36′

▼ 8.6	SO	Track on right.
1.3 ▲	SO	Track on left.

▼ 9.9	SO	Track on left is Southwest #42: Wolverine Loop. Zero trip meter.
0.0 ▲		Continue east to Capitol Reef National Park.
		GPS: N 37°55.46′ W 111°13.19′

▼ 0.0		Continue west to Boulder Town.
7.9 ▲	SO	Track on right is Southwest #42: Wolverine Loop. Zero trip meter.

▼ 0.3	SO	Track on right. Road passes through Circle Cliffs.
7.6 ▲	SO	Track on left. Road passes through Circle Cliffs.

▼ 1.1	SO	Track on left.
6.8 ▲	SO	Track on right.

▼ 1.6	SO	Cattle guard and turnout on left. Road descends Long Canyon.
6.3 ▲	SO	Cattle guard and turnout on right. Top of Long Canyon.
		GPS: N 37°55.12′ W 111°14.34′

▼ 7.4	SO	Cross over The Gulch on bridge.
0.5 ▲	SO	Cross over The Gulch on bridge. Road ascends Long Canyon.

▼ 7.9	SO	The Gulch hiking trail parking on right. Zero trip meter.
0.0 ▲		Continue up Long Canyon.
		GPS: N 37°51.00′ W 111°18.83′

▼ 0.0		Continue toward Boulder Town.
9.6 ▲	SO	The Gulch hiking trail parking on left. Zero trip meter.

▼ 0.7	SO	Top of The Gulch. Track on right.

THE MORMON MIGRATION

In 1820, 14-year-old Joseph Smith journeyed into the woods of upstate New York in order to find the answer to a lingering religious question and experienced the first in a series of spiritual epiphanies. An angel named Moroni appeared to him, telling him that he was a prophet and revealing hidden scriptures on golden tablets, which Smith translated from an unknown language. In 1830, Smith published these revealed writings as the Book of Mormon, and along with six other men, he formed the Church of Christ, later known as the Church of Jesus Christ of Latter-day Saints (LDS).

Brigham Young

Due to religious opposition, Smith and his growing number of followers left New York for Kirtland, Ohio, a year later. Shortly after, in 1832, a young follower named Brigham Young was baptized into the faith and began his movement up the ranks of the church.

The Mormons experienced increasing animosity from settlers in Ohio, so even as their church grew there, they established new settlements in Missouri. In 1835, Brigham Young was appointed to the Council of the Twelve Apostles, the highest governing group in the church.

In 1838, Missouri issued an "extermination order" against the Mormons. The animosity toward them resulted from exaggerated rumors of violence and the fear among original settlers that they would lose control of the area to the increasing number of Mormons. With harassment continuing in Ohio, the church moved to Nauvoo, Illinois, where things improved only temporarily. Here as well, non-Mormon settlers eventually began to persecute and even kill church members, mostly over their claims of religious superiority and espousal of polygamy. While jailed in Carthage, Illinois, in 1844, Joseph Smith and one of his followers were murdered by a furious mob.

Shortly before Smith's assassination, he had commissioned Young to lead an expedition west in order to find a place where the church could build a community free of persecution. In April of 1847, Young, now the president of the Church of Latter-day Saints, led a large group of followers on a 111-day journey to find their new home. When he arrived in the Salt Lake Valley near Emigrant Canyon on July 24, 1847, Young declared to his people, "This is the right place."

One of the most significant colonizers in U.S. history, Brigham Young began his settlement of Utah in 1849 by moving 30 families south of the Salt Lake Valley. Young's idea was to establish communities along each of the eight major Utah streams. Any region that contained a water source was open for colonization.

During the next 20 years, over 80,000 Mormons emigrated to the Utah Territory, while approximately 6,000 perished along the way. The church endeavored to find places to live for arriving families as well as to establish livelihoods for its followers. Throughout this time, Young continually expanded Mormon colonies into such areas as the Sanpete Valley and Little Salt Lake Valley in southern Utah.

In 1850, the Mormon leader helped found Parowan, the first iron enterprise of the LDS. Until this time, most Mormon colonies had been farming and livestock communities. Parowan began a trend of establishing mining towns based on natural resources, such as coal, silver, lead, and zinc.

Under the leadership of Brigham Young, the LDS devised two main types of colonization: direct and nondirect. The direct method was the most popular, and it consisted of

Continued on next page

Continued from previous page

establishing colonies with the full planning and guidance of the church. Religious leaders organized, formed, and financially backed the community, deciding which families would go, what their livelihoods would be, and any other long-term goals of the town.

In contrast, nondirect settlements occurred when individual families ventured out in small groups to establish their own communities. They were not under the guidance of the LDS and did not receive any financial aid. However, the church encouraged nondirect settlements, especially for younger families.

When the transcontinental railroad was completed in 1869, it allowed for larger numbers of settlers to migrate than ever before, and Young and the church welcomed this growth. However, in the early 1870s, overpopulation emerged as an obstacle for Utah settlers. Consequently, many families began migrating to the outlying states of Nevada, Arizona, Colorado, Idaho, and Wyoming.

Perhaps as a result of this rapid growth, the U.S. government began to feel the Mormons were becoming a threat. In 1857, President James Buchanan sent 3,000 soldiers from Fort Leavenworth to infiltrate the Salt Lake Valley in what became known as the Utah War. There was no bloodshed during the "war," but the army ultimately succeeded in its mission—the removal of Brigham Young as leader of the territory and the appointment of a new, non-Mormon governor.

In the two decades spanning 1858 to 1877, the Mormons managed to establish 205 additional settlements. Areas such as Bear Lake, Cache Valley, Pahvant Valley, and the valleys along the Sevier, Virgin, and Muddy Rivers blossomed with Mormon communities. Despite the popularity of the LDS in Utah, the federal government continued to keep a tight hold on the territory. In 1887, Congress passed legislation that unincorporated the church, made voting for women illegal, and more strongly enforced the law against polygamy. The new laws forced church leaders to renounce their doctrine encouraging plural marriages, which had been in effect since 1843.

By the early 1900s, very few regions in Utah did not have Mormon settlements, and church leaders changed their focus from colonization to building up previously established communities. The public view of the LDS has changed through the years from one of apprehension to one of acceptance. The growth of the church continues today in Utah as well as in many countries around the world.

8.9 ▲	SO	Top of The Gulch. Second entrance to track on left.

▼ 0.8	SO	Second entrance to track on right.
8.8 ▲	SO	Track on left.

▼ 1.4	SO	Cattle guard.
8.2 ▲	SO	Cattle guard.

▼ 2.0	SO	Small track on right.
7.6 ▲	SO	Small track on left.

▼ 2.3	SO	Small track on right.
7.3 ▲	SO	Small track on left.

▼ 3.6	SO	Deer Creek Campground (fee area) on right, then cross over Deer Creek, followed by hiking trail on left.

6.0 ▲	SO	Hiking trail on right, then cross over Deer Creek, followed by Deer Creek Campground (fee area) on left.
		GPS: N 37°51.29' W 111°21.28'

▼ 6.1	SO	Small track on right.
3.5 ▲	SO	Small track on left.

▼ 7.2	SO	Cattle guard.
2.4 ▲	SO	Cattle guard.

▼ 7.7	SO	Road on right.
1.9 ▲	SO	Road on left.

▼ 8.2   SO   Exiting Grand Staircase–Escalante
National Monument.
1.4 ▲   SO   Entering Grand Staircase–Escalante
National Monument.
GPS: N 37°53.49′ W 111°24.25′

▼ 8.8   SO   Boulder Pines Road on right.
0.8 ▲   SO   Boulder Pines Road on left.

▼ 9.2   SO   Intersection on edge of Boulder Town.
0.4 ▲   SO   Intersection on edge of Boulder Town.
Follow sign for Circle Cliffs and Henry
Mountains.

▼ 9.6   Trail ends at Utah 12 at the Burr Trail
Trading Post. Information board at cor-
ner in Boulder Town.
0.0 ▲   From Utah 12 at the Burr Trail Trading
Post in Boulder Town, zero trip meter
and turn east on the paved Burr Trail.
Information board at corner.
GPS: N 37°54.03′ W 111°25.42′

Spectacular Double Arch

Upper Muley Twist Trail

STARTING POINT   Southwest #40: Burr Trail, 2.9
miles west of Southwest #39: Notom Road
FINISHING POINT   Trailhead for the Strike Valley
Overlook
TOTAL MILEAGE   2.7 miles
UNPAVED MILEAGE   2.7 miles
DRIVING TIME   45 minutes (one-way)
ELEVATION RANGE   5,700–5,900 feet
USUALLY OPEN   Year-round
DIFFICULTY RATING   3
SCENIC RATING   8
REMOTENESS RATING   +0

Special Attractions

■ Moderate trail completely within Capitol
Reef National Park.
■ Strike Valley Overlook viewpoint.

Description

This interesting spur trail is contained within Capitol Reef National Park. It leads off
from Southwest #40: Burr Trail, 2.9 miles
west of Southwest #39: Notom Road. The
start of the trail is signed for Upper Muley
Twist. The first 0.4 miles can be used by
passenger vehicles down to a small parking
lot for the Muley Twist trail. From here, the
trail becomes 4WD and enters the narrow,
rocky wash. Caution is needed during flash
flood seasons.

The next half mile of the trail, the lump-
iest, has several large boulders. Drivers
should place their wheels carefully. The trail
follows along Muley Twist Creek wash,
passing under Peek-a-boo Rock. There are
several large arches up in the cliff walls,
including the large Double Arch near the
end of the trail.

The trail finishes at a small parking area,
which is the trailhead for the Strike Valley
Overlook. The hiking trail is a half-mile
round trip and provides outstanding views of
the Waterpocket Fold and surrounding area.

Current Road Information

Capitol Reef National Park
HC-70 Box 15
Torrey, UT 84775
(435) 425-3791

Map References
BLM Escalante
USGS 1:24,000 Wagon Box Mesa, Bitter
 Creek Divide
 1:100,000 Escalante
Maptech CD-ROM: Escalante/Dixie
 National Forest
Other: Recreation Map of the Henry
 Mountains Area (incomplete)

Route Directions

▼ 0.0 From Southwest #40: Burr Trail, 2.9
 miles west of Southwest #39: Notom
 Road, turn northeast onto signed road
 for Upper Muley Twist. Zero trip meter.
 GPS: N 37°51.21′ W 111°02.51′

▼ 0.2 SO Cross through tight small wash.
▼ 0.4 SO Passenger car parking area for hiking
 trail. Continue and enter narrow, rocky
 wash.
▼ 1.1 SO Trail leaves wash.
▼ 1.2 SO Trail rejoins wash; wash is wider with
 rising sandstone folds on either side.
▼ 1.5 SO Cave under overhang under cliff on
 right.
 GPS: N 37°52.17′ W 111°02.47′

▼ 1.8 SO Trail re-enters narrows.
▼ 2.1 SO Large double arch up on left.

SW Trail #41: Upper Muley Twist Trail

GPS: N 37°52.43′ W 111°02.61′

▼ 2.2 SO Large arch high up at top of cliff on
 left.
▼ 2.3 SO Large double arch at top of cliff on left.
▼ 2.7 Trail ends at parking area for Strike
 Valley Overlook.
 GPS: N 37°52.88′ W 111°02.74′

SOUTHWEST REGION TRAIL #42

Wolverine Loop

STARTING POINT Southwest #40: Burr Trail, 3.6
 miles west of Southwest #41: Upper
 Muley Twist Trail
FINISHING POINT Southwest #40: Burr Trail, 20
 miles east of Boulder Town
TOTAL MILEAGE 20.9 miles
UNPAVED MILEAGE 20.9 miles
DRIVING TIME 2 hours
ELEVATION RANGE 5,900–6,700 feet
USUALLY OPEN Year-round
DIFFICULTY RATING 3
SCENIC RATING 9
REMOTENESS RATING +1

Special Attractions
- Wolverine Petrified Wood Natural Area.
- Slot canyons in Wolverine Canyon.
- Spectacular canyon scenery in the Grand
 Staircase–Escalante National Monument.

History
President Clinton, issuing a proclamation
under the provisions of the Antiquities Act
of 1906, established the Grand Staircase–
Escalante National Monument on September
18, 1996. From the first, the designation of
the national monument has been controver-
sial. It encompasses about 1,870,800 acres of
federal land in south-central Utah and is managed by the Bureau of Land Management.
Created to protect a vast array of historic sites
and natural resources, the monument has
been vigorously protested by a variety of in-
terested parties: local ranchers and miners
who see their livelihood threatened, recre-

The Wolverine Loop climbs out of the wash along a loose, shaley surface

ationalists who see their access restricted, and some people who feel that the creation of a formalized park will increase traffic to the area. The new monument is supported by the Sierra Club and a group called the Southern Utah Wilderness Alliance (SUWA). Opposition to SUWA is strong in the towns surrounding the monument.

Access to 4WD trails in the new monument has been somewhat restricted. Vehicles are required to remain on designated roads, though to date the trails that have been closed are predominantly dead-end trails that see little use. ATV use is permitted on designated trails within the monument. It is hoped that responsible users will continue to be able to access trails in this area. A vehicle travel map is available from the BLM office in Escalante.

There has been some vandalism of the petrified wood along this trail. Please help keep access to this area open by not taking samples, especially of the less common crystal grottos in some of the logs.

Description

This loop trail, contained entirely within the Grand Staircase–Escalante National Monument, runs south of the Burr Trail, west of Capitol Reef National Park. For the most part, the route follows a loop trail that has been graded by the BLM. However, at the farthest end of the graded loop, the route breaks away from the graded trail in favor of a smaller ungraded sandy track that follows a

small wash and runs briefly along a ridge top offering excellent views.

The trail leaves from Southwest #40: Burr Trail 3.6 miles west of Southwest #41: Upper Muley Twist Trail at the BLM signpost for the Wolverine Petrified Wood Natural Area. For the first 2 miles it follows the BLM graded route and then turns off onto a rough, unmarked track heading southwest. It follows a small wash, which can be loose and sandy, for a couple of miles. A small section of ridge top gives great views to the south and southwest toward the Circle Cliffs, Death Hollow, and Bitumen Mesa. A couple of secluded campsites in this section offer wide-ranging views but little shade.

The smaller trail crosses the wash repeatedly before rejoining the graded route 6.5

Looking down into Wolverine Slot Canyon

Petrified logs along the trail

miles after leaving it. A small wash just before you rejoin the main road can wash out, which may cause longer vehicles to drag their rear bumpers. Drivers who do not wish to tackle this smaller trail may remain on the BLM graded road and continue around the loop.

After rejoining the BLM route, the trail winds down to Wolverine Canyon. After 10.7 miles, you will start to see petrified wood along the trail, even in the rocks thrown up by the grader! The long, sloping bench of rock to the east of the trail hides a secret world that's open to those willing to hike into it. Tributaries of Wolverine Creek have eroded deeply into the earth's surface, forming narrow, twisting slot canyons that are all but invisible from above. They can be difficult to enter, and once inside, you should expect to do a lot of scrambling and sloshing through mud and water. As always, do not enter slot canyons if there is any chance of rain or thunderstorms; there is little chance of escape in a flash flood.

The Wolverine Petrified Wood Natural Area is reached 3 miles after rejoining the main track. A hiking trail leads into the protected area, where you can find many examples of the ancient fossilized wood. Many millions of years ago, these trees were buried under soil, and over time the wood dissolved and was replaced with a silica material. Erosion has uncovered the resulting mineral wood.

From here, the trail climbs gradually to rejoin Southwest #40: Burr Trail. The graded road crosses many creeks, and washouts are common.

Current Road Information
Grand Staircase–Escalante National
   Monument Office
190 East Center St.
Kanab, UT 84741
(435) 644-4300

BLM Escalante Field Station
PO Box 225
Escalante, UT 84726
(435) 826-5600

Escalante Interagency Office
755 West Main
Escalante, UT 84726
(435) 826-5499

Map References
BLM   Escalante
USFS Dixie National Forest: Escalante
      Ranger District
USGS 1:24,000   Lampstand, Pioneer
      Mesa, Wagon Box Mesa
      1:100,000 Escalante
Maptech CD-ROM: Escalante/Dixie
      National Forest
Trails Illustrated, #213
Utah Atlas & Gazetteer, p. 28
Utah Travel Council #5
Other: BLM Map of the Grand Staircase–
      Escalante National Monument

Route Directions

▼ 0.0   On Southwest #40: Burr Trail, 3.6
         miles west of Southwest #41: Upper
         Muley Twist Trail, turn southeast at
         BLM sign for Wolverine Petrified Wood
         Area and zero trip meter.
1.9 ▲   Trail finishes at Southwest #40: Burr
         Trail. Turn left for Boulder Town, right
         for Capitol Reef National Park.
         GPS: N 37°51.93′ W 111°06.19′

▼ 0.8   SO Cross through wash.

1.1 ▲ SO Cross through wash.

▼ 0.9 SO Cross through wash.
1.0 ▲ SO Cross through wash.

▼ 1.0 SO Cross through wash.
0.9 ▲ SO Cross through wash.

▼ 1.8 SO Cross through Death Hollow wash.
0.1 ▲ SO Cross through Death Hollow wash.

▼ 1.9 TR Turn onto the small ungraded track and zero trip meter.
0.0 ▲ Continue on main graded track.
GPS: N 37°50.51' W 111°06.98'

▼ 0.0 Continue on small track.
6.5 ▲ TL Rejoin the main graded route. Zero trip meter.

▼ 0.1 SO Pass through wire gate, then cross through wash.
6.4 ▲ SO Cross through wash, then pass through wire gate.

▼ 0.2 SO Enter wash.
6.3 ▲ SO Exit wash.

▼ 0.6 SO Exit wash on right.
5.9 ▲ SO Enter wash.
GPS: N 37°50.26' W 111°07.46'

▼ 0.9 SO Old dam on left, then cross through wash.
5.6 ▲ SO Cross through wash, then old dam on right.

▼ 1.2 SO Track on right.
5.3 ▲ SO Track on left.

▼ 1.6 SO Cross through wash.
4.9 ▲ SO Cross through wash.

▼ 1.8 SO Cross through wash.
4.7 ▲ SO Cross through wash.

▼ 1.9 SO Faint track on right.
4.6 ▲ SO Faint track on left.

▼ 2.0 SO Trail crests rise; excellent views of Circle Cliffs and Death Hollow.

4.5 ▲ SO Trail crests rise; excellent views of Circle Cliffs and Death Hollow.

▼ 3.4 SO Enter wash.
3.1 ▲ SO Exit wash.

▼ 4.0 BR Leave wash up loose shale rise.
2.5 ▲ BL Descend loose shale to enter wash.

▼ 4.5 SO Old track on right to old mine on mesa, then cross through wash.
2.0 ▲ BR Cross through wash, then old track on left to old mine on mesa.
GPS: N 37°48.93' W 111°10.10'

▼ 4.7 SO Cross through wash.
1.8 ▲ SO Cross through wash.

▼ 5.0 SO Cross through wash.
1.5 ▲ SO Cross through wash.

▼ 5.2 SO Cross through wash.
1.3 ▲ SO Cross through wash.

▼ 5.6 SO Track on left to dam.
0.9 ▲ SO Track on right to dam.
GPS: N 37°47.94' W 111°10.26'

▼ 6.1 SO Cross through slightly washed out wash.
0.4 ▲ SO Cross through slightly washed out wash.

▼ 6.3 SO Old dam on left.
0.2 ▲ SO Old dam on right.

▼ 6.4 SO Slightly washed out wash crossing; longer vehicles should exercise care.
0.1 ▲ SO Slightly washed out wash crossing; longer vehicles should exercise care.

▼ 6.5 TR T-intersection, rejoin BLM graded track and zero trip meter.
0.0 ▲ Continue northeast.
GPS: N 37°47.26' W 111°10.25'

▼ 0.0 Continue along graded track.
3.0 ▲ TL Turn left onto unsigned small sandy trail.

▼ 0.3   SO   Track on left to campsite.
2.7 ▲   SO   Track on right to campsite.

▼ 0.5   SO   Cross through sandy wash, then track on left goes past corral to Little Death Hollow hiking trail. Cross second wash. Little Bown Bench is directly ahead.
2.5 ▲   SO   Cross through wash, then track on right goes past corral to Little Death Hollow hiking trail. Cross second sandy wash. Little Bown Bench is directly behind.
     GPS: N 37°47.06' W 111°10.78'

▼ 0.7   SO   Cross through wash.
2.3 ▲   SO   Cross through wash.

▼ 1.2   SO   Track on left.
1.8 ▲   SO   Track on right.

▼ 1.4   SO   Track on right.
1.6 ▲   SO   Track on left.

▼ 1.5   SO   Cross through wash.
1.5 ▲.   SO   Cross through wash.

▼ 2.0   SO   Cross though wash, followed by track on left.
1.0 ▲   SO   Track on right, then cross through wash.

▼ 2.3   SO   Large piece of petrified wood on right and other chunks scattered over the slab. Walk past large piece to look down into the slot canyons, tributaries of Wolverine Creek.
0.7 ▲   SO   Large piece of petrified wood on left and other chunks scattered over the slab. Walk past large piece to look down into the slot canyons, tributaries of Wolverine Creek.
     GPS: N 37°48.17' W 111°11.65'

▼ 2.4   SO   Track on left.
0.6 ▲   SO   Track on right.

▼ 2.5   SO   Track on left, then cross through wash. Access slot canyon by scrambling down on foot following the wash to the right.
0.5 ▲   SO   Cross through wash, followed by track on right. Access slot canyon by scram-bling down on foot following the wash to the left.

▼ 3.0   TR   Track on left to Wolverine hiking trail and the major petrified wood area. Zero trip meter.
0.0 ▲   Leave Wolverine Creek.
     GPS: N 37°48.27' W 111°12.31'

▼ 0.0   Continue north along Wolverine Creek. Entrance to slot canyon on right. The wash can be loose and sandy.
9.5 ▲   TL   Track on right to Wolverine hiking trail and the major petrified wood area. Entrance to slot canyon on the left. Zero trip meter.

▼ 0.5   SO   Leave wash.
9.0 ▲   SO   Enter Wolverine Creek. The wash can be loose and sandy.

▼ 0.6   SO   Cross through wash.
8.9 ▲   SO   Cross through wash.

▼ 0.8   SO   Cross through wash twice.
8.7 ▲   SO   Cross through wash twice.

▼ 0.9   SO   Cross through wash.
8.6 ▲   SO   Cross through wash.

▼ 1.3   SO   Cross through small, tight wash.
8.2 ▲   SO   Cross through small, tight wash.

▼ 1.4   SO   Cross through small, tight wash.
8.1 ▲   SO   Cross through small, tight wash.

▼ 1.8   SO   Cross through small, tight wash.
7.7 ▲   SO   Cross through small, tight wash.

▼ 3.6   SO   Enter wash.
5.9 ▲   SO   Leave wash.

▼ 3.7   SO   Cattle guard.
5.8 ▲   SO   Cattle guard.

▼ 3.8   SO   Old mine remains up cliff on right.
5.7 ▲   SO   Old mine remains up cliff on left.
     GPS: N 37°50.93' W 111°12.94'

▼ 3.9   SO   Leave wash.

SW Trail #42: Wolverine Loop

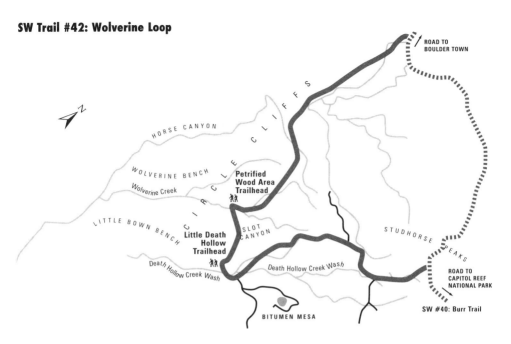

5.6 ▲ SO Enter wash.

▼ 4.0 SO Enter wash.
5.5 ▲ SO Leave wash.

▼ 4.3 BR Track swings right into larger wash.
5.2 ▲ BL Track swings left into smaller wash.
        GPS: N 37°51.06' W 111°13.36'

▼ 4.5 SO Track on left at fork in wash. There are
            multiple small splits in the wash for
            the next mile depending on the current
            washouts and the graded route. Select
            the best line.
5.0 ▲ BL Track on right at fork in wash.

▼ 5.5 SO Exit wash.
4.0 ▲ SO Trail enters wash. There are multiple
            small splits in the wash for the next
            mile depending on the current
            washouts and the graded route. Select
            the best line.

▼ 6.8 SO Track on left, then cross through small
            creek.
2.7 ▲ SO Cross through small creek, then track
            on right.

▼ 8.1 SO Track on left is old mining track.

1.4 ▲ SO Track on right is old mining track.

▼ 8.4 SO Track on left.
1.1 ▲ SO Track on right.

▼ 8.9 SO Cross through small wash.
0.6 ▲ SO Cross through small wash.

▼ 9.0 SO Cross through small wash.
0.5 ▲ SO Cross through small wash.

▼ 9.1 SO Cross through small wash.
0.4 ▲ SO Cross through small wash.

▼ 9.2 SO Cross through small wash.
0.3 ▲ SO Cross through small wash.

▼ 9.4 SO Campsite area on right.
0.1 ▲ SO Campsite area on left.

▼ 9.5   Cross through wash, then trail ends at
            Southwest #40: Burr Trail. Turn right
            for Capitol Reef National Park, turn left
            for Boulder Town.
0.0 ▲   On Southwest #40: Burr Trail, 20
            miles east of Boulder Town, turn south
            at the BLM sign and zero trip meter.
        GPS: N 37°55.46' W 111°13.18'

Clay Point Road

STARTING POINT Utah 276, 10 miles north of Ticaboo

FINISHING POINT Southwest #40: Burr Trail, 18.4 miles from Utah 276

TOTAL MILEAGE 24.9 miles

UNPAVED MILEAGE 24.9 miles

DRIVING TIME 1.5 hours

ELEVATION RANGE 4,200–6,300 feet

USUALLY OPEN Year-round

DIFFICULTY RATING 2

SCENIC RATING 7

REMOTENESS RATING +0

Special Attractions

■ Varied desert scenery.
■ Alternative backcountry leg of the Burr Trail.
■ Historic Starr Springs Ranch.

History

The Starr Ranch, which today is a National Forest Service recreation area, dates back to the 1880s. The ranch was owned by Al Starr, who eked out a living raising cattle. When miners started coming into the area to work the mines at Bromide Basin, Starr diversified and sold mules and horses to the miners.

A butte rises high above this old corral at the start of Coal Bed Mesa

He hired Franz Weber of Hanksville to build him a stone house and cellar, which you can see today just before the entrance to the campground. Franz Weber was an accomplished stone mason, who was responsible for several ranch buildings in the region as well as the stone church at Hanksville. However, before the house at Starr Ranch was finished, the mining operations at Bromide Basin wound down. Al Starr's livelihood disappeared, and Franz Weber had to stop working at Starr Ranch. The house was never finished and was abandoned. The stone cellar was completed; it is behind the house, built into the hillside.

Description

This trail provides an interesting alternative route to starting Southwest #40: Burr Trail on a paved road. The trail leaves Utah 276, 10 miles north of Ticaboo at the sign for the Starr Springs Recreation Area (fee required). The road is good graded gravel to the recreation site, which is at the start of the historic Starr Ranch. Camping and picnic areas are set in some shade, and you can view the remains of the stone cabin on the ranch.

From Starr Springs, the road becomes graded dirt and crosses the Copper Creek Benches. As it wraps around the base of Mount Hillers, the road surface has a higher rock content, but then it becomes clay as it heads toward Coal Bed Mesa. This section is fine for a passenger car, although after rain it is likely to be impassable. You pass connections to Southwest #45: Stanton Pass Trail and Southwest #44: Shootering Canyon Trail.

The route passes Coal Bed Mesa on the right as it wraps down to cross Hansen Creek in a deep V. The desert scenery is a mixture of steep-sided buttes and mesas to the north and gently sloping benches dropping to the south.

View along a small wash to the Distant Dials Knob

As the route descends toward Clay Point, it passes through badlands scenery composed of very soft blue shale. Water runoff has eroded the sides of the buttes into deep channels. The trail crosses through Saleratus Wash and Bullfrog Wash before finishing at Southwest #40: Burr Trail.

Current Road Information
BLM Henry Mountain Field Station
PO Box 99
Hanksville, UT 84734
(435) 542-3461

Map References
BLM   Hite Crossing
USGS 1:24,000   Copper Creek Benches,
    Ant Knoll, Clay Point, The Post
    1:100,000 Hite Crossing
Maptech CD-ROM: Moab/Canyonlands
Trails Illustrated, #213
Utah Atlas & Gazetteer, pp. 20, 21, 29
Utah Travel Council #5
Other: Recreation Map of the Henry
    Mountains Area

Route Directions

▼ 0.0   On Utah 276, 10 miles north of
    Ticaboo, turn northwest on Clay Point
    Road at the sign for Starr Springs
    Recreation Area and zero trip meter.
3.1 ▲   Trail ends at Utah 276. Turn left for
    Hanksville, right for Ticaboo.
    GPS: N 37°48.61′ W 110°37.77′

▼ 0.5   SO Track on right.
2.6 ▲   SO Track on left.

▼ 1.9   SO Track on left.
1.2 ▲   SO Track on right.

▼ 2.4   SO Track on right.
0.7 ▲   SO Track on left.

▼ 3.1   SO Track on right to Starr Springs
    Recreation Area (fee area), a National
    Forest Service campground and picnic
    area. Zero trip meter.
0.0 ▲   Continue toward highway.
    GPS: N 37°50.73′ W 110°39.56′

▼ 0.0   Continue west.
1.8 ▲   SO Track on left to Starr Springs
    Recreation Area (fee area), a National
    Forest Service campground and picnic
    area. Zero trip meter.

▼ 0.1   SO Track on left to cattletank.
1.7 ▲   SO Track on right to cattletank.

▼ 0.7   SO Track on left.
1.1 ▲   SO Track on right.

▼ 1.0   SO Track on left, then track on right.
0.8 ▲   SO Track on left, then track on right.

▼ 1.8   SO Track on right is Southwest #45:
    Stanton Pass Trail. Zero trip meter.
0.0 ▲   Continue east toward Starr Springs.
    GPS: N 37°50.35′ W 110°41.30′

▼ 0.0   Continue west.
4.6 ▲   SO Track on left is Southwest #45:
    Stanton Pass Trail. Zero trip meter.

SW Trail #43: Clay Point Road

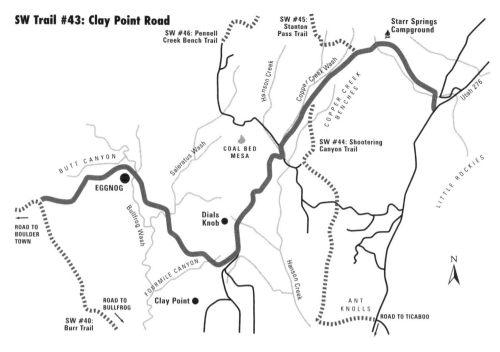

▼ 2.3   SO   Track on left is Southwest #44:
Shootering Canyon Trail.

2.3 ▲   SO   Track on right is Southwest #44:
Shootering Canyon Trail.

     GPS: N 37°48.88′ W 110°43.12′

▼ 2.4   SO   Track on right.

2.2 ▲   SO   Track on left.

▼ 2.8   SO   Track on right to corral.

1.8 ▲   SO   Track on left to corral.

▼ 4.3   SO   Cross through Copper Creek Wash, followed by small tracks on left and right.

0.3 ▲   SO   Small tracks on left and right, then cross through Copper Creek Wash.

▼ 4.6   SO   Cross through Hansen Creek, followed by track on left to Shootering Canyon. Zero trip meter.

0.0 ▲   Continue east.

     GPS: N 37°47.08′ W 110°44.30′

▼ 0.0   Continue west.

5.5 ▲   SO   Track on right to Shootering Canyon, then cross through Hansen Creek. Zero trip meter.

▼ 0.4   SO   Cross through wash.

5.1 ▲   SO   Cross through wash.

▼ 1.9   SO   Track on left.

3.6 ▲   SO   Track on right.

▼ 2.3   SO   Cattle guard.

3.2 ▲   SO   Cattle guard.

▼ 3.1   SO   Cross through wash.

2.4 ▲   SO   Cross through wash.

▼ 3.4   SO   Track on right.

2.1 ▲   SO   Track on left.

▼ 3.5   SO   Cross through wash.

2.0 ▲   SO   Cross through wash.

▼ 4.1   SO   Cross through wash. Dials Knob on right.

1.4 ▲   SO   Cross through wash. Dials Knob on left.

▼ 4.3   SO   Cross through wash.

1.2 ▲   SO   Cross through wash.

▼ 4.8   SO   Track on left.

0.7 ▲   SO   Track on right.

▼ 5.5	SO	Clay Point Road on left. Zero trip meter.
0.0 ▲		Continue southeast.
		GPS: N 37°43.49′ W 110°46.85′

▼ 0.0		Continue northwest.
5.9 ▲	SO	Clay Point Road on right. Zero trip meter.

▼ 0.8	SO	Cross through wash at head of Fourmile Canyon.
5.1 ▲	SO	Cross through wash at head of Fourmile Canyon.

▼ 3.4	SO	Descend to cross through Saleratus Wash.
2.5 ▲	SO	Descend to cross through Saleratus Wash.

▼ 5.7	TL	T-intersection. Swing sharply left. Track on right crosses through Bullfrog Wash and continues to the north.
0.2 ▲	BR	Swing sharply away from Bullfrog Wash. Track ahead crosses through Bullfrog Wash again and continues to the north.

▼ 5.8	SO	Cross through Bullfrog Wash.
0.1 ▲	SO	Cross through Bullfrog Wash.

▼ 5.9	BR	Track on left to Eggnog. Zero trip meter.
0.0 ▲		Continue along main route.
		GPS: N 37°46.37′ W 110°50.69′

▼ 0.0		Continue toward the Burr Trail.
4.0 ▲	SO	Track on right to Eggnog. Zero trip meter.

▼ 0.1	SO	Track on right to corral in small canyon.
3.9 ▲	SO	Track on left to corral in small canyon.

▼ 0.7	SO	Cattle guard.
3.3 ▲	SO	Cattle guard.

▼ 1.6	SO	Track on left.
2.4 ▲	SO	Track on right.

▼ 3.0	SO	Track on left on right-hand bend.

1.0 ▲	SO	Track on right on left-hand bend.

▼ 3.5	SO	Track on left.
0.5 ▲	SO	Track on right.

▼ 4.0		Trail finishes at Southwest #40: Burr Trail. Turn left for Bullfrog, right to continue along Burr Trail to Boulder Town.
0.0 ▲		On Southwest #40: Burr Trail, 18.4 miles from Utah 276, zero trip meter and turn east toward Starr Spring.
		GPS: N 37°45.58′ W 110°54.42′

SOUTHWEST REGION TRAIL #44

Shootering Canyon Trail

STARTING POINT Utah 276, 1.7 miles north of Ticaboo Gas Station

FINISHING POINT Southwest #43: Clay Point Road, 7.2 miles west of Utah 276

TOTAL MILEAGE 12.3 miles

UNPAVED MILEAGE 12.3 miles

DRIVING TIME 1.5 hours

ELEVATION RANGE 4,200–5,200 feet

USUALLY OPEN Year-round

DIFFICULTY RATING 3

SCENIC RATING 8

REMOTENESS RATING +1

Special Attractions

- Tony M Mine and uranium mining relics.
- Driving through a very narrow canyon.
- Loose sandy track with many dry wash crossings.

History

Shootering Canyon has a long and colorful history, starting with early ranching days and continuing to its present-day mining operations. You may notice that the name of this canyon changes depending on who you talk to and which maps you read. It seems the original name, the one printed on the USGS maps, is Shitamaring Canyon. The local explanation for this name, one that has a "ring" of truth surrounding it, is that the water in the canyon has a laxative effect. The immediate results of this water on the cattle in the narrow, echoing canyon supplied the name!

The mill, however, goes by the name "Shootaring," while the BLM prefer the designation "Shootering." Whatever you call it, it's still the same canyon.

The mine in the canyon is recent compared to most uranium mines in the area. The construction of Shootaring Mill by Plateau Resources Limited was completed in 1979. Its purpose was to concentrate the ore for easier shipment. Ticaboo was established at that time as the company town. After three years of construction, the mill ran for only three months before being shut down. The price of uranium had dropped to the point where it was uneconomical to produce. For 20 years, a skeleton crew has remained at the mine, waiting for the price of uranium to rise, and currently it is working toward opening the mine for production some time in 2000.

The mine in the canyon was originally

An open uranium adit sits at the foot of a canyon wall

called the Lucky Strike; today it goes by the name Tony M Mine.

Description

The trail leaves west from Utah 276 at an unmarked turn 1.7 miles north of Ticaboo Gas Station. After 0.8 miles, you can see the distinctive conical Ant Knolls to the north, and a little farther on, the Shootaring Uranium Mill stands out below the bluff. Passing by a corral, the trail descends to join the Shitamaring Creek wash. Both the descent and the trail along the wash can be very loose and sandy. You will need a 4WD and may need to deflate your tires slightly for better flotation in the deeper sand sections.

After 4.6 miles, the trail joins the graded gravel road that follows Lost Spring Wash. This good road does not last long, however; after passing the Tony M Mine 2.3 miles later, the standard drops again.

There are many uranium adits visible in the cliff faces on either side of the trail, plus piles of tailings and mining machinery. Care is needed around the workings.

The trail then enters the extremely narrow Shootering Canyon. There is just enough room for a vehicle to squeeze through between the towering rocky walls. After a mile, the trail leaves the canyon and climbs up to cross the Copper Creek Benches, finally joining Southwest #43: Clay Point Road. From here, turn left to head toward Southwest #40: Burr Trail or turn right to return to Utah 276.

The Little Rockies rise up in the background as the trail leaves Shootering Canyon

Current Road Information

BLM Henry Mountain Field Station
PO Box 99
Hanksville, UT 84734
(435) 542-3461

Map References

BLM   Hite Crossing
USGS 1:24,000   Lost Spring, Copper
       Creek Benches
       1:100,000 Hite Crossing
Maptech CD-ROM: Moab/Canyonlands
Trails Illustrated, #213 (incomplete)
Utah Atlas & Gazetteer, p. 28
Utah Travel Council #5
Other: Recreation Map of the Henry
        Mountains Area

Route Directions

▼ 0.0   On Utah 276, 1.7 miles north of
           Ticaboo Gas Station, turn west onto
           unmarked dirt track and zero trip meter.
2.6 ▲   Trail ends at Utah 276, 1.7 miles north
           of Ticaboo. Turn right for Bullfrog
           Marina, left for Hanksville.
           GPS: N 37°41.65' W 110°40.36'

▼ 0.2   SO Cross through small wash.
2.4 ▲   SO Cross through small wash.

▼ 0.8   SO The Ant Knolls, large conical domes,
            on right.
1.8 ▲   SO The Ant Knolls, large conical domes,
            on left.

▼ 1.4   SO Track on left. Shootaring Uranium Mill
            is visible on right.
1.2 ▲   SO Track on right. Shootaring Uranium Mill
            is visible on left.

▼ 1.6   SO Track on right at corral.
1.0 ▲   SO Track on left at corral.
            GPS: N 37°41.65' W 110°41.87'

▼ 1.7   SO Track on right is second entrance to
            corral, followed by track on left. Trail
            descends to Shitamaring Creek wash.
0.9 ▲   SO Track on right, followed by track on left
            to corral.

▼ 2.6   SO Track on left to Hansen Creek. Zero trip
            meter.
0.0 ▲   Trail climbs out of Shitamaring Creek
           wash.
           GPS: N 37°41.76' W 110°42.75'

▼ 0.0   Continue along Shitamaring Creek wash.
2.0 ▲   SO Track on right to Hansen Creek. Zero
            trip meter.

▼ 0.1   SO Cattle guard. Trail crosses though
            Shitamaring Creek wash nine times in
            the next 1.9 miles.
1.9 ▲   SO Cattle guard.

▼ 2.0   SO Join graded gravel road and zero trip
            meter.
0.0 ▲   Continue along sandy track. Trail
           crosses Shitamaring Creek wash nine
           times in the next 1.9 miles.
           GPS: N 37°43.48' W 110°42.45'

▼ 0.0   Continue along gravel road.
4.1 ▲   BR Turn onto small, unmarked sandy track
            and zero trip meter.

▼ 2.1   SO Row of uranium adits halfway up cliff
            face on left.
2.0 ▲   SO Row of uranium adits halfway up cliff
            face on right.

▼ 2.3   SO Entrance to Tony M Mine on left.
1.8 ▲   SO Entrance to Tony M Mine on right.
            GPS: N 37°45.33' W 110°42.12'

▼ 2.5   SO Cross over Shitamaring Creek wash on
            bridge, then pass through area of old
            mining activity, tailings piles, old
            machinery, and large mine adits in the
            cliff walls on both sides.
1.6 ▲   SO Pass through area of old mining activi-
            ty, tailings piles, old machinery, and
            large mine adits in the cliff walls on
            both sides, then cross over
            Shitamaring Creek wash on bridge.

▼ 2.8   SO Cross through wash three times in the
            next 0.2 miles.
1.3 ▲   SO Cross through wash a few times.

SW Trail #44: Shootering Canyon Trail

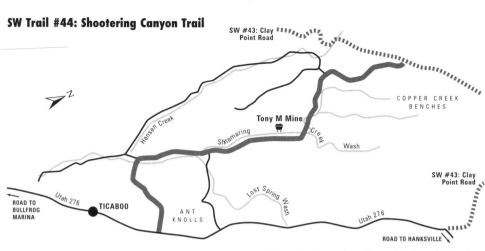

▼ 3.1   SO   Enter wash.

1.0 ▲   SO   Leave wash, then cross through wash three times in the next 0.2 miles.

▼ 3.2   BL   Faint track goes up Shitamaring Creek bed on right. Continue in main canyon and enter narrow part of canyon.

0.9 ▲   BR   Faint track goes up Shitamaring Creek bed on left. Continue in main canyon, narrow section ends.
         GPS: N 37°45.89' W 110°42.10'

▼ 4.0   SO   Track climbs out of wash.

0.1 ▲   SO   Track descends into wash. Canyon becomes very narrow.
         GPS: N 37°46.35' W 110°42.59'

▼ 4.1   TR   Unsigned T-intersection. Zero trip meter.

0.0 ▲   Continue down toward canyon.
         GPS: N 37°46.36' W 110°42.62'

▼ 0.0   Continue northeast.

3.6 ▲   TL   Turn left onto unsigned track and zero trip meter.

▼ 0.1   SO   Cross through wash, then track on right.

3.5 ▲   SO   Track on left, then cross through wash.

▼ 0.4   SO   Cross through wash.

3.2 ▲   SO   Cross through wash.

▼ 0.5   SO   Cross through wash.

3.1 ▲   SO   Cross through wash.

▼ 0.6   SO   Cross through wash. Mount Hillers is visible to the north.

3.0 ▲   SO   Cross through wash. Mount Hillers is visible to the north.

▼ 0.7   SO   Cross through wash.

2.9 ▲   SO   Cross through wash.

▼ 0.9   SO   Faint track on left. Trail rises up to Copper Creek Benches.

2.7 ▲   SO   Faint track on right.

▼ 1.2   BR   Fork.

2.4 ▲   SO   Track on right.
         GPS: N 37°46.98' W 110°43.55'

▼ 2.2   SO   Track on right.

1.4 ▲   SO   Track on left.

▼ 2.8   SO   Cross through wash.

0.8 ▲   SO   Cross through wash.

▼ 3.4   SO   Cross through wash.

0.2 ▲   SO   Cross through wash.

▼ 3.6   Trail ends at Southwest #43: Clay Point Road. Turn right for Utah 276, left to continue along Clay Point Road.

0.0 ▲   On Southwest #43: Clay Point Road, 7.2 miles west of Utah 276, turn south at sign for Shootering Canyon and zero trip meter.
         GPS: N 37°48.89' W 110°43.12'

Stanton Pass Trail

STARTING POINT Southwest #47: Bull Creek
Pass Trail, 6 miles west of Utah 276
FINISHING POINT Southwest #43: Clay Point
Road, 4.9 miles from Utah 276
TOTAL MILEAGE 14.3 miles
UNPAVED MILEAGE 14.3 miles
DRIVING TIME 2 hours
ELEVATION RANGE 5,300–7,470 feet
USUALLY OPEN June to November
DIFFICULTY RATING 2
SCENIC RATING 8
REMOTENESS RATING +1

Special Attractions

- Scenic pass with a range of backcountry scenery.
- Links two major 4WD roads, Southwest #47: Bull Creek Pass Trail and Southwest #43: Clay Point Road.

Description

This very pretty route links Southwest #47: Bull Creek Pass Trail in the north to Southwest #43: Clay Point Road in the south. It leaves Bull Creek Pass Trail 2.7 miles west of Trachyte Ranch and heads generally southwest, gradually ascending the benches alongside Benson Creek. There are panoramic views of Mount Hillers, Big Ridge, and the conical Cass Creek Peak to the southwest, of Mount Pennell to the west, and of Mount Ellen to the northwest.

After 4 miles, the trail passes Quaking Aspen Spring on the right, which is fenced to prevent cattle from damaging the source; but you can see the spring trickling from under a rock ledge. A popular campsite is set under large oaks near the spring, a short way down a small track.

After 5 miles, the trail crests Stanton Pass, passing between Cass Creek Peak and Bulldog Peak, and then descends toward Clay Point Road. The descent through juniper vegetation is rough, but the graded trail should pose no difficulties to a high-clear-

ance vehicle in dry weather. Good tires are an advantage; the rocks can be very sharp and can easily puncture a sidewall.

After 9 miles, the trail winds across the top of Cow Flat, a long dry valley that marks the vegetation change from juniper and small pine to the sagebrush of the lower elevations. Southwest #46: Pennell Creek Bench Trail leads off from here.

The trail climbs briefly to run around the south flank of Mount Hillers, dominated by red rocky fins. On a clear day, you can see Lake Powell to the south as you descend through Copper Creek near the end of the trail, and you can always see the Little Rockies range, the southernmost peaks of the Henry Mountains: Mount Holmes and the higher Mount Ellsworth south of it, separated by Freds Ridge. This part of the trail is

Blue Ridge stands off in the distance beyond this old corral

particularly lovely in early evening, as the light catches the Little Rockies and paints them red-purple.

The trail finishes on Southwest #43: Clay Point Road, 4.9 miles from its junction with Utah 276.

Current Road Information
BLM Henry Mountain Field Station
PO Box 99
Hanksville, UT 84734
(435) 542-3461

Map References
BLM   Hanksville, Hite Crossing
USGS 1:24,000   Cass Creek Peak, Copper
        Creek Benches, Ant Knoll
        1:100,000 Hanksville, Hite Crossing
Maptech CD-ROM: Moab/Canyonlands
Trails Illustrated, #213
Utah Atlas & Gazetteer, pp. 28, 29
Utah Travel Council #5
Other: Recreation Map of the Henry
        Mountains Area

Route Directions

▼ 0.0   On Southwest #47: Bull Creek Pass
             Trail, 6 miles from Utah 276, zero
             trip meter and turn west toward

             Quaking Aspen Spring.

6.0 ▲   Trail finishes on Southwest #47: Bull
             Creek Pass Trail. Turn right to join Utah
             276; turn left to return to Henry
             Mountains.
             GPS: N 37°57.88' W 110°39.61'

▼ 0.1   SO Second entrance from Bull Creek Pass
             Trail on right.
5.9 ▲   SO First exit to Bull Creek Pass Trail on left.

▼ 0.3   SO Cross through creek. Track starts to
             climb.
5.7 ▲   SO End of descent from pass. Cross
             through creek.

▼ 1.0   SO Old corral on left. Views ahead to
             Mount Hillers, Big Ridge, Cass Creek
             Peak, and Mount Pennell.
5.0 ▲   SO Old corral on right. Views back to
             Mount Hillers, Big Ridge, Cass Creek
             Peak, and Mount Pennell.
             GPS: N 37°57.25' W 110°40.20'

▼ 1.7   SO Cattle guard.
4.3 ▲   SO Cattle guard.

▼ 2.6   SO Track on left.
3.4 ▲   SO Track on right.
             GPS: N 37°56.25' W 110°41.46'

SW Trail #45: Stanton Pass Trail

▼ 3.2   SO   Track on right.
2.8 ▲   SO   Track on left.

▼ 3.9   SO   Track on left.
2.1 ▲   SO   Track on right.

▼ 4.0   SO   Track on right to campsite under large oaks. Quaking Aspen Spring on right.
2.0 ▲   SO   Quaking Aspen Spring on left, followed by track on left to campsite under large oaks.
    GPS: N 37°55.45' W 110°42.43'

▼ 4.5   SO   Track on left.
1.5 ▲   SO   Track on right.

▼ 4.8   SO   Old track on left.
1.2 ▲   SO   Old track on right.

▼ 5.1   SO   Stanton Pass (7,470 feet). Bulldog Peak on the right, Cass Creek Peak on the left. Track descends.
0.9 ▲   SO   Stanton Pass (7,470 feet). Bulldog Peak on the left, Cass Creek Peak on the right. Track descends.
    GPS: N 37°54.77' W 110°43.41'

▼ 5.8   SO   Track on left.
0.2 ▲   SO   Track on right.

▼ 6.0   SO   Track on right to Mud Spring and Southwest #47: Bull Creek Pass Trail. Zero trip meter.
0.0 ▲   Continue climbing Stanton Pass.
    GPS: N 37°54.04' W 110°43.81'

▼ 0.0   Continue descent from Stanton Pass.
2.8 ▲   SO   Track on left to Mud Spring and the Horn. Zero trip meter.

▼ 0.8   SO   Track on left.
2.0 ▲   SO   Track on right.

▼ 0.9   SO   Small dam on right.
1.9 ▲   SO   Small dam on left.

▼ 2.5   SO   Cattle guard.
0.3 ▲   SO   Cattle guard.

▼ 2.8   TL   Track on right is Southwest #46: Pennell Creek Bench Trail. Zero trip meter, then cross through Saleratus Wash.
0.0 ▲   Continue toward Stanton Pass.
    GPS: N 37°51.99' W 110°45.25'

▼ 0.0   Continue east.
5.5 ▲   TR   Cross through Saleratus Wash, then track on left is Southwest #46: Pennell Creek Bench Trail. Zero trip meter.

▼ 0.7   SO   Track on right.
4.8 ▲   BR   Track on left.

▼ 1.3   SO   Track on right.
4.2 ▲   SO   Track on left.

▼ 2.3   SO   Views southeast over Mount Holmes, Freds Ridge, and Mount Ellsworth, and views south to Lake Powell and Waterpocket Fold.
3.2 ▲   SO   Views southeast over Mount Holmes, Freds Ridge, and Mount Ellsworth, and views south to Lake Powell and Waterpocket Fold.

▼ 3.1   SO   Track on right, followed by cattle guard.
2.4 ▲   SO   Cattle guard, followed by track on left.

▼ 4.5   SO   Track on left, then cross through Copper Creek Wash, followed by old stone ruin on left and campsite on right.
1.0 ▲   SO   Old stone ruin on right and campsite on left, cross through Copper Creek Wash, then track on right.
    GPS: N 37°50.85' W 110°42.00'

▼ 4.8   SO   Track on left.
0.7 ▲   SO   Track on right.

▼ 5.5   Trail ends on Copper Creek Benches at Southwest #43: Clay Point Road. Turn right to continue along Clay Point Road, left to Utah 276.
0.0 ▲   On Southwest #43: Clay Point Road, 4.9 miles from Utah 276, zero trip meter and follow sign to Stanton Pass and the Horn.
    GPS: N 37°50.35' W 110°41.32'

Pennell Creek Bench Trail

STARTING POINT Southwest #45: Stanton Pass Trail, 5.5 miles from southern end of trail

FINISHING POINT End of Pennell Creek Bench/ Cow Flat

TOTAL MILEAGE 5.2 miles (all three legs)

UNPAVED MILEAGE 5.2 miles

DRIVING TIME 1.5 hours (all three legs)

ELEVATION RANGE 5,700–5,800 feet

USUALLY OPEN April to December

DIFFICULTY RATING 3

SCENIC RATING 8

REMOTENESS RATING +2

Special Attractions

■ Very remote, little-traveled spur tracks.

■ Stunning views over No Mans Mesa and Glen Canyon National Recreation Area.

Description

This short spur trail consists of three legs, each leading to a different viewpoint, and can be done in conjunction with Southwest #45: Stanton Pass Trail.

The trail starts 5.5 miles from the south end of Stanton Pass Trail, immediately west of Saleratus Wash. Turn south and follow the rough wheel tracks. There are no signs along the route, and tracks can be faint, so navigation can be very tricky. After 0.8 miles, fork right and cross through Saleratus Wash. This is normally dry, but can wash out quite badly, so care is needed on the crossing. Watch for other wheel tracks and pick your line carefully; there may be more than one option.

After the wash, there is a short climb onto Pennell Creek Bench, which is narrow and can have deep washouts. Once on top of the bench, the trail winds through juniper bushes, passing the turn to the west leg and continuing south. It dead-ends at 2.5 miles with a panoramic view to the south and west over the Glen Canyon area, Waterpocket Fold, and back over the bench to the Henry Mountains.

Though the trail continues from this point, descending to cross the wash, at the time of research the climb up the far side had deep washouts and was beyond the scope of this book.

The west leg goes a short way to the edge of the Bench and gives unparalleled views over No Mans Mesa and the Pennell Creek Roughs badlands far below.

The third leg is the least dramatic of the three and continues down onto Cow Flat, past a fenced spring to stop at a rise.

Current Road Information

BLM Henry Mountain Field Station
PO Box 99
Hanksville, UT 84734
(435) 542-3461

View of No Mans Mesa, Castle Rock, and the Pennell Creek Roughs from the overlook at the end of the trail's second leg

Map References

BLM   Hite Crossing (incomplete)
USGS 1:24,000   Ant Knoll
       1:100,000 Hite Crossing
       (incomplete)
Maptech CD-ROM: Moab/Canyonlands
Trails Illustrated, #213 (incomplete)
Utah Atlas & Gazetteer, p. 28
Other: Recreation Map of the Henry
        Mountains Area (incomplete)

Route Directions

▼ 0.0   5.5 miles from the south end of
         Southwest #45: Stanton Pass Trail,
         zero trip meter and turn south 0.1
         miles west of Saleratus Wash. The
         turn is unmarked.
         GPS: N 37°51.99' W 110°45.25'

▼ 0.2   SO Track on left.
▼ 0.3   SO Track on left. Trail now crosses the
            open Cow Flat and becomes ungraded
            dirt track.
▼ 0.8   TR Turn is unmarked and faint. Look for
            the trail cutting up the bench on your
            right. Straight ahead is the start of the
            third leg (Cow Flat).
            GPS: N 37°51.33' W 110°45.69'

▼ 0.9   SO Cross through small wash. Follow wheel
            tracks and pick your route carefully.
▼ 1.0   SO Cross through Saleratus Wash and
            climb up to Pennell Bench.
▼ 1.3   SO End of climb, trail undulates through
            junipers.
▼ 1.5   BL Faint track on right; this is start of sec-
            ond leg of trail.
            GPS: N 37°51.49' W 110°46.31'

▼ 1.9   BR At cattletank and small dam, swing
            southwest. Tracks are faint.
            GPS: N 37°51.21' W 110°46.52'

▼ 2.5   First leg ends as the trail runs out to a
         point. Trail continues but is badly
         washed out just past the wash. Retrace
         your steps to the 1.5-mile point.
         GPS: N 37°50.77' W 110°46.85'

SW Trail #46: Pennell Creek Bench Trail

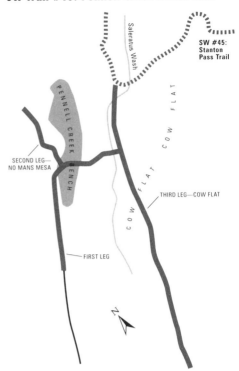

Second Leg: No Mans Mesa

▼ 0.0   At the 1.5-mile mark on first leg, zero
         trip meter and turn west.
▼ 0.2   SO Cross through small wash.
▼ 0.4   SO Cross through small wash.
▼ 0.7   SO Trail finishes at a panoramic viewpoint
            overlooking No Mans Mesa and the
            Pennell Creek Roughs. Note the small
            castle-shaped rocky outcrop slightly to
            the south. Retrace your steps down
            from the mesa and return to the 0.8-
            mile mark on first leg.
            GPS: N 37°52.06' W 110°46.36'

Third Leg: Cow Flat

▼ 0.0   At the 0.8-mile mark on first leg, zero
         trip meter and turn right (south) if
         coming from Pennell Creek Bench.
         Track on left (north) leads back to the
         start of the trail and Southwest #45:
         Stanton Pass Trail.

▼ 0.2   SO   Faint track on left.
▼ 0.7   SO   Faint track on right.
▼ 1.0   SO   Spring and corral below trail on left.
GPS: N 37°50.35' W 110°45.86'

▼ 1.5   SO   Cross through small wash.
GPS: N 37°50.02' W 110°46.14'

▼ 2.0   Trail finishes at point with view over
             Saleratus Wash directly below, Mount
             Hillers to the north, and Mount Holmes
             and Mount Ellsworth to the east.
GPS: N 37°49.64' W 110°46.23'

SOUTHWEST REGION TRAIL #47

Bull Creek Pass Trail

STARTING POINT Utah 95, 21 miles south of
Hanksville
FINISHING POINT Utah 276, 5 miles south of
junction with Utah 95
TOTAL MILEAGE 52.3 miles
UNPAVED MILEAGE 52.3 miles
DRIVING TIME 7 hours
ELEVATION RANGE 4,800–10,485 feet
USUALLY OPEN Early June to late November
DIFFICULTY RATING 2
SCENIC RATING 10
REMOTENESS RATING +2

Special Attractions
■ Long, remote backcountry byway with
varied scenery and elevation changes.
■ Bull Creek Pass at 10,485 feet.
■ Rare chance to see a wild bison herd.

History
The Henry Mountains are a geologic anom-
aly: frustrated volcanoes that were unable to
reach the surface due to a thick, tough layer
of sedimentary rock that prevented their
erupting. The sedimentary layer bent up-
ward instead, forming the domes of the
Henry Mountains. The overlying sedimentary rock has eroded in places, exposing the ig-
neous rock underneath. This geologic formation is called a stock. The Henry Mountains

have five stocks: Mount Pennell, Mount
Hillers, Mount Ellen, Mount Holmes, and
Mount Ellsworth. In 1871, John Wesley
Powell first named the mountain range after
Joseph Henry, a professor at the Smithsonian
Institute. However, it was not until 1875
that the Henry Mountains were first sur-
veyed by geologist Grove Karl Gilbert. This
late date of exploration stands as a testimony
to the rugged remoteness of the Henry
Mountains.

The history of the Henry Mountains
region includes tales of lost mines, ghost
towns, and more recently, wild buffalo.
Human habitation dates back about eight
thousand years to Archaic and Fremont
Indian cultures, although there are few visible remains.

The Bull Creek Pass Trail passes the
remains of Eagle City along Crescent Creek.
All that is left now are the remains of a log
cabin, collapsed in a grove of aspens. But
Eagle City, founded in the 1890s, was once
a thriving mining community, boasting cook
houses, boarding houses, and saloons. The
mines were located farther up Crescent
Creek in Bromide Basin. When the mines
ran dry, the people moved on to more prof-
itable ventures. Eagle City dwindled, and by
1900 it was deserted.

A more recent introduction to the area is
a herd of buffalo, one of the only free-roam-
ing buffalo herds left in the United States. In
1941, 18 head of buffalo were transported
from Yellowstone National Park to the Robbers Roost area, east of Utah 276, in order to
safeguard the survival of the Yellowstone
herd. The herd gradually migrated west of
the highway over a period of a few years, first
to the eastern slopes of the Henry Mountains and then to the western slopes, where it
has remained. Best chances of seeing the buffalo are in the meadows surrounding the
McMillan Springs Campground and south
as far as Aeroplane Spring. The herd today
numbers approximately 450 animals. Since
1950, there have been approximately 60
hunting permits granted annually, though
exact numbers vary, and the season is broken
into three hunts each fall. The permits are

distributed via a lottery system and competition is fierce.

Trachyte Ranch, on the southeastern lowlands of this trail, dates back to 1913 when uranium was first discovered in the area. You can see a log cabin and associated buildings close to Trachyte Creek, and the ranch dam is just upstream. Mining adits can also be seen in the cliff walls surrounding Trachyte Creek.

Description

This trail is entirely on BLM land and is a designated scenic backcountry byway. The trail turns off Utah 95, 21 miles south of Hanksville. The turn is unsigned except for the small circular byway sign. It is graded dirt over the full 52.3 miles; the standard varies from a smooth surface suitable for a passenger car to rough, rocky sections and washouts that require high clearance. Snow closes the higher portions of the trail any time from late October onward, but the lower parts are traversable most times of the year in dry conditions. Fall is a particularly beautiful time of year for the drive—the extreme summer heat has passed, the leaves are turning, and the weather is generally dry. Rain can render most of this trail impassable.

After 1.6 miles, the trail passes by the Little Egypt Geologic Site. Entrada sandstone columns banded with limestone form strange columnar formations that early set-

Crescent Creek wash crossing

tlers compared to the Sphinx of Egypt. The trail crosses Crescent Creek and winds through the lower elevations and badlands scenery. The vistas are desolate at this stage, with scrubby sage giving way to stunted juniper as the trail climbs. The sparse ruins of Eagle City are visible after 11.7 miles; an old log cabin is about all that remains. The trail then climbs up to the first of three passes, Wickiup Pass, and connects with Southwest #49: Town Wash and Bull Mountain Trail. There are stunning views east over the Burr Desert as the trail wraps around the hill.

You reach Bull Creek Pass, the high point of the trail at 10,485 feet, after 18.2 miles. There are wide-ranging views to the northeast over the tributaries of the Dirty Devil River and Canyonlands National Park. On a clear day you can see the bulk of the La Sal Mountains east of Moab and the Abajo Mountains near Monticello. To the northwest are Waterpocket Fold, Circle Cliffs, and Boulder Mountain. The pass is the start of

The remains of a miner's stone cabin near Crescent Creek

the hiking trail to the top of Mount Ellen, a 5-mile round trip.

From the pass you will begin a long descent, past the intersection with Southwest #48: Copper Ridge Trail, to the developed campground at McMillan Springs. The wild bison herd that inhabits the Henry Mountains can often be seen grazing the grassy meadows just west of Bull Creek Pass. Remember that these are wild animals and can be aggressive if approached too closely. The trail then undulates down from the higher elevations, crossing Pennellen Pass, passing by the steep cliffs of the Horn, and traversing the sloping Coyote Benches before dropping back down into the arid badlands again. There are some good undeveloped campsites along this section at a variety of elevations, some sheltered in the shade of pines, others more open with good vistas. You get some of the best views of the entire trail while descending to Coyote Benches. To the east, distant views extend over the red rock of the Robbers Roost area to the Abajo Mountains. The distinctive shapes of Gunsight Butte and Sewing Machine Butte can be seen on a clear day.

After passing the connection with Southwest #45: Stanton Pass Trail and the remains of Trachyte Ranch, the trail finishes at Utah 276. With the exception of the starting and finishing points, this trail is well signed along its length. However, the region is very remote, and except during hunting season, you are unlikely to see any other vehicles. The BLM officials only occasionally travel the trails, so outside help should not be relied upon. Gas, accommodations, and limited supplies are available in Hanksville, Ticaboo, and Bullfrog Marina.

Current Road Information
BLM Henry Mountain Field Station
PO Box 99
Hanksville, UT 84734
(435) 542-3461

Map References
BLM   Hanksville, Hite Crossing
USGS 1:24,000   Turkey Knob, Raggy

Canyon, Mt. Ellen, Steele Butte, Mt. Pennell, Cass Creek Peak, Black Table
1:100,000 Hanksville, Hite Crossing
Maptech CD-ROM: Moab/Canyonlands; Escalante/Dixie National Forest
Trails Illustrated, #213 (incomplete)
Utah Atlas & Gazetteer, pp. 28, 29
Utah Travel Council #5
Other: Recreation Map of the Henry Mountains Area

Route Directions

▼ 0.0   Turn west off Utah 95 onto unsigned, graded dirt road, 21 miles south of Hanksville, and zero trip meter.
3.5 ▲   Trail ends at Utah 95. Turn left for Hanksville, right for Bullfrog Marina.
GPS: N 38°05.84′ W 110°37.28′

▼ 0.2   BL   Follow main track left at sign to Little Egypt Geologic Site.
3.3 ▲   BR   Track on left.

▼ 1.6   SO   Little Egypt area on right; red Entrada columns banded with white limestone.
1.9 ▲   SO   Little Egypt area on left; red Entrada columns banded with white limestone.

▼ 3.5   TR   Turn right at sign toward Sawmill Basin and the Horn, and zero trip meter.
0.0 ▲   Continue toward Utah 95.
GPS: N 38°02.98′ W 110°37.87′

▼ 0.0   Continue toward Sawmill Basin.
9.0 ▲   TL   Turn left at sign for Utah 95 and zero trip meter.

▼ 0.6   TR   Cross through Crescent Creek wash, normally dry.
8.4 ▲   TL   Cross through Crescent Creek wash, normally dry.
GPS: N 38°02.76′ W 110°38.46′

▼ 0.7   SO   Cross through Crescent Creek wash; old crane on left of track.
8.3 ▲   SO   Cross through Crescent Creek wash; old crane on right of track.

▼ 0.9　SO　Track on left. Trail follows Crescent Creek.

8.1 ▲　SO　Track on right. Trail follows Crescent Creek.

▼ 1.4　SO　Track on right.

7.6 ▲　SO　Track on left.

▼ 2.6　SO　Faint track on left.

6.4 ▲　SO　Faint track on right.

▼ 3.0　SO　Track on left to active mine (Martinique Mining Co.).

6.0 ▲　SO　Track on right to active mine (Martinique Mining Co.).
　　　　　GPS: N 38°04.50′ W 110°39.62′

▼ 3.1　SO　Cross through Crescent Creek wash.

5.9 ▲　SO　Cross through Crescent Creek wash.

▼ 3.3　SO　Single-room stone miner's cabin on right.

5.7 ▲　SO　Single-room stone miner's cabin on left.
　　　　　GPS: N 38°04.69′ W 110°39.69′

▼ 3.8　SO　Cattle guard.

5.2 ▲　SO　Cattle guard.

▼ 4.0　SO　Timber miner's cabin on left under cottonwoods next to Crescent Creek.

5.0 ▲　SO　Timber miner's cabin on right under cottonwoods next to Crescent Creek.
　　　　　GPS: N 38°04.75′ W 110°40.40′

▼ 4.6　SO　Track on left is closed for mining reclamation. Entering juniper forest.

4.4 ▲　SO　Track on right is closed for mining reclamation. Leaving juniper forest.

▼ 5.6　SO　Helipad on right, track on left.

3.4 ▲　SO　Helipad on left, track on right.

▼ 6.2　SO　Track on right.

2.8 ▲　SO　Track on left.
　　　　　GPS: N 38°05.02′ W 110°42.60′

▼ 6.6　SO　Cattle guard, tracks on right and left along fence line.

2.4 ▲　SO　Tracks on right and left along fence line, followed by cattle guard.

▼ 8.0　SO　Helipad on right, track on left.

1.0 ▲　SO　Helipad on left, track on right.

▼ 8.1　BR　Track on left.

0.9 ▲　BL　Track on right.
　　　　　GPS: N 38°04.43′ W 110°44.58′

▼ 8.2　SO　Eagle City site—old log cabin on right.

0.8 ▲　SO　Eagle City site—old log cabin on left.

▼ 8.4　SO　Cattle guard.

0.6 ▲　SO　Cattle guard.

▼ 8.6　SO　Track on left is closed with wire.

0.4 ▲　SO　Track on right is closed with wire.

▼ 9.0　TR　Sharp U-turn back; follow signs to Wickiup Pass and Sawmill Basin. Track on left is Southwest #48: Copper Ridge Trail. Zero trip meter.

0.0 ▲　　　Continue east.
　　　　　GPS: N 38°04.40′ W 110°45.61′

▼ 0.0　　　Climb up shelf road.

3.1 ▲　TL　Sharp U-turn back; follow along Crescent Creek. Ahead is Southwest #48: Copper Ridge Trail. Zero trip meter.

▼ 2.2　SO　Cattle guard, sign "Granite Ridges" and track on left.

0.9 ▲　SO　Cattle guard, sign "Granite Ridges" and track on right.

▼ 2.5　SO　Cross through Granite Creek.

0.6 ▲　SO　Cross through Granite Creek.

▼ 3.1　SO　Wickiup Pass (9,360 feet). At intersection, go straight, bearing slightly left. The road on right is Southwest #49: Town Wash and Bull Mountain Trail to Utah 24 and Hanksville. Shady campsite at junction. Zero trip meter.

0.0 ▲　　　Continue downhill.
　　　　　GPS: N 38°05.70′ W 110°46.65′

▼ 0.0　　　Climb toward Bull Creek Pass.

9.7 ▲　SO　Wickiup Pass (9,360 feet). At intersection, go straight, bearing slightly right.

The road on left is Southwest #49: Town Wash and Bull Mountain Trail to Utah 24 and Hanksville. Shady campsite at junction. Zero trip meter.

▼ 2.6   SO   Bull Creek Pass (10,485 feet), high point of route. Hiking trail to the summit of Mount Ellen leads off to the north. Extensive views.

7.1 ▲   SO   Bull Creek Pass (10,485 feet), high point of route. Hiking trail to the summit of Mount Ellen leads off to the north. Extensive views. End of climb from McMillan Springs Campground.
GPS: N 38°05.16′ W 110°48.11′

▼ 2.8   SO   Track on right to Burned Ridge.
6.9 ▲   SO   Track on left to Burned Ridge.

▼ 4.6   BL   Track on right.
5.1 ▲   BR   Track on left.

▼ 4.9   SO   Track on left joins Southwest #48: Copper Ridge Trail. Follow sign toward McMillan Springs Campground. Shady campsite in the aspens to the right.

4.8 ▲   SO   Track on right joins Southwest #48: Copper Ridge Trail. Shady campsite in the aspens to the left.

▼ 5.5   SO   Track on right to campsite.
4.2 ▲   SO   Track on left to campsite.

▼ 5.7   SO   Track on left to viewpoint on a rise.
4.0 ▲   SO   Track on right to viewpoint on a rise.

▼ 6.9   BL   Track on right to log cabin; pass Willow Spring on right.
2.8 ▲   BR   Pass Willow Spring on left, followed by a track on left to log cabin.

▼ 7.5   BL   Track on right to Dugout Creek and Cedar Creek. Entrance to McMillan Springs Campground on right (fee required).
2.2 ▲   BR   Track on left to Dugout Creek and Cedar Creek. Entrance to McMillan Springs Campground on left (fee required). Leaving juniper and pinyon vegetation and entering ponderosa pines and aspens.
GPS: N 38°04.31′ W 110°50.84′

SW Trail #47: Bull Creek Pass Trail

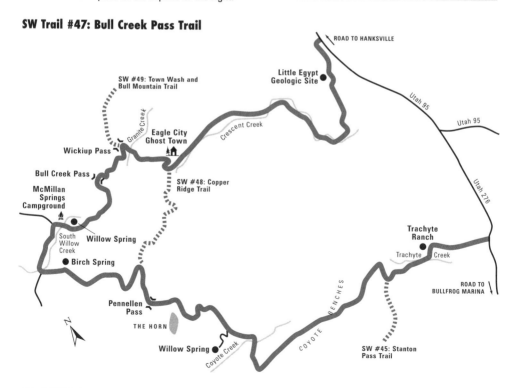

▼ 9.7 TL Cross through South Willow Creek, then turn left, following signs for Birch Spring and the Horn. Straight on goes to Southwest #39: Notom Road. End of descent from Bull Creek Pass. Zero trip meter.

0.0 ▲ Trail climbs to Bull Creek Pass
GPS: N 38°03.15′ W 110°52.33′

▼ 0.0 Trail starts to climb.
6.3 ▲ TR Turn right, following signs for Bull Creek Pass. Left goes to Southwest #39: Notom Road. Zero trip meter.

▼ 0.2 SO Cattle guard.
6.1 ▲ SO Cattle guard.

▼ 1.5 SO Birch Spring on left of trail on a right-hand bend.
4.8 ▲ SO Birch Spring on right of trail on a left-hand bend.
GPS: N 38°02.87′ W 110°51.06′

▼ 2.7 SO Cattle guard; trail passes by junipers.
3.6 ▲ SO Cattle guard.

▼ 3.9 SO Track on right to viewpoint. Views southeast to the Horn.
2.4 ▲ SO Track on left to viewpoint. Views southeast to the Horn.

▼ 6.3 TR T-intersection. Track on left is Southwest #48: Copper Ridge Trail. Zero trip meter.
0.0 ▲ Continue north.
GPS: N 38°01.76′ W 110°48.22′

▼ 0.0 Continue south toward the Horn.
9.3 ▲ TL Turn left. Track ahead is Southwest #48: Copper Ridge Trail. Zero trip meter.

▼ 1.2 SO Track on left to Box Spring.
8.1 ▲ SO Track on right to Box Spring.

▼ 1.4 TL T-intersection at Pennellen Pass (7,912 feet).
7.9 ▲ TR Pennellen Pass (7,912 feet).
GPS: N 38°00.61′ W 110°48.50′

▼ 2.0 SO Trail passes the Horn.
7.3 ▲ SO Trail passes the Horn.

▼ 3.0 SO Campsite on left.
6.3 ▲ SO Campsite on right.

▼ 4.5 SO Track on right, then cattle guard. Views of the Horn and Ragged Mountain.
4.8 ▲ SO Cattle guard, then track on left. Views of the Horn and Ragged Mountain.
GPS: N 37°59.67′ W 110°46.52′

▼ 6.3 SO Track on right to Willow Spring.
3.0 ▲ SO Track on left to Willow Spring.
GPS: N 37°58.76′ W 110°45.88′

▼ 6.4 SO Camping areas on right and left, then corral on left.
2.9 ▲ SO Corral on right, then camping areas on right and left.

▼ 7.7 BR Track on left to campsite with view.
1.6 ▲ BL Track on right to campsite with view.

▼ 8.8 SO Turkey Haven undeveloped BLM campsite on left.
0.5 ▲ SO Turkey Haven undeveloped BLM campsite on right.
GPS: N 37°57.61′ W 110°45.43′

▼ 9.3 TL T-intersection. Turn left, following sign to Coyote Benches and Trachyte Ranch. Track on right is Southwest #45: Stanton Pass Trail. Zero trip meter.
0.0 ▲ Continue north.
GPS: N 37°57.16′ W 110°45.36′

▼ 0.0 Continue northeast.
5.4 ▲ TR Turn right, following sign to the Horn. Track on left is Southwest #45: Stanton Pass Trail. Zero trip meter.

▼ 0.9 SO Cattle guard. Spectacular views east.
4.5 ▲ SO Cattle guard. Spectacular views east.

▼ 1.7 SO Track on right to Coyote Benches. Views of Mount Hillers on right.
3.7 ▲ SO Track on left to Coyote Benches. Views of Mount Hillers on left.
GPS: N 37°57.60′ W 110°43.58′

▼ 4.7	SO	Cattle guard.
0.7 ▲	SO	Cattle guard.

▼ 4.9	SO	Track on left is signposted to North Wash, but is washed out after a couple of miles.
0.5 ▲	SO	Track on right is signposted to North Wash, but is washed out after a couple of miles.
		GPS: N 37°57.85' W 110°40.31'

▼ 5.4	SO	Track on right is Southwest #45: Stanton Pass Trail to Quaking Aspen Spring. Zero trip meter.
0.0 ▲		Continue along main track.
		GPS: N 37°57.88' W 110°39.61'

▼ 0.0		Continue along main track.
6.0 ▲	BR	Track on left is Southwest #45: Stanton Pass Trail to Quaking Aspen Spring. Continue toward Coyote Benches. Zero trip meter.

▼ 1.2	SO	Mine shaft visible on far side of creek.
4.8 ▲	SO	Mine shaft visible on far side of creek.

▼ 1.4	SO	Track on left to sheds—remains of Trachyte Ranch.
4.6 ▲	SO	Track on right to sheds—remains of Trachyte Ranch.

▼ 1.6	SO	Cross through creek.
4.4 ▲	SO	Cross through creek.

▼ 1.8	SO	Track on right.
4.2 ▲	BR	Track on left.

▼ 2.0	SO	Track on right.
4.0 ▲	SO	Track on left.

▼ 2.1	SO	Cross through creek.
3.9 ▲	SO	Cross through creek.

▼ 2.2	TL	Track on right to private property (Cat Ranch).
3.8 ▲	TR	Track ahead to private property (Cat Ranch).
		GPS: N 37°57.88' W 110°37.78'

▼ 2.3	SO	Track on right.
3.7 ▲	SO	Track on left.

▼ 2.7	SO	Track on left to camping area and old log cabin, remains of Trachyte Ranch. Cross through Trachyte Creek, then track on right to camping area, wooden cabin, and remains of old truck.
3.3 ▲	SO	Track on left to camping area, wooden cabin, and remains of old truck. Cross through Trachyte Creek, then track on right to camping area and old log cabin, remains of Trachyte Ranch.

▼ 3.0	SO	Track on right.
3.0 ▲	SO	Track on left.

▼ 3.1	SO	Old corral on right, dam on left.
2.9 ▲	SO	Dam on right, old corral on left.

▼ 5.8	SO	Track on right.
0.2 ▲	SO	Track on left.

▼ 6.0		Trail ends at Utah 276, 4.4 miles south of the junction with Utah 95. Turn left for Hanksville, right for Bullfrog Marina.
0.0 ▲		On Utah 276, 4.4 miles south of junction with Utah 95, turn onto trail, following Scenic Backcountry Byway sign.
		GPS: N 37°57.66' W 110°34.47'

Copper Ridge Trail

STARTING POINT Southwest #47: Bull Creek Pass Trail near Crescent Creek

FINISHING POINT Southwest #47: Bull Creek Pass Trail, 1.4 miles north of Pennellen Pass

TOTAL MILEAGE 6.3 miles

UNPAVED MILEAGE 6.3 miles

DRIVING TIME 1 hour

ELEVATION RANGE 8,200–9,100 feet

USUALLY OPEN November to June

DIFFICULTY RATING 2

SCENIC RATING 8

REMOTENESS RATING +1

Special Attractions
- Spectacular views east over the Robbers Roost area.
- Long length of comfortable shelf road.
- Access to the higher elevation trails in Bromide Basin.

History
The Henry Mountains and Bromide Basin, in particular, have a long mining history. The most intriguing tale related to the mountains may have even occurred at Bromide Basin—though it may not have, depending on which version of the story you believe. Part truth, part legend, the tale of the Lost Mine of the Henry Mountains begins when the Spanish extensively explored this area as an offshoot of the Spanish Trail. According to the tale, they found an incredibly rich mine somewhere in the Henry Mountains and extracted the gold using the local Indians as slaves. One day, the Indians rebelled and a battle was fought with great loss of life on both sides. The Indians prevailed, and before they left the mine, they filled in the shaft and the medicine man placed a curse on the mine, so that all who attempted to work it would meet with disaster and death. The mine lay dormant for many years, its location known only to the Indians, who passed it down in their tales.

In 1853, John Frémont explored this area of Utah. He discovered steps cut into the wall at Spanish Bottoms that the Spanish had used to get their mules and men up to the Henry Mountains from the Colorado River. Along the old trail near the Henry Mountains, he found the bones of a pack mule with piles of gold ore on either side, spilled out from panniers long rotted away. Some of his men were very excited about the find, and some years later one of them, John Burke, returned to seek the lost mine. He was gone for several weeks, and then one day he staggered into the Desert Springs stage station with some ore samples he said came from an old Spanish mine. He said that Indians had stolen his horse and all of his gear and told him to leave the area.

The owner of the stage station, Ben Bowen, teamed up with him, and they hired a man named Blackburn to guide them and tend to the cooking and horses. En route to the mountains, they stopped at a ranch in Blue Valley for supplies. The rancher warned them against proceeding, saying that a hired Indian boy had told him that his grandfather had been forced to work in the mines and that there was a curse on anyone who went there. Undaunted, the three men proceeded, entering the Henry Mountains from the north and crossing the headwaters of Crescent Creek and Copper Creek before climbing up to what is now the Bromide Basin area. There they located the mine Burke had found before, a mine with the shafts filled in but much gold ore on the surface. They filled their sacks and began their return to the town of Pleasant Dale. In cutting across unknown desert terrain, they got

Looking east along Copper Ridge Trail late in the day

hopelessly lost and against the advice of Blackburn, Burke and Bowen drank from a pool of stagnant water. They got very sick, but reached Pleasant Dale and recovered—only to die a few days later, after learning that the gold they had recovered had assayed out at over $6,000 a ton. Blackburn did go back to the mountain, but before he could locate the mine, a messenger caught up with him saying one of his children had died. He never went back.

Another possible victim of the Indian curse on the mine was Edgar Wolverton, who worked several smaller mines on Crescent Creek. He built a mill with a 18-feet-high waterwheel on the eastern flanks of Mount Pennell that took water from Straight Creek to help grind ore. This mill has been removed from the mountain for preservation and is now located next to the BLM office in Hanksville.

In 1911, his mines were flooded, leaving him with time on his hands to locate the lost Spanish mine. Wolverton spent 10 years searching for the mine and kept a detailed diary of his efforts. The entry for July 21, 1921, records that he "found the old Mexican mill today whilst panning the hill south of camp." Shortly after that he had an accident with his horse—exact details vary—and was taken to Fruita, Colorado, for surgery. He survived the surgery, only to die a few days later. He is buried in the cemetery at Elgin, Utah. Wolverton's diary puts the location of the lost mine on the flanks of Mount Pennell rather than near Bromide Basin.

The area north of Copper Ridge was named Bromide Basin by early prospectors because it reminded them of bromide ore they had known in Colorado. In 1889, a small gold rush to Bromide Basin launched the growth of Eagle City, 2 miles below on Crescent Creek. The Bromide Mine was in full swing by 1891, and a five-stamp mill was constructed to process the ore. Between 1891 and 1893, $15,000 worth of gold was removed, and the Denver & Rio Grande Western Railroad was considering a branch line from the main line at Green River to Eagle City. However, the vein played out before any work could be started, and by 1900 both Eagle City and Bromide Basin were deserted.

There were sporadic attempts at mining after that, although nothing of great worth was ever found. The private lands up at Bromide Basin are now closed to the public.

Description

This short, easy trail offers an alternative to driving the complete Southwest #47: Bull Creek Pass Trail, as it cuts across and shaves 19 miles off the full loop. However, it is a worthwhile trail in its own right, as it provides unparalleled views east over the Robbers Roost area, Gunsight Butte, and Canyonlands National Park, as well as to the La Sal and Abajo Mountains.

The gradients are mild and the surface is graded dirt the entire way; in dry weather there should be no problems for high-clearance vehicles. In wet weather the trail, like most in this region, should be avoided.

The trail is shelf road for almost its entire length, but is a comfortable width for a full-size vehicle, and there are adequate passing places. It gives access up to the mining areas of Bromide Basin high on the flanks of Mount Ellen. Campsites are few along this trail, but there are good campsites at either end, particularly near Pennellen Pass.

Current Road Information

BLM Henry Mountain Field Station
PO Box 99
Hanksville, UT 84734
(435) 542-3461

Map References

BLM Hanksville
USGS 1:24,000 Mt. Ellen
      1:100,000 Hanksville
Maptech CD-ROM: Moab/Canyonlands;
      Escalante/Dixie National Forest
Trails Illustrated, #213
Utah Atlas & Gazetteer, p. 28
Utah Travel Council #5
Other: Recreation Map of the Henry
      Mountains Area

Route Directions

▼ 0.0   9 miles from the north end of Southwest #47: Bull Creek Pass Trail, zero trip meter and proceed southeast along the Copper Ridge Trail. Immediately cross through Crescent Creek, swing left and start to climb. Track on right is reclamation area; please stay out.

2.2 ▲   Track on left is reclamation area; please stay out. Swing right and cross through Crescent Creek. Trail ends at Southwest #47: Bull Creek Pass Trail. Turn right for Utah 95.
    GPS: N 38°04.40' W 110°45.61'

▼ 0.2   SO   Track on left.
2.0 ▲   SO   Track on right.

▼ 0.9   SO   Track on left.
1.3 ▲   SO   Track on right.

▼ 1.7   SO   Track on left to flat camping area with excellent views.
0.5 ▲   SO   Track on right to flat camping area with excellent views.

▼ 2.2   SO   Intersection. Track on right to Bromide Basin; track on left runs out on Copper Ridge. Zero trip meter.
0.0 ▲   Continue northeast as trail climbs.

▼ 0.0   Continue southwest as trail descends.
4.1 ▲   SO   Intersection. Track on left to Bromide Basin; track on right runs out on Copper Ridge. Zero trip meter.

▼ 0.1   SO   Views southwest to Mount Hillers, the Horn, Ragged Mountain, and Mount Pennell.
4.0 ▲   SO   Views southwest to Mount Hillers, the Horn, Ragged Mountain, and Mount Pennell.

▼ 1.3   SO   Track on left.
2.8 ▲   SO   Track on right.

▼ 2.6   SO   Cross through Slate Creek in grove of small aspens.
1.5 ▲   SO   Cross through Slate Creek in grove of small aspens.

▼ 4.1   Trail finishes at Southwest #47: Bull Creek Pass Trail, 1.4 miles north of Pennellen Pass.
0.0 ▲   On Southwest #47: Bull Creek Pass Trail, 1.4 miles north of Pennellen Pass, turn left onto Copper Ridge Trail and zero trip meter.
    GPS: N 38°01.76' W 110°48.22'

SW Trail #48: Copper Ridge Trail

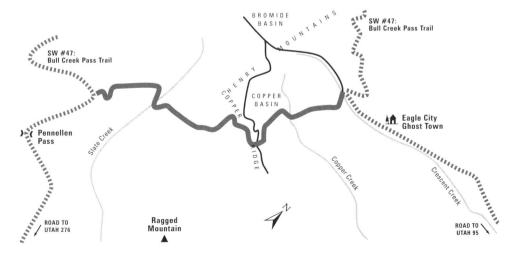

Town Wash and Bull Mountain Trail

STARTING POINT Utah 24, 9 miles west of Hanksville
FINISHING POINT Southwest #47: Bull Creek Pass Trail at Wickiup Pass
TOTAL MILEAGE 35.9 miles
UNPAVED MILEAGE 35.9 miles
DRIVING TIME 3.5 hours
ELEVATION RANGE 4,575–9,300 feet
USUALLY OPEN May to November
DIFFICULTY RATING 3
SCENIC RATING 7
REMOTENESS RATING +1

Special Attractions

- Ghost town site of Giles.
- Panoramic views of the Henry Mountains.
- Remote, seldom traveled desert track.
- Desolate badlands and moonscape scenery.

Fording the Fremont River

History

The township of Giles, near the start of this trail, was first established in 1883; it was originally called Blue Valley, after the blue-gray barren clay hills in this desolate region. Founded by Mormons as an agricultural community, Blue Valley was divided by the Fremont River, which was used for irrigation, and the two halves were connected by a narrow wooden bridge. The Mormon church provided the town's social life and leadership. Originally it was a branch of the ward in the upper valley, but in 1885 a new ward was formed, which included Blue Valley and nearby Hanksville.

Most of the irrigated farming took place south of the Fremont River on the river flats. Nearly three thousand acres of corn, alfalfa, cabbages, and other fruits and vegetables were irrigated by canals and ditches that diverted water from the river.

In 1895, Blue Valley changed its name to Giles after a prominent resident, Bishop Henry Giles, who died in 1892. He is buried in the Giles cemetery.

The major reason for the formation of Giles also proved its undoing. In 1897, the Fremont River flooded, wiping out the bridge and most of the irrigation canals. The town of 200 people rallied to repair the damage, but in 1909 a second flood once again washed out their farms. The town never recovered and was officially disbanded in 1910.

Today little remains of Giles. On the north side of the river, next to milepost 109, just east of the start of this trail, is a stone house that was originally the Abbot Cabin, a rest house for travelers. On the south side, just as the trail swings around Steamboat Point, there are some stone foundations in the undergrowth. The cemetery is found just off the trail to the east.

The Spanish Trail also came close to the Henry Mountains and early settlers established many mines in the area. An old folk legend places a supposed battle between the Spanish and the Indians at the north end of the mountain range. As the story goes, the site and graves were marked by a Latin cross dated 1777.

Description

This alternate route into the Henry Mountains from the north is little traveled; most visitors take the major dirt road leading directly south from Hanksville. The trail starts 9 miles west of Hanksville; turn south from Utah 24 on an unsigned dirt trail. You almost immediately cross a concrete ford through the Fremont River, which can be deep and fast flowing, and silt can build up on the concrete, leading to a sticky trap for the unwary. If in doubt, walk the crossing first and engage 4WD. Do not attempt if the river is in flood stage.

The trail passes the ghost town of Giles set underneath Steamboat Point, a prominent butte that resembles a funneled steamship. Little is left of Giles these days; you can find the graveyard with a bit of hunting to the east of Steamboat Point— look for an old fence line.

The trail swings around Steamboat Point and heads south up Town Wash. It is narrow graded dirt, rough in places but traversable with a high-clearance vehicle in dry weather. Navigation along the trail is tricky; there are no signs, and junctions are often faint and easy to miss.

After 4 miles, the trail leaves Town Wash and climbs up onto the mesa, affording good views north over the wash and south toward the massive Henry Mountains, which rear up out of the flat land. The trail winds over the flat Blue Valley Benches, crossing many small washes and passing a myriad of small, unmarked two-track trails. There are some spectacular areas of badlands, a desolate moonscape with no vegetation, and patches of salt creeping up through the poor soil.

After almost 20 miles, the trail joins the graded road from Hanksville, and the worst of the difficult navigation is over, although the upper reaches of this road are rougher than anything encountered so far. The trail climbs steadily through large junipers and stunted pines toward Bull Mountain, visible east of the trail. The scenery changes dramatically as the trail climbs and winds around the slope of Bull Mountain and Bull Creek Wash. There is a small section of

The trail runs along the canyon wall as it descends into Town Wash

shelf road, but it is a comfortable width for a full-size vehicle, and there are adequate passing places.

You pass the picnic area of Dandelion Flat after 34 miles, where there are picnic tables set in a shady pine grove. The hiking trail to Log Flat and East Saddle starts here. Half a mile farther is the developed BLM campground of Lonesome Beaver (fee required). Many secluded campsites are set under tall pines and aspens.

The trail finishes on Wickiup Pass, where it intersects Southwest #47: Bull Creek Pass Trail.

Current Road Information

BLM Henry Mountain Field Station
PO Box 99
Hanksville, UT 84734
(435) 542-3461

Map References

BLM   Hanksville (incomplete)
USGS 1:24,000   Steamboat Point, Town
      Point, Hanksville, Bull Mt., Dry
      Lakes Peak, Mt. Ellen
      1:100,000 Hanksville (incomplete)
Maptech CD-ROM: Moab/Canyonlands
Trails Illustrated, #213 (incomplete)
Utah Atlas & Gazetteer, pp. 28, 29
Utah Travel Council #5 (incomplete)
Other: Recreation Map of the Henry
        Mountains Area

Route Directions

▼ 0.0   On Utah 24, 9 miles west of Hanksville,
           turn south onto unmarked dirt road lead-
           ing down through the tamarisks. Trail
           leads off just before a left-hand bend.
9.6 ▲   Trail ends on Utah 24. Turn right for
           Hanksville, left for Capitol Reef
           National Park.
           GPS: N 38°21.56′ W 110°52.39′

▼ 0.1   SO Cross through Fremont River on con-
           crete ford.
9.5 ▲   SO Cross through Fremont River on con-
           crete ford.

▼ 1.0   SO Track on left.
8.6 ▲   SO Track on right.

▼ 1.5   SO Track swings south around Steamboat
           Point and commences up Town Wash.
8.1 ▲   SO Track leaves Town Wash and swings
           west around Steamboat Point.

▼ 1.6   SO Fence line in scrub on left marks Giles
           graveyard.
8.0 ▲   SO Fence line in scrub on right marks
           Giles graveyard.

▼ 2.6   SO Cross through Town Wash.
7.0 ▲   SO Cross through Town Wash.

▼ 2.9   SO Track on left.
6.7 ▲   SO Track on right.
           GPS: N 38°20.09′ W 110°51.67′

▼ 3.7   SO Pass through wire gate in fence line.

5.9 ▲   SO Pass through wire gate in fence line.

▼ 3.8   SO Drop down to enter Town Wash.
5.8 ▲   SO Trail leaves Town Wash.

▼ 4.1   SO Trail leaves Town Wash and climbs
           mesa.
5.5 ▲   SO Enter Town Wash.

▼ 4.7   SO Top of mesa, trail levels off.
4.9 ▲   SO Trail descends mesa to enter Town
           Wash. Views north over wash.

▼ 6.1   SO Track on right.
3.5 ▲   SO Track on left.
           GPS: N 38°17.75′ W 110°52.58′

▼ 6.3   SO Track on right.
3.3 ▲   SO Track on left.

▼ 6.9   SO Pass through wire gate in fence line.
2.7 ▲   SO Pass through wire gate in fence line.

▼ 7.4   SO Track on left to viewpoint over wash.
2.2 ▲   SO Track on right to viewpoint over wash.

▼ 7.6   SO Track on left.
2.0 ▲   BL Track on right.

▼ 8.0   SO Track on right.
1.6 ▲   SO Track on left.

▼ 8.1   SO Cross through Cottonwood Creek.
1.5 ▲   SO Cross through Cottonwood Creek.

▼ 9.6   TL T-intersection. Junction is unmarked.
           Zero trip meter.
0.0 ▲   Continue north.
           GPS: N 38°15.11′ W 110°51.25′

▼ 0.0   Continue northeast.
6.3 ▲   TR Junction is unmarked. Zero trip meter.

▼ 0.4   SO Cross through Coaly Wash.
5.9 ▲   SO Cross through Coaly Wash.

▼ 0.6   SO Track on right. Trail crosses Blue Valley
           Benches.
5.7 ▲   SO Track on left. Trail crosses Blue Valley
           Benches.

SW Trail #49: Town Wash and Bull Mountain Trail

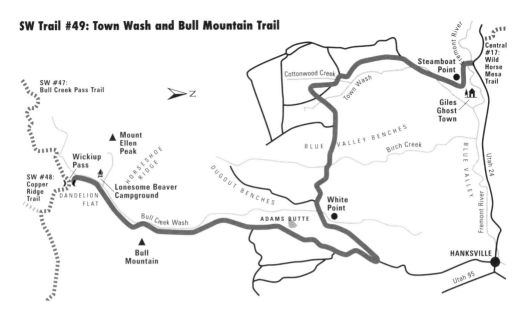

▼ 0.8   SO   Cross through small wash.
5.5 ▲   SO   Cross through small wash.

▼ 1.9   SO   Small tracks on left and right.
4.4 ▲   SO   Small tracks on left and right.

▼ 2.2   SO   Cattle guard, then cross wash.
4.1 ▲   SO   Cross wash, then cattle guard.

▼ 2.6   SO   Cross through small wash.
3.7 ▲   SO   Cross through small wash.

▼ 2.7   SO   Track on left.
3.6 ▲   SO   Second entrance to track on right.

▼ 2.8   SO   Second entrance to track on left.
3.5 ▲   SO   Track on right.

▼ 3.9   SO   Cross through Birch Creek.
2.4 ▲   SO   Cross through Birch Creek.

▼ 4.3   SO   Cattle guard.
2.0 ▲   SO   Cattle guard.

▼ 4.5   SO   Trail runs down small wash.
1.8 ▲   SO   Leave wash.

▼ 5.3   SO   Leave wash.
1.0 ▲   SO   Trail runs along small wash.

▼ 6.3   SO   Major track on right to Dugout Benches and Birch Creek. Zero trip meter.
0.0 ▲   Continue southeast.
        GPS: N 38°15.41' W 110°45.66'

▼ 0.0   Continue northwest.
3.9 ▲   SO   Major track on left to Dugout Benches and Birch Creek. Zero trip meter.

▼ 0.5   SO   Cross through Bull Creek Wash, followed by track on right.
3.4 ▲   SO   Track on left, then cross through Bull Creek Wash.

▼ 1.0   SO   White Point rocks on left.
2.9 ▲   SO   White Point rocks on right.

▼ 2.5   SO   Small track on left.
1.4 ▲   SO   Small track on right.

▼ 3.9   TR   T-intersection, follow sign to Lonesome Beaver Campground. Left goes to Hanksville. Trail standard improves to wider graded dirt. Zero trip meter.
0.0 ▲   Continue southwest.
        GPS: N 38°17.65' W 110°42.86'

▼ 0.0   Continue south.

| 5.7 ▲ | TL | Turn onto unmarked dirt road. Trail standard drops. Straight on goes to Hanksville. Zero trip meter. |

| ▼ 3.4 | SO | Cattle guard. |
| 2.3 ▲ | SO | Cattle guard. |

| ▼ 4.0 | SO | Adams Butte on right. |
| 1.7 ▲ | SO | Adams Butte on left. |

| ▼ 4.2 | SO | Corral on left. |
| 1.5 ▲ | SO | Corral on right. |

| ▼ 4.3 | SO | Cattle guard. |
| 1.4 ▲ | SO | Cattle guard. |

| ▼ 4.8 | SO | Cattle guard. |
| 0.9 ▲ | SO | Cattle guard. |

| ▼ 5.7 | SO | Track on left to Utah 95. Continue straight, following signs for Lonesome Beaver Campground. Zero trip meter. |
| 0.0 ▲ | | Continue north. |

GPS: N 38°12.90' W 110°44.44'

| ▼ 0.0 | | Continue south. |
| 8.8 ▲ | SO | Track on right to Utah 95. Continue straight, following signs for Hanksville. Zero trip meter. |

| ▼ 1.1 | SO | Track on right to private property. |
| 7.7 ▲ | SO | Track on left to private property. |

| ▼ 3.3 | SO | Two tracks on right to campsites. |
| 5.5 ▲ | SO | Two tracks on left to campsites. |

| ▼ 4.6 | SO | Some campsites on right as trail winds around Bull Mountain. Trail becomes rougher. |
| 4.2 ▲ | SO | Some campsites on left as trail winds around Bull Mountain. Trail standard improves. |

| ▼ 5.1 | SO | Cattle guard, start of shelf road. |
| 3.7 ▲ | SO | Cattle guard, end of shelf road. |

| ▼ 5.5 | SO | Track on left to viewpoint. |
| 3.3 ▲ | BL | Track on right to viewpoint. |

GPS: N 38°08.53' W 110°44.61'

| ▼ 6.0 | SO | End of shelf road. |
| 2.8 ▲ | SO | Start of shelf road. |

| ▼ 7.4 | SO | Trail drops to cross through Bull Creek Wash. |
| 1.4 ▲ | SO | Cross through Bull Creek Wash. |

GPS: N 38°07.34' W 110°45.52'

| ▼ 7.7 | SO | Cross through Bull Creek Wash. |
| 1.1 ▲ | SO | Cross through Bull Creek Wash. |

| ▼ 7.8 | SO | Sign, "Entering Sawmill Basin." |
| 1.0 ▲ | SO | Leaving Sawmill Basin. |

| ▼ 8.4 | SO | Dandelion Flat Picnic Area on right. Hiking trailhead to Log Flat and East Saddle on right. |
| 0.4 ▲ | SO | Dandelion Flat Picnic Area on left. Hiking trailhead to Log Flat and East Saddle on left. |

GPS: N 38°06.87' W 110°46.33'

| ▼ 8.6 | SO | Small track on right. |
| 0.2 ▲ | SO | Small track on left. |

| ▼ 8.8 | SO | Track on right is main entrance to Lonesome Beaver Campground (fee required). Zero trip meter. |
| 0.0 ▲ | | Continue north. |

GPS: N 38°06.56' W 110°46.65'

| ▼ 0.0 | | Continue south. |
| 1.6 ▲ | SO | Track on left is main entrance to Lonesome Beaver Campground (fee required). Zero trip meter. |

| ▼ 0.1 | SO | Side entrance to campground on right. |
| 1.5 ▲ | SO | Side entrance to campground on left. |

| ▼ 1.6 | | Trail ends at Wickiup Pass at Southwest #47: Bull Creek Pass Trail. Turn right to Bull Creek Pass, left to Utah 95. |
| 0.0 ▲ | | At Wickiup Pass on Southwest #47: Bull Creek Pass Trail, zero trip meter and turn north, downhill, from the pass. |

GPS: N 38°05.70' W 110°46.65'

Selected Further Reading

Alexander, Thomas G. *Utah, the Right Place.* Salt Lake City: Gibbs M. Smith, Inc., 1996.

American Park Network, Utah's National Parks. San Francisco: American Park Network, 1998.

Athearn, Robert. *The Denver and Rio Grande Western Railroad.* Lincoln, Nebr.: University of Nebraska Press, 1962.

Arizona. Salt Lake City: Gibbs M. Smith, Inc., 1983.

Baars, Donald L. *The Colorado Plateau, A Geologic History.* Albequerque, N.Mex.: University of New Mexico Press, 1972.

Bennett, Cynthia Larsen. *Roadside History of Utah.* Missoula, Mont.: Mountain Press Publishing Company, 1999.

Benson, Joe. *Scenic Driving Utah.* Helena, Mont.: Falcon Publishing, Inc., 1996.

Best Western: Utah Fun Tours. N.p, n.d.

Boren, Kerry Ross, and Lisa Lee Boren. *The Gold of Carre-Shinob.* Salt Lake City: Bonneville Books, 1998.

Canyon Legacy: A Journal of the Dan O'Laurie Museum—Moab, Utah. No. 8, 9, 10, 18, 22.

Carr, Stephen L. *The Historical Guide to Utah Ghost Towns.* Salt Lake City: Western Epics, 1972.

Carr, Stephen L., and Robert W. Edwards. *Utah Ghost Rails.* Salt Lake City: Western Epics, 1989.

Chronic, Halka. *Roadside Geology of Utah.* Missoula, Mont.: Mountain Press Publishing Co., 1990.

Clark, Carol. *Explorers of the West.* Salt Lake City: Great Mountain West Supply, 1997.

Colclazer, Suasan. *In Pictures-Bryce Canyon: The Continuing Story.* Las Vegas: KC Publications, 1989.

Colwell, Joseph I. *Boulder Mountain, Throne of the Colorado Plateau.* Salt Lake City: Dixie Interpretive Association, 1992.

DeCourten, Frank. *Dinosaurs of Utah.* Salt Lake City: University of Utah Press, 1998.

Dixie National Forest...Land of Many Uses!. Blackner Card and Souvenir Co, n.d.

Egan, Ferol. *Frémont: Explorer for a Restless Nation.* Reno, Neva.: University of Nevada Press, 1985.

Fife, Carolyn Perry, and Wallace Dean Fife, eds. *Travelers' Choice: A Guide to the Best of Utah's National Parks, Monuments, and Recreation Areas.* Salt Lake City: D and C Publishing, 1998.

Godfrey, Andrew E. *A Guide to the Paiute ATV Trail.* N.p.: Fishlake Discovery Association, n.d.

Harris, Edward D. *John Charles Frémont and the Great Western Reconnaissance.* New York: Chelsea House Publishers, 1990.

Heck, Larry E. *The Adventures of Pass Patrol. Vol. 1, In Search of the Outlaw Trail.* Aurora, Colo.: Outback Publications, Inc., 1996.

—-. *The Adventures of Pass Patrol. Vol. 2, 4-Wheel Drive Trails and Outlaw Hideouts of Utah.* Aurora, Colo.: Outback Publications, Inc., 1999.

—-. *The Adventures of Pass Patrol. Vol. 6, 4-Wheel Drive Roads to Hole in the Rock.* Aurora, Colo.: Outback Publications, Inc., 1998.

Hemingway, Donald W. *Utah and the Mormons.* Salt Lake City: Great Mountain West Supply, 1994.

Hinton, Wayne K. *Utah: Unusual Beginning to Unique Present.* New York: Windsor Publications, Inc., 1988.

Huegel, Tony. *Utah Byways: Backcountry Drives for the Whole Family.* Idaho Falls, Idaho: Post Company, 1996.

Kelly, Charles. *The Outlaw Trail: A History of Butch Cassidy and His Wild Bunch.* Lincoln, Nebr.: University of Nebraska Press, 1996.

Kelsey, Michael R. *Hiking and Exploring the Paria River*, 3rd ed. Provo, Utah: Kelsey Publishing, 1998.

—. *Hiking and Exploring Utah's Henry Mountains and Robbers Roost*, rev. ed. Provo, Utah: Kelsey Publishing, 1990.

Korns, J. Roderic, and Dale L. Morgan, eds. *West from Fort Bridger: The Pioneering of Immigrant Trails across Utah, 1846-1850*. Logan, Utah: Utah State University Press, 1994.

May, Dean L. *Utah: A People's History*. Salt Lake City: University of Utah Press, 1987.

McGrath, Roger D. *Gunfighters, Highwaymen and Vigilantes*. Los Angeles: University of California Press, 1984.

Miller, David E. *Hole in the Rock*. N.p.: University of Utah Press, 1998.

The Outlaw Trail Journal, 1992-1999.

Patterson, Richard. *Historical Atlas of the Outlaw West*. Boulder, Colo.: Johnson Publishing Co., 1997

Peterson, Charles S. *Utah: A Bicentennial History*. New York: W. W. Norton and Co., Inc., 1977.

Poll, Richard D., ed. *Utah's History*. Logan, Utah: Utah State University Press, 1989.

Powell, Allan Kent. *The Utah Guide*. Golden, Colo.: Fulcrum Publishing, 1995.

—. *The Utah History Encyclopedia*. Salt Lake City: University of Utah Press, 1994.

Rutter, Michael. *Utah: Off the Beaten Path*. Guilford, Conn.: The Globe Pequot Press, 1999.

Thompson, George A. *Some Dreams Die: Utah's Ghost Towns and Lost Treasures*. Salt Lake City: Dream Garden Press, 1999.

Thrapp, Dan L. *Encyclopedia of Frontier Biography*. 3 vols. London: University of Nebraska Press, 1988.

Utah Historical Quarterly. Spring 2000, vol. 68, no. 2.

Utah State Historical Society. Utah History Suite CD-ROM. Provo, Utah: Historical Views, 1998-99.

Van Cott, John W. *Utah Place Names*. Salt Lake City: University of Utah Press, 1990.

Weibel, Michael R. *Utah Travel Smart*. Santa Fe, N.Mex.: John Muir Publications, 1999.

—. *Utah: Travel Smart*. Santa Fe, N.Mex.: John Muir Publications, 1999.

Wharton, Gayen, and Tom Wharton. *It Happened in Utah*. Helena, Mont.: Falcon Publishing, 1998.

—. *Utah*. Oakland, Cali.: Fodor's Travel Publications, 1995.

—. *Utah*. Oakland, Cali.: Compass American Guides, 1950.

About the Authors

Peter Massey grew up in the outback of Australia, where he acquired a life-long love of the backcountry. After retiring from a career in investment banking in 1986 at the age of thirty-five, he served as a director of a number of companies in the United States, the United Kingdom, and Australia. He moved to Colorado in 1993.

Jeanne Wilson was born and grew up in Maryland. After moving to New York City in 1980, she worked in advertising and public relations before moving to Colorado in 1993.

After traveling extensively in Australia, Europe, Asia, and Africa, the authors covered more than 80,000 miles touring the United States and the Australian outback between 1993 and 1997. Since then they have traveled more than 25,000 miles doing research for their two guidebook series: *Backcountry Adventures* and *4WD Trails*.

Photo Credits

Unless otherwise indicated in the following list of acknowledgments (which is organized by page number), all photographs were taken by Bushducks—Maggie Pinder and Donald McGann.

66 Utah State Historical Society; **72** Utah State Historical Society; **106** Utah State Historical Society; **173** Utah State Historical Society.

Front cover photography: Bushducks—Maggie Pinder and Donald McGann

california trails
backroad guides

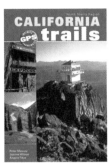
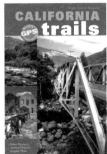

California Trails–Northern Sierra This book outlines detailed trail information for 55 off-road routes located near the towns of Sacramento (east), Red Bluff (east), Truckee, South Lake Tahoe, Sonora, Susanville, Chico, Oroville, Yuba City, Placerville, Stockton (east), Jackson, and Sonora. **ISBN-10, 1-930193-23-8; ISBN-13, 978-1-930193-23-9; Price $19.95**

California Trails–High Sierra This guidebook navigates and describes 50 trails located near the towns of Fresno (north), Oakhurst, Lone Pine, Bishop, Bridgeport, Coulterville, Mariposa, and Mammoth Lakes. **ISBN-10, 1-930193-21-1; ISBN-13, 978-1-930193-21-5; Price $19.95**

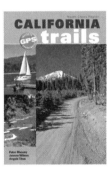
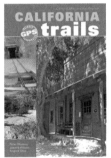

California Trails–North Coast This guide meticulously describes and rates 47 off-road routes located near the towns of Sacramento, Redding (west), Red Bluff, Clear Lake, McCloud, Mount Shasta, Yreka, Crescent City, and Fort Bidwell. **ISBN-10, 1-930193-22-X; ISBN-13, 978-1-930193-22-2; Price $19.95**

California Trails–Central Mountains This guide is comprised of painstaking detail and descriptions for 52 trails located near the towns of Big Sur, Fresno, San Luis Obispo, Santa Barbara, Bakersfield, Mojave, and Maricopa. **ISBN-10, 1-930193-19-X; ISBN-13, 978-1-930193-19-2; Price $19.95**

California Trails–South Coast This field guide includes meticulous trail details for 50 trails located near the towns of Los Angeles, San Bernardino, San Diego, Salton Sea, Indio, Borrego Springs, Ocotillo and Palo Verde. **ISBN-10, 1-930193-24-6; ISBN-13, 978-1-930193-24-6; Price $19.95**

California Trails–Desert This edition of our Trails series contains detailed trail information for 51 off-road routes located near the towns of Lone Pine (east), Panamint Springs, Death Valley area, Ridgecrest, Barstow, Baker and Blythe. **ISBN-10, 1-930193-20-3; ISBN-13, 978-1-930193-20-8; Price $19.95**

to order
call 800-660-5107 or
visit 4WDbooks.com

arizona trails
backroad guides

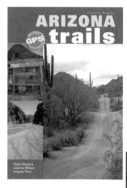

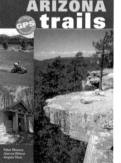

Arizona Trails–Northeast
This guidebook consists of meticulous details and directions for 47 trails located near the towns of Flagstaff, Williams, Prescott (northeast), Winslow, Fort Defiance and Window Rock. **ISBN-10, 1-930193-02-5; ISBN-13, 978-1-930193-02-4; Price $19.95**

Arizona Trails–West
This volume consists of comprehensive statistics and descriptions for 33 trails located near the towns of Bullhead City, Lake Havasu City, Parker, Kingman, Prescott (west), and Quartzsite (north). **ISBN-10, 1-930193-00-9; ISBN-13, 978-1-930193-00-0; Price $19.95**

Arizona Trails–Central
This field guide includes meticulous trail details for 44 off-road routes located near the towns of Phoenix, Wickenburg, Quartzsite (south), Payson, Superior, Globe and Yuma (north). **ISBN-10, 1-930193-01-7; ISBN-13, 978-1-930193-01-7; Price $19.95**

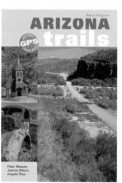

Arizona Trails–South
This handbook is composed of comprehensive statistics and descriptions for 33 trails located near the towns of Tucson, Douglas, Mammoth, Reddington, Stafford, Yuma (southeast), Ajo and Nogales. **ISBN-10, 1-930193-03-3; ISBN-13, 978-1-930193-03-1; Price $19.95**

colorado trails
backroad guides

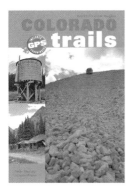

Colorado Trails–North-Central
This guidebook is composed of comprehensive statistics and descriptions of 28 trails, including 8 trails additional to those profiled in the Adventures Colorado book, around Breckenridge, Central City, Fraser, Dillon, Vail, Leadville, Georgetown, and Aspen. **ISBN-10, 1-930193-11-4; ISBN-13, 978-1-930193-11-6; Price $16.95**

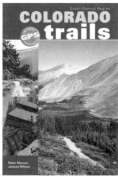

Colorado Trails–South-Central
This edition of our Trails series includes meticulous trail details for 30 off-road routes located near the towns of Gunnison, Salida, Crested Butte, Buena Vista, Aspen, and the Sand Dunes National Monument. **ISBN-10, 1-930193-29-7; ISBN-13, 978-1-930193-29-1; Price $16.95**

Colorado Trails–Southwest
This field guide is comprised of painstaking details and descriptions for 31 trails, including 15 trails additional to those described in the Adventures Colorado book. Routes are located around Silverton, Ouray, Telluride, Durango, Lake City, and Montrose. **ISBN-10, 1-930193-32-7; ISBN-13, 978-1-930193-32-1; Price $19.95**

to order
call 800-660-5107 or
visit 4WDbooks.com

for information on all
adler publishing
guides

call 800-660-5107 or
visit 4WDbooks.com